Spiritual Interventions and Attachment

Spiritual Interventions and Attachment offers a variety of models of lay minister-driven spiritual interventions to which clergy from diverse religious backgrounds might consider referring their congregants. Each chapter reviews a specific model, providing a history, a description, inclusion and exclusion criteria, training requirements, and a clinical illustration. The author also provides a critique of each model using attachment theory as the organizing framework.

All these models are designed to ease the overwhelming burden of clergy who are unable to provide appropriately matched pastoral care to all their congregants who experience spiritual and emotional struggles. University course instructors, clergy, chaplains, pastoral counselors, lay ministers, and mental health professionals will benefit from this insightful book.

Geoff Goodman, PhD, ABPP, is professor of psychiatry and behavioral sciences in the Emory University School of Medicine and associate professor of psychology and spiritual care in Emory University's Candler School of Theology in Atlanta, Georgia, USA. He holds board certifications in clinical psychology and psychoanalysis from the American Board of Professional Psychology.

Let's be real: pastoral care can feel like trying to stop a flood with a paper towel. We weren't meant to carry every burden alone. This book is a lifeline for clergy who know they're human and still want to serve with wisdom and love. Geoff Goodman doesn't give us more guilt about what we can't do. He gives us companions, tools, and models that remind us care isn't a solo act. It's a sacred collaboration. And Goodman reminds us, there are collaborators already waiting … trained, trusted, and ready to help.

Tony Sundermeier, *senior pastor,*
First Presbyterian Church of Atlanta

Geoff Goodman brings his considerable expertise in attachment theory to examine seven different approaches to spiritual care, how each approach might affect a care receiver's experience of God, and how that relational experience with God changes everything. This work will be helpful to clergy, spiritual directors, psychotherapists, and others, professional and not, who care about helping other people develop spiritually.

Russell Siler Jones, *ThD, LCMHCS, author of*
Spirit in Session: Working with Your Client's Spirituality
(and Your Own) in Psychotherapy

Geoff Goodman has brought a fresh look to spiritually integrated work through the lens of attachment theory. Clergy and mental health professionals would do well to add this book to their professional shelves!

Carol Z.A. McGinnis, *PhD, SIP, BC-TMH, NCC,*
LCPC (MD), professor of counseling, Messiah University

In this book, Geoff Goodman offers a thoroughgoing exploration of applications of attachment theory in the caregiving work of a wide range of practitioners of pastoral and spiritual care. With careful attention to detail and drawing upon his own life experience, case studies as well as psychodynamic theory and practice, Professor Goodman's lucid and accessible text is an exceedingly useful handbook for both teachers and practitioners.

Emmanuel Y. Lartey, *PhD, DD (Honoris Causa),*
Charles Howard Candler Professor of Pastoral Theology & Spiritual
Care, Candler School of Theology & Graduate Division of Religion;
Affiliate Faculty, African American Studies, Emory University;
Inaugural Bishop, North America Diocese, Methodist Church, Ghana

Spiritual Interventions and Attachment

Seven Models for Clergy, Lay Ministers, and Mental Health Professionals

Geoff Goodman

NEW YORK AND LONDON

Designed cover image: Käthe Kollwitz (1920), "Hands Cradling a Child's Head," Allison Mulholland, Weschler's Auctioneers & Appraisers

First published 2026
by Routledge
605 Third Avenue, New York, NY 10158

and by Routledge
4 Park Square, Milton Park, Abingdon, Oxon, OX14 4RN

Routledge is an imprint of the Taylor & Francis Group, an informa business

© 2026 Geoff Goodman

The right of Geoff Goodman to be identified as author of this work has been asserted in accordance with sections 77 and 78 of the Copyright, Designs and Patents Act 1988.

All rights reserved. No part of this book may be reprinted or reproduced or utilised in any form or by any electronic, mechanical, or other means, now known or hereafter invented, including photocopying and recording, or in any information storage or retrieval system, without permission in writing from the publishers.

For Product Safety Concerns and Information please contact our EU representative GPSR@taylorandfrancis.com. Taylor & Francis Verlag GmbH, Kaufingerstraße 24, 80331 München, Germany.

Trademark notice: Product or corporate names may be trademarks or registered trademarks, and are used only for identification and explanation without intent to infringe.

ISBN: 978-1-041-01959-6 (hbk)
ISBN: 978-1-041-01951-0 (pbk)
ISBN: 978-1-003-61711-2 (ebk)

DOI: 10.4324/9781003617112

Typeset in Times New Roman
by KnowledgeWorks Global Ltd.

Jesus of Nazareth

It is not the healthy who need a doctor, but the sick. I have not come to call the righteous, but sinners.

(Mark 2:17, New International Version;
see also Matthew 9:12–13; Luke 5:31–32)

Contents

Acknowledgments	ix
1 Introduction	1

PART I
Models of Spiritual Intervention Conducted by Lay Ministers — 31

2 Stephen Ministry: Carrying Each Other's Burdens — 33

3 Spiritual Direction: An Invitation to the Practice of Contemplation — 49

4 Twelve-Step Programs: Surrendering to the God of Our Understanding — 82

5 Godly Play: Suffer the Little Children to Come Unto Me — 107

PART II
Models of Spiritual Intervention Conducted by Licensed Professionals — 125

6 Using Drawing in a Spirituality Group to Discuss Mental Representations of God — 127

7 Spiritually Integrated Psychotherapy: Introducing Spirituality and Working Through Spiritual Struggles — 142

8 Attachment-Informed Psychotherapy: Transforming Attachment Relationships to a Higher Power and to Parents   178

9 Final Reflections   208

Author Index   *220*
Subject Index   *224*

Acknowledgments

I want to thank all my instructors and mentors for training me in each of the seven models of spiritual intervention presented in this book. Pastor Susannah Wade at Marble Collegiate Church in New York City, along with many Stephen Leaders at Marble (especially Abby Shue and Ted Gregory), came alongside me in my Stephen Ministry training. The always jovial Lori Kem at Stephen Ministries St. Louis trained me to become a Stephen leader. I also want to thank Pastors Katie Sundermeier and Rob Sparks for accepting me as a Stephen Minister at First Presbyterian Church of Atlanta. My care receiver graciously agreed to allow me to present our work together.

Two spiritual directors, Florida Ellis and Julie Johnson, urged me to become a spiritual director at a party on behalf of the Samaritan Counseling Center of Atlanta (SCCA), where they are on staff. I thank these women for supporting my application to the Shalem Institute. I want to thank Phillip C. Stephens (the Shalem Institute program director), Kathleen Talvacchia (my peer group staff contact), and my peer group supervision members (Mary Bieter, John Edwards, Cindy Enger, Erlinda Perlado-Mertens, and Ann Folwell Stanford) for their wisdom, encouragement, and gentle challenge during my spiritual director training. My faith tradition did not provide me with a context to practice contemplation, so the learning curve was at times uncomfortably steep. Having these spiritual lights in my life illuminated my path. My spiritual directee graciously agreed to allow me to present our work together.

I entered a 12-step program in 2009, got sober six months later, and became a sponsor after a year. I want to thank my sponsor, my two sponsees, and my weekly meeting for helping me daily to turn my will and my life over to the care of God. My 12-step program enables me to have close relationships and maintain a work–life balance.

I would like to express gratitude to my two Godly Play instructors, Cynthia Insko and Mary Hunter Maxwell, for their patience with me and my fellow trainees. I would also like to thank all the children who have given me on-the-job training. I dedicate Chapter 5 to the memory of Godly Play founder Jerome Berryman, who died on August 6, 2024.

My group co-leader, Amy Manierre, MDiv, provided me with an opportunity to organize a spirituality group on a psychiatric unit dedicated to the treatment of inpatients diagnosed with borderline personality disorder. I also want to express appreciation to the nursing staff who worked on this unit and to the group participants who graciously shared their beliefs and feelings. Neil Madero and Dolores Burns assisted with the preparation of the patient illustrations (Figures 6.1 and 6.2). I also gratefully acknowledge the assistance of Marcia Miller, chief librarian at this teaching hospital, in locating and obtaining reference materials for Chapter 6.

Carol Pitts, the clinical director of SCCA, urged me to train as a spiritually integrated psychotherapist, which I pursued at the Association for Clinical Pastoral Education (ACPE). I want to acknowledge Russell Siler Jones, Wayne Gustafson, Tere Canzoneri, and Carol McGinnis for their consultation during my spiritually integrated psychotherapy (SIP) training. Russell conducted the SIP curriculum training Modules 1 and 2. In addition to Wayne and Tere, Carol T. Smith and Jamie DeRuyter Swart participated in my SIP training final presentation. Carol McGinnis continues as my community of practice leader. Three of my patients graciously agreed to allow me to present our work together.

As a graduate student at Columbia University in the fall of 1985, Larry Aber introduced me to attachment theory and research, which resulted in a lifelong love affair with studying the development of relationships of all kinds. The following semester, in Ann Belford Ulanov's Union Theological Seminary course, Religion and the Unconscious, I read the classic *Birth of the Living God* by Ana-Maria Rizzuto, which blew my mind. Rizzuto's book is where my psychological understanding of human relationships to God began. Pehr Granqvist, especially through his *Attachment in Religion and Spirituality: A Wider View*, has mentored me in applying attachment theory to the development of human relationships to God. I have appreciated our e-mail correspondence over the past couple of years. Other notable attachment theorists and researchers who have helped me think about the application of attachment theory to clinical practice include John Bowlby, Mary Main, Inge Bretherton, Arietta Slade, Jeremy Holmes, and Peter Fonagy. Each of these persons has left their indelible mark on my clinical understanding. I also need to acknowledge the tremendous supervisors during my adult and child and adolescent psychoanalytic training at the Contemporary Freudian Society in New York City: John Rosegrant, William Greenstadt, Phyllis Sloate, Delia Battin, and the clinically flexible Thomas Lopez. This is the all-star team of psychoanalytic supervisors.

Of course, I must also acknowledge all my patients through the years, who have taught me how to be a more effective therapist and a better version of myself.

I want to thank John Morgenstern at Emory University and Allison Mulholland at Weschler's Auctioneers & Appraisers for helping me to acquire a digital copy of Käthe Kollwitz's (1920) drawing, *Hands Cradling a Child's Head*, for the cover image. Kollwitz's artwork has been a mainstay, covering four of my other books, and I feel grateful to have another of her drawings grace the cover of this book.

I want to express gratitude to my psychoanalyst, Dr. Marvin Markowitz, Andy Phillips, and my spiritual director, Juarlyn Gaiter, for their personal support of me during the writing process. I want to thank Routledge (especially Anna Moore) for believing in my work, and Leonard Rosenbaum, who provided the skill and precision necessary to compile the author and subject indexes. He has contributed his excellent work for all my first-authored books. I appreciate his energy and positivity. My personal editor, Donna Freitas, made some key suggestions early in my writing that transformed the book's entire character. It is now accessible to a wider audience—those who might be seeking help as well as offering it. I appreciate her attention to detail as well as purpose. She also made me believe that my writing meant something to her. I now consider her a friend as well as a colleague. Uli Guthrie contributed her editorial skills to Chapter 2.

On a personal note, I want to thank my close colleagues at Emory University, Wendy Jacobson, Andy Miller, and John Snarey for their support, and Ian McFarland and Ed Phillips, Beth Corrie, and Emmanuel Lartey for their mentorship at the Candler School of Theology. First Presbyterian Church of Atlanta, including pastors Tony and Katie Sundermeier, Rob Sparks, and Barry Gaeddert, continues to provide me every week with spiritual nourishment, encouragement, resources, and support.

My wife, Valeda Dent, reproduced Figure 8.1 in PowerPoint and procured many journal articles for me. She believed that I could write three books in 2 years when I had my doubts. I feel grateful for her encouragement and patience. Finally, my daughter, Carlyn, gives me hope. I thank you for being you.

Geoff Goodman
April 5, 2025

Chapter 1

Introduction

The Purpose of Writing This Book

When I was a first-year student at MIT, I was trying to find my way at an intellectual powerhouse in a bustling urban setting. I was no longer crushing it at a public high school in my dying town in rural Pennsylvania. An addiction that started in high school became much more problematic for me at MIT, probably owing to the stresses of living away from home in an urban environment for the first time as well as having to compete with certifiable geniuses who already knew electromagnetism and differential equations.

In the song, "California," Chappell Roan's (2023) ode to homesickness and failure, she repeats the bridge with a mixture of desperation and resignation no fewer than four consecutive times: "Come get me out." Is she singing these words to herself? To her parents? To God? I get tearful every time I listen to this song, because I know these feelings at a cellular level. Come get me out of this dorm, this university, this big city, this addiction, this life—I thought so often while a student at MIT. Too ashamed to return home, I fantasized about dropping out of school and disappearing into the Salvation Army. I increasingly relied on my addiction to cope with these feelings.

Then I joined a student Christian group on campus called Seekers. Seekers was the name of the college youth group at Park Street Church, a historic Congregational church located in downtown Boston. In many ways, this group saved my life, because I became part of a community who believed in Jesus like I did. Feeling supported by this church and this community, I approached one of the associate pastors and opened up for the first time about my addiction. I was desperately seeking help. This man was completely nonjudgmental and caring, but his recommendation disappointed me: I was to pray to God to take away the addiction. He would also be praying for me. That was it—the sum total of the conversation. There was no follow-up, no other support offered. So I prayed mightily for the addiction to stop. But, like Paul's tormenting "thorn in my flesh" (II Corinthians 12:7, New International Version [NIV]), which he pleaded with God to take away three times (II Corinthians 12:8, NIV), it did not stop. Another

29½ years would pass before I joined a 12-step program that put me on the path of recovery.

Of course, pastoral resources were far fewer in 1980, when I was in college. The pastoral staff at Park Street Church were probably overwhelmed with more serious issues in the congregation such as suicidal behaviors, cancer diagnoses, and family losses. I would have cherished the opportunity to have talked with someone on a regular basis—someone who cared not only about my addiction but also about my feeling homesick and not measuring up academically for the first time in my life. I would have benefited from talking with a Stephen Minister, a spiritual director, a sponsor, a therapist—anybody who could help me carry the burden of my addiction. Fortunately, we now have more spiritual resources at our disposal. This book discusses some of the most significant spiritual resources currently available.

The idea for this book came out of writing my first two books in this series: *Using Psychoanalytic Techniques to Transform the Attachment Relationship to God: Our Refuge and Strength* (Goodman, 2025b) and *Practical Applications of Transforming the Attachment Relationship to God: Using Attachment-Informed Psychotherapy* (Goodman, 2025a; both books published by Routledge). Psychotherapy is not the only model of spiritual intervention available to which clergy can refer congregants. On the contrary, there is a whole array of spiritual interventions that have their own separate literatures, but no one place where these spiritual interventions have been discussed, compared, and contrasted. I wanted to write a book for both clergy and licensed mental health professionals as a primary source for what is available to persons seeking spiritual meaning for their lives.

I selected each of the seven models of spiritual intervention presented in this book because I have had the good fortune of having been trained in each one. Thus, I discuss each of these models from the inside out—an insider's look at each model, if you will.

I wrote this book for my 18-year-old self, the self who had no spiritual resources to lean on other than my weekly college youth group. I wrote this book to inform not only seekers of spiritual help but also clergy, lay ministers, and licensed mental health professionals (i.e., "allies") about seven models of spiritual intervention aimed specifically at seekers of spiritual meaning. Clergy and lay ministers can learn and conduct four of these models, while licensed mental health professionals can learn and conduct the other three. I also wrote this book to identify models of spiritual intervention that might be unfamiliar to some clergy, lay ministers, and licensed mental health professionals. This book not only describes each model but also demonstrates how each one works and how to receive training in each one.

I view these seven models of spiritual intervention as extensions of pastoral care, which consists of direct contact between a lay minister or professional, serving in a helping capacity, and a congregant, presenting as a care seeker. I believe in the importance of highlighting these models because there is ample anecdotal evidence that some clergy can feel burned out by the overwhelming spiritual, emotional, and physical needs of their congregations.

A clergy member courageous enough to share her experience, Karen Scheib (2018) discusses what it was like to pastor her dream church:

> I was the always-available pastor who didn't take a day off and couldn't say no to anyone in need. At one point, I even took into the parsonage a homeless woman with two children under the age of five. Even at the time I knew it was not a good idea. After six years of being in ministry, I was burned-out, my marriage had come to an end, and I had decided to begin a doctoral program as a way of escape. ... I felt like a failure in my personal and professional life. (pp. 43–44)

Scheib eventually realized, perhaps too late, that her way of doing ministry was not sustainable.

Scheib is not alone in feeling alone. J. R. Briggs (2014) reports that many clergy feel pressure to meet benchmarks of success, established by their diocese or denominational conference, that consist of the three Bs—*"buildings, bodies and budget* [emphasis in original], marked by three questions: How many? How often? How much?" (p. 63). According to Briggs (2014), clergy "feel sky-high expectations and unbearable pressures and believe it impossible to meet the demands so many place on them" (p. 48). As church attendance is dramatically declining (Jones, 2024), church leaders nevertheless expect clergy to maintain their operating expenses (including their own salaries) and congregational services with less revenue. Clergy are now chafing under these new financial pressures like the ancient enslaved Israelites whom Pharaoh commanded to make bricks without straw while still maintaining their daily brick quota (Exodus 5:6–9, NIV). This problem needs creative solutions to maintain the spiritual, emotional, and financial well-being of our clergy. The creative solution proposed in this book is the clergy's expanded reliance on partners and allies to meet their congregations' needs, consistent with the New Testament's declaration that all believers are "a chosen people, a royal priesthood" (I Peter 2:9, NIV). Models of spiritual intervention conducted by lay ministers and licensed mental health professionals can help to relieve the enormous burden experienced by today's clergy. Clergy do not have to go it alone. Help is available, and these models more than pay for themselves in clergy peace of mind and overall congregational well-being. I could have benefited from spiritual resources offered by a lay minister or licensed professional, if only I had known about them.

Definition of Spiritual Intervention and Related Constructs

As you begin reading this book, you might be interested in knowing what I mean by the constructs "spirituality," "spiritual intervention," "religion," "lay minister," "licensed professional," and "pastoral care." According to two pioneers of Spiritually Integrated Psychotherapy (SIP), Kenneth Pargament and Julie Exline (2022), the essence of spirituality is "the capacity to see domains of life ... through a sacred lens, imbuing them with deeper divine-like character and significance" (p. 6). Earlier in his career, Pargament (1999) defined "spirituality" as "a search for the sacred" (p. 12). In Chapter 7, I note how this definition risks circularity because it begs for a definition of "sacred." Despite the circularity, it does provide a starting point for a definition of a spiritual intervention:

> A spiritual intervention consists of an intentional action based on a caregiver's body of knowledge, skills, and training for the purpose of facilitating a care receiver's search for the sacred.

Consistent with the framework of attachment theory that I use to discuss each of the seven models of spiritual intervention introduced in this book, caregivers use spiritual interventions to restore a secure attachment relationship to a Higher Power. My intended audience consists of caregivers who believe in a monotheistic, personified Higher Power as well as receivers of this care. Although my intended audience does not consist of persons who believe in pantheism or practice nontheistic religions, even these persons might believe in a Higher Power. One school of Buddhism (a traditionally nontheistic religion) believes that "human, physical, moral, and spiritual capacities were so corrupted that men and women needed to rely on some other power, the Buddha, to save them" (Kennedy, 1995, p. 24). Pehr Granqvist (2020) also indicates that "one of the most common Buddhist prayers is 'I take refuge in the Buddha'" (p. 67). Thus, the seven models of spiritual intervention discussed here could have a wider application than for those persons who adhere to a belief in a monotheistic, personified Higher Power.

Religion and spirituality experience a "tenuous coexistence" (Griffith, 2010, p. 36). I define religion as consisting of the institutions that espouse a particular set of doctrines related to worship of the sacred. By contrast, spirituality is a personal experience of the sacred in a person's life. This book focuses on the restoration of a care receiver's spirituality as viewed through the lens of attachment theory. Spirituality and spiritual interventions designed to restore a secure attachment relationship to the sacred are what this book is about. My pastor at Park Street Church, for example, prescribed petitionary prayer without getting to know me or my personal spirituality. The caregivers using the spiritual interventions described herein strive to get to know a care receiver's personal spirituality, to make a connection with the care receiver that ultimately points to a Higher Power Who cares deeply for that care receiver and wants nothing but to love this person.

I categorize these seven models of spiritual intervention in a 2 × 2 typology, with the type of caregiver (lay minister vs. licensed professional) and the type of spiritual intervention (explicit vs. implicit) intersecting along two orthogonal

Table 1.1 Typology Presenting Models of Spiritual Intervention Based on Type of Caregiver and Type of Spiritual Intervention

Type of Spiritual Intervention	Type of Caregiver	
	Lay Minister	Licensed Professional
Explicit	Stephen Ministry Spiritual Direction 12-step programs Godly Play	Spirituality groups Spiritually Integrated Psychotherapy Attachment-Informed Psychotherapy
Implicit	Community outreach (e.g., Habitat for Humanity*) Humanistic organizations (e.g., New York Society for Ethical Culture,* Up with People*)	Spiritually Integrated Psychotherapy Attachment-Informed Psychotherapy

* Not covered in this book.

axes (see Table 1.1). *I define a lay minister as someone who has not necessarily received formal ministerial training but nevertheless implements models of spiritual intervention.* Lay ministers can implement these models explicitly (i.e., addressing relationship to a Higher Power) or implicitly (i.e., addressing meaning in one's life). Examples of lay ministers addressing spirituality explicitly include Stephen Ministry (see Chapter 2), Spiritual Direction (see Chapter 3), 12-step programs (see Chapter 4), and Godly Play (see Chapter 5). Examples of "lay ministers" addressing spirituality implicitly include community outreach programs such as Habitat for Humanity and humanistic organizations such as the New York Society for Ethical Culture and Up with People. I do not cover this lower left quadrant, primarily because the term "lay minister" does not accurately depict these organizations' membership. These organizations, however, do represent models of quasi-spiritual intervention overseen by nonclergy.

By contrast, *I define a licensed professional as someone who has received specialized training in a mental health profession (e.g., psychiatry, clinical or counseling psychology, social work, psychiatric nursing practice) and holds a state license in their profession to practice psychotherapy.* Licensed professionals can address spirituality explicitly or implicitly, depending on the patient's needs (see Chapters 7 and 8). Spirituality groups address spirituality explicitly because that is their stated purpose (see Chapter 6). SIP (see Chapter 7) and attachment-informed psychotherapy (AIP; see Chapter 8), however, take place with an ear firmly pressed to the ground to listen for spiritual vibrations in the patient's narrative, which the therapist can make manifest or allow to lie dormant. SIP and AIP therapists must be skilled at knowing when to make spirituality explicit and when to keep it implicit. A lay minister does not typically cultivate the awareness of such nuance.

Models of Pastoral Care

How do these seven models of spiritual intervention overlap with pastoral care? *I define pastoral care as a pastor's direct or indirect provision of spiritual care to a congregant or group of congregants that often overlaps with emotional and social support.* In this book, I discuss seven models of pastoral care that do *not* include a pastor's direct provision of spiritual care. The interested reader can find many other excellent resources about pastoral care such as Cooper-White (2011), Doehring (2015), Dykstra (2005), Lartey (2003), Patton (1993), Ramsay (2004), and Scheib (2016).

John Patton (1993) discusses three paradigms of pastoral care. The clinical paradigm of pastoral care, which is most relevant here, has ascended in popularity in the past 80 years, since the advent of modern psychology, and focuses on the knowledge, skills, and training of clergy to meet the spiritual and emotional needs of congregants (Patton, 1993). This paradigm focuses on the mystical authority of Carl Rogers (1980), a clinical psychologist best known for developing person-centered psychotherapy. Rogers (1957) identifies three simple ingredients of psychotherapy: empathy, genuineness, and unconditional positive regard. Models of spiritual intervention such as Stephen Ministry (see Chapter 2) and Spiritual Direction (see Chapter 3) rely on the use of these three ingredients in their interactions with care receivers. Jesus, however, relies on a wider range of intervention tools in communicating empathy than does Rogers (Goodman, 1991). Because of its nearly ubiquitous use in pastoral care settings, Lartey (2003) points out that "the tried-and-tested person-centered values of humanistic counseling, baptized with healthy doses of liberal Western theology, become the underlying premises upon which the practice of universal pastoral counseling is based" (p. 164). As I emphasize in Chapter 2, person-centered spiritual intervention might be transformative for some care receivers, but, for others (perhaps having grown up in a non-Western culture), a one-size-fits-all approach might fail.

In addition to the clinical paradigm, Patton (1993) articulates two other paradigms that have characterized pastoral care in the history of the Christian church: the classical paradigm and the communal contextual paradigm. The classical paradigm predominated from the time of Jesus to the advent of modern psychology. This paradigm focused on "the caring elements in Christian theology and tradition" (p. 10). A caricature of this paradigm would be a pastor telling a congregant having an affair to "leave your life of sin," which Jesus said to the woman caught in adultery (John 8:11, NIV). Again, the pastor of Park Street Church was using the classical paradigm of pastoral care in responding to my disclosure of addiction.

The communal contextual paradigm of pastoral care emphasizes an egalitarian approach that supports lay ministers as a viable caring community. This caring also includes a keen awareness of the care receiver's positionality, including their age, race and ethnicity, gender and gender identity, sexual orientation, socioeconomic status, citizenship status, and cultural background. This third paradigm enables lay ministers to provide pastoral care. Patton (1993) argues that clergy need all three paradigms of pastoral care "to rethink and carry out the pastoral care of the church at this point in history" (p. 11). The seven models of spiritual intervention emphasize the clinical paradigm of pastoral care, but some of them also draw on other paradigms such as the classical (e.g., Stephen Ministry; see Chapter 2) and the communal contextual (e.g., spirituality group; see Chapter 6).

A fourth paradigm, the intercultural paradigm, emphasizes the interconnection among three aspects of humanity. Lartey (2003) explains that human beings are "1) like all others, 2) like some others, and 3) like no other" (p. 34). According to Lartey (2003), "Interculturality ... speaks of living in the three spheres—being centered in the intersection of the universal, the cultural and the individual within living, colourful persons" (p. 35). Although all humans share sociality, language, and a host of other traits, group differences also exist in which experiences are not universally shared. Race, class, gender, sexual orientation, religion, and culture represent group experiences not shared by other groups. Humans also have unique experiences not shared by anyone else. Lartey (2003) argues that intercultural caregivers must attend to all three spheres to respond to the total needs of the care receiver.

Thus, caregivers like me who are members of the dominant culture (or race or gender or religion) must take exquisite care to examine our own cultural norms, especially our individualism and privilege (Ramsay, 2004), to protect our care receivers from unexamined assumptions that we can easily make about them. On my own intercultural journey, I learned through first-hand experience that, no matter how empathic I think I am, I will never know what it means to be black, to be a woman, or to be gay in the society in which I live. In 2020, Black Lives Matter was staging protests across the country, and my wife, Valeda, who is black, and I participated in these protests, catalyzed by the murder of George Floyd, a black man who suffocated to death at the hands of a white police officer, Derek Chauvin. It was in this fraught sociopolitical context that Valeda and I had some frank conversations about race and what it means to be black in America. I learned things about Valeda's experience I never knew before in our 12 years of marriage. She told me that, while she is shopping in clothing stores, store clerks often follow her around. I have never had that experience. Whenever a police officer stops her in her car, for a minor infraction such as a rolling stop at a stop sign, Valeda immediately puts her sweaty palms on the steering wheel at 10 and 2. I have never had to do that. I have never had to *think* to do that. My survival in these situations has never been at stake—and not because I have never been pulled over. In our conversations, Valeda recounted many such frustrating and frightening experiences living in this country that I have never experienced. Why is that the case?

At some point in one of our conversations, I had a sudden realization: no matter how empathic and loving and understanding and well-meaning I am as Valeda's husband and friend, I will never—in my gut—know what it is like to be a black person in America. The reason, of course, is that I am not black, and I will never be black. That realization came with a profound feeling of sadness—there will always be a barrier to my understanding of Valeda's experience as a black woman living in this country. The best I can do is to imagine what her experience might be like. To try to understand her experience, I can conjure up moments from my life where I felt ostracized. But I know that my imagination and my memories will never allow me to comprehend fully her experience as a black woman living in America.

Upon further reflection, I also feel sadness that, because I will never fully understand Valeda's experience as a black woman living in America, I will never fully understand my own privilege as a member of the dominant race and gender. It is only through the loss of something that the something can be truly known. Therefore, I would only fully know my privilege as a white man in this society if it were taken away from me. Of course, my whiteness and my maleness are permanent characteristics of who I am, so I will never know the loss of these characteristics. Not knowing their loss, I can never fully know the privilege attached to their presence.

I bring up the limitations of my empathy for Valeda because the sobering reality of these limitations bears directly on who I am as a caregiver. Humility is essential to the caregiving relationship. If I think I know someone's experience—I mean really know it in my gut—I am fooling myself, and so would you be if you thought the same. Curiosity for a care receiver's experience is an essential feature of all transformative caregiving relationships, but I must simultaneously realize that I will never know—in my gut—their experience. My comprehension is always relative, never absolute. Even though this book primarily explores Patton's (1993) clinical paradigm, I never want to lose sight of the communal contextual and intercultural paradigms, because they point us to the larger sociocultural context in which both caregivers and care receivers live. The cultivation of my humility came out of a sociopolitical movement that prompted frank conversations with Valeda about her experience as a black woman living in this country. I know that my realization in 2020 has made me a more humble, more effective caregiver in each of the seven models of spiritual intervention that I both practice and write about in this book.

Images of Pastoral Care

I want to discuss briefly Robert Dykstra's (2005) *Images of Pastoral Care*, because the mental representations of pastoral care that we hold critically influence how we implement pastoral care. I am offering a new image of pastoral care that undergirds the seven models of spiritual intervention. Dykstra (2005) presents a compendium of images of pastoral care, beginning with the founder of pastoral care, Anton Boisen. These images of pastoral care tell us something about the historical epoch in which each image emerged as well as the prevailing priorities of clergy caring for their congregants during that epoch. Writing in the early 20th century, Boison viewed a person as a living human document (Dykstra, 2005), which emphasizes the value of narrative in spiritual intervention. In subsequent epochs, other images of pastoral care have emerged (Dykstra, 2005): the living human web (Miller-McLemore), the solicitous shepherd (Hiltner), the wounded healer (Nouwen), the wise fool (Campbell), the intimate stranger (Dykstra), the midwife (Hanson), and the gardener (Kornfeld). What does each model imply about the pastoral caregiver? What does each model imply about the care receiver?

None of these images emphasizes the attachment relationship between the pastoral caregiver and the care receiver. Miller-McLemore's pastoral image of the living human web comes closest, but it implies that all relationships are egalitarian. Can a person say that one thread of a spider's web is more important than the others? Yet attachment theory clearly articulates a hierarchy of relationships from most to least important (see below). Infants attach to caregivers whom they perceive as "stronger and/or wiser" (Bowlby, 1988, p. 120) and therefore meet their attachment needs for protection and comfort. Infants establish a hierarchy of caregivers—primary, secondary, tertiary—on whom they rely when they experience distress. The pastoral image of the living human web does not adequately capture this hierarchy of caregiving relationships.

How do we know that congregants form attachment relationships to their pastoral caregivers, whether clergy or nonclergy? Pastoral theologian James Dittes (Dykstra, 2005) suggests that the ideal pastoral image is that of the ascetic witness. He believes that the pastoral encounter with a congregant "is decidedly *not* [emphasis in original] an occasion for building a 'relationship.' ... The pastoral counselor maintains the same studied aloofness and nonchalance without the buffer of screen or notepad" (p. 145). This pastoral image suggests that the pastoral caregiver is simply a witness or observer, never a participant. Interpersonal psychiatrist Harry Stack Sullivan (1953) discovered that the effective psychotherapist is not only a passive observer of the patient but also an active participant in the construction of a therapeutic relationship with the patient, which serves as the vehicle of transformation. This transformation takes place not only in the patient but also in the therapist. Influenced by attachment theory, later clinical theorists and researchers identified the presence of "interaction structures" in the study of the psychotherapy process. Interaction structures are patterns of reciprocal interaction in which both therapist and patient participate, often outside their awareness. The therapist is responsible for becoming aware of these interaction structures and sharing this awareness with the patient (Jones, 2000).

Persons, spiritual or nonspiritual, tend to relate (or refuse to relate) to God in a manner that reflects how they relate (or refuse to relate) to significant others, especially caregivers during childhood. In psychoanalytic theory, we refer to this phenomenon as "transference" (Freud, 1912)—we transfer onto another person the feelings, attitudes, fantasies, wishes, and fears that we experienced with our caregivers during childhood. We typically consider these persons to whom we transfer our mental states stronger and wiser when they offer caregiving to us. When I was in first grade, my teacher, Mrs. Wolf, helped me put on my bulky winter coat. I immediately said, "Thanks, Mommy," then quickly corrected myself. I felt embarrassed that I had called her "Mommy," but such is the power of transference. In that moment, she was behaving like my mother. Our responses to people who behave like caregivers in our lives can vary widely.

We must also filter our images of pastoral care through our sociocultural lens. If my image of God, received from my religious tradition, is "KING OF KINGS AND LORD OF LORDS" (Revelation 19:16, NIV), and the ruler of my country is literally a king who detains and kills political prisoners, steals the wealth of his people to enrich himself, and instigates tensions between various factions to maintain control of the masses, I might not want to believe in such a God, much less worship Him. I might, therefore, reject approaches to pastoral care that embrace this God imagery. If I view God as a colonizer who forces people to submit to His will, then I will not trust God to protect me; rather, God might actually victimize me (Lartey & Moon, 2020). Main and Hesse (1990) discuss the dilemma of the disorganized/disoriented infant in the Strange Situation procedure (see below): during reunion episodes, the infant perceives the caregiver as "*at once the source of and the solution to [their] alarm* [emphasis in original]" (p. 163). We can imagine a disorganized/disoriented relationship to God developing if a person's only choice offered by their religious tradition is to believe in an image of God that raises alarm while simultaneously offering solace from that alarm. Caregivers need to be aware of the damaging images of God and of pastoral care that could prevent someone from seeking that care in the first place.

Every model of spiritual intervention described in the chapters that follow includes a caregiver and a care receiver. The caregiver is always vulnerable to the care receiver's transference, which is not always one of gratitude for the care provided. Transference occurs in practically every caregiving relationship and can arouse peculiar emotional reactions in the caregiver in direct response to the care receiver's transference. This phenomenon is known as countertransference (Wallin, 2007). The resulting transference–countertransference matrix is another way of describing interaction structures, which form in every caregiving relationship. Thus, Dittes's "aloofness and nonchalance" (Dykstra, 2005, p. 145) could be a countertransference reaction to the care receiver's attitude toward the caregiver.

As a long-time patient in my own therapy, I would not want an aloof or nonchalant therapist. I did not need an aloof or nonchalant pastor at Park Street Church. These qualities might also trigger an iatrogenic effect—the emergence of certain transference feelings directly related to my therapist's or pastor's unfortunate interaction style and not my past caregiving relationships. Thus, the causality between transference and countertransference reactions is bidirectional. These interaction structures emerge, however, only in a consciously (or unconsciously) recognized attachment relationship that consists of a stronger, wiser caregiver trying to help a less-strong, less-wise care receiver.

I would like to offer a new image of pastoral care that incorporates these insights. The ideal image of pastoral care is the spiritually responsive attachment figure. This image acknowledges the attachment relationship that inevitably forms between a pastoral caregiver and a care receiver. The pastoral caregiver responds to the spiritual needs of the care receiver in the context of an attachment relationship. The pastoral caregiver does not meet these spiritual needs but rather responds to them by bearing witness. That can include making the care receiver aware that their spiritual needs exist, in an explicit or even implicit spiritual intervention that a SIP therapist might implement (see Chapter 7). Only a Higher Power can satisfy spiritual needs. Stephen Ministry often points out in its literature and training that God is the "Curegiver" (Bretscher, 2020; Haugk, 2020). The responsibility of the spiritually responsive attachment figure is to recognize the presence of the attachment relationship and to use this relationship to respond to the care receiver's spiritual needs. These spiritual needs include the need to restore or enhance the security of the care receiver's attachment relationship to a Higher Power. Only the grace of God can satisfy a care receiver's spiritual needs, but the spiritually responsive attachment figure can facilitate this restored or enhanced connection.

Application of Attachment Theory as an Organizing Framework

I use attachment theory to evaluate critically each of the seven models of spiritual intervention, because attachment theory has much to offer in helping us to understand pastoral care. Attachment theory helps us to clarify the meaning of a person's relationship to a caregiver and to a Higher Power. Under specific conditions, a caregiver serves as an attachment figure. According to Bowlby (1988),

> As a rule careseeking is shown by a weaker and less experienced individual towards someone regarded as stronger and/or wiser. A child, or older person in the careseeking role, keeps within range of the caregiver, the degree of closeness or of ready accessibility depending on circumstances: hence the concept of attachment behaviour. (p. 120)

Attachment behavior is activated when the care receiver "seeks protection and/or comfort" (p. 123) from the caregiver. Elsewhere, Bowlby (1977) proclaims that attachment behavior "is held to characterize human beings from the cradle to the grave" (p. 203). Thus, even adults need the protection and comfort of someone stronger and wiser. In a different book (Goodman, 2025b), I argue that a Higher Power is ideally suited to serve this purpose for human beings.

The attachment concept of a secure base contains the idea that a caregiver provides protection for the care receiver in the background as the care receiver explores the environment. Traditionally in attachment theory, this care receiver is represented as an infant, but, as Bowlby (1977) indicates, we never outgrow the need for a secure base. A safe haven, a complementary attachment concept, contains the idea that a caregiver provides comfort for the care receiver when internal or external threats to homeostasis cause the care receiver to become distressed. Thus, a caregiving relationship proceeds when the care receiver (e.g., patient, client, spiritual directee, sponsee) uses the caregiver to explore themselves and their relationships and to seek proximity to receive comfort when confronted by distressing internal and external threats. Not only spiritually responsive attachment figures but also a Higher Power can provide these attachment functions (see below and Chapter 8).

The Role of Attachment Theory in Individualizing Spiritual Care

Attachment theory is the lens through which I evaluate these seven models of spiritual intervention. Attachment theory gained prominence in the 1950s through the pioneering work of British psychiatrist and psychoanalyst John Bowlby (e.g., 1958), who observed orphaned children during the London Blitz and in the aftermath of World War II. Bowlby also became acquainted with the ethological research of Harry Harlow (e.g., 1958) and applied all these insights to form a new theory of how and why infants become attached to their caregivers. For Bowlby (1982), infants spend the first year of their life developing expectations of their caregivers' behavior that help them to seek proximity and maintain contact during moments when they feel frightened or fatigued or upset. According to Bowlby (1982), infants evolved to seek proximity to and maintain contact with their caregivers to protect themselves from predators or other unknown dangers in the environment.

The attachment system is a behavioral control system that alerts the infant to these dangers and prompts the infant to reduce the physical distance between them and the caregiver. When the environment does not pose any danger, the infant's exploratory system is activated, allowing the infant to extend their physical distance from the caregiver to explore and learn from the environment. The degree to which the caregiver provides a secure base from which the infant can explore the environment and a safe haven to which the infant can return in times of perceived danger determines how securely attached the infant is to the caregiver.

Mary Ainsworth, a Canadian developmental psychologist and doctoral student of Bowlby's, studied individual differences in infant attachment

(Goodman, 2014). For her doctoral dissertation, Ainsworth (1967) conducted an ethnographic study of Ugandan caregivers and infants and then assumed a position at Johns Hopkins University, where she created a procedure for studying these individual differences systematically (Karen, 1998). Using what she called the Strange Situation procedure, Ainsworth (Ainsworth & Wittig, 1969) published her first study on 23 infants and caregivers recruited from the Baltimore area. In this procedure, the infant and caregiver participate in a series of eight 3-minute episodes that include two separations from and two reunions with the caregiver. What Ainsworth discovered from this first study revolutionized the fields of developmental and clinical psychology. Approximately 65% of the infants expressed distress during the caregiver separations and proximity-seeking and contact-maintenance during the reunions (i.e., activation of the attachment system), with a prompt return to play (i.e., activation of the exploratory system). She labeled this attachment pattern "secure" (type B). Approximately 20% of the infants expressed only moderate distress during the caregiver separations and a slight turning away from or snubbing of the caregiver during the reunions, continuing their play. She labeled this attachment pattern "anxious-avoidant" (type A). Approximately 15% of the infants expressed intense distress during the caregiver separations and an ambivalent response to the caregiver during the reunions, alternately seeking contact and resisting it when offered. Ainsworth labeled this attachment pattern "anxious-resistant" or "anxious-ambivalent" (type C). These different patterns of attachment organization were unanticipated and produced subsequent theoretical advances (Ainsworth et al., 1978).

Ainsworth and her colleagues (Ainsworth et al., 1978) also identified routine caregiving patterns during the first 12 months associated with these three attachment patterns. Caregivers of securely attached infants were emotionally responsive to their infants' cries of distress and immediately gratified their needs. Caregivers of anxious-avoidant infants often rejected their infants' needs for physical contact. Caregivers of anxious-resistant infants were often inconsistent in meeting their infants' needs.

Mary Main, a doctoral student of Ainsworth's, identified a fourth attachment pattern that she labeled "disorganized/disoriented" (type D). Infants who display this attachment pattern appear disorganized and disoriented during the Strange Situation reunion episodes with the caregiver—running around in circles, freezing in place for 30 or more seconds, and lying prone on the floor, to name just a few observed behaviors of infants in this category (Main & Solomon, 1990). Approximately 15% of infants meet criteria for this classification (van IJzendoorn et al., 1999) but are also assigned a secondary attachment classification from one of the traditional attachment categories (i.e., A, B, C). Researchers have identified several caregiver antecedents of disorganized attachment: caregiver history of childhood abuse and general maltreatment (Carlson et al., 1989a, 1989b; Lyons-Ruth et al., 1989), caregiver depression (Lyons-Ruth et al., 1986, 1990, 1997), caregiver unresolved childhood trauma (Ainsworth & Eichberg, 1991), and caregiver frightening behavior directed toward the infant (Hesse & Main, 1999; Lyons-Ruth et al., 1999; Main & Hesse, 1990; Schuengel et al., 1999). Disorganized attachment has been associated with more severe forms of psychopathology such as dissociative identity disorder (e.g., Carlson, 1998).

Main also developed an interview method of assessing attachment patterns in adolescence and adulthood (Main et al., 1985). She reasoned that infants begin to develop repositories of these expectations of caregiver behavior in their minds that she called "internal working models" (see also Bowlby, 1980) or "attachment representations." According to Main and her colleagues (1985): "Individual differences in these internal working models will therefore be related not only to individual differences in patterns of nonverbal behavior but also to patterns of language and structures of mind" (p. 67). Main and her colleagues developed the Adult Attachment Interview (AAI; George et al., 1996) and a companion classification system (Main & Goldwyn, 1994) that yields the three traditional attachment patterns and a fourth attachment pattern associated with childhood abuse and trauma, which is the adult analogue of disorganized/disoriented attachment in infancy. Main argued that the patterns of behavior identified by Ainsworth in infancy could predict patterns of behavior as well as language in adulthood, which was demonstrated in a 20-year longitudinal study (Waters et al., 2000). In adulthood, behavioral assessments of attachment break down; it is doubtful that anyone reading this book right now is scanning the environment in search of their primary caregiver.

Thus, researchers use the AAI classification system to analyze how a person discusses their relationships, particularly relationships with caregivers during childhood (ages 5–12). Slade (1999) extended this thinking about attachment patterns to what she calls a person's "primary mode of relatedness" (p. 588), in which the internal working model governs their patterns of interaction with significant others. Daniel (2015) explored these primary modes of relatedness as they relate to the four attachment patterns from the research of Main (Hesse & Main, 2000). Daniel identified nine "interpersonal markers" (p. 115) that characterize each of the four primary modes of relatedness. These markers include proximity/distance, trust/expectations of others, attitude to seeking and receiving help, expression and regulation of emotions, self-image/self-esteem, openness and self-disclosure, dependence/independence, conflict management, and empathy.

The Role of Attachment Theory Across Cultures

Ever since Ainsworth (1967) completed her groundbreaking doctoral dissertation in rural Uganda almost 60 years ago, attachment research has withstood cross-cultural scrutiny. Researchers have identified the same four attachment patterns in many Western and non-Western cultures, although the percentages sometimes differ from culture to culture (Mesman et al., 2018). In every culture studied thus far, children "were observed to show attachment behavior in stressful circumstances and to have a preferential bond with one or more caregivers" (Mesman et al., 2018, p. 866). Socioeconomic hardship and other adverse circumstances seem to attenuate the percentage of attachment security in many cultures. In addition, the percentages of the type of attachment insecurity (i.e., anxious-avoidance or anxious-resistance) can vary by cultural milieu. For example, compared with US samples, Anglo-Saxon and European samples tend to feature higher percentages of anxious-avoidance and lower percentages of anxious-resistance, while Asian samples tend to feature higher percentages of anxious-resistance and lower percentages of anxious-avoidance (Mesman et al., 2018).

Nevertheless, in every culture studied thus far, researchers have identified all four attachment patterns. Attachment behavior is a universal phenomenon, not a cultural one. Culture seems to play a role, however, in the relative percentages of attachment insecurity. Thus, in attachment theory, we find that the human is both "like all others" and "like some others" (Lartey, 2003, p. 34).

Of all the psychoanalytic theories that I have studied, attachment theory has been the most serious about earnestly investigating these cultural differences and their meaning. I argue elsewhere (Goodman, 2025b) that these group differences in attachment patterns require different therapeutic techniques to address the relational problems that care receivers often seek to address in psychotherapy. A one-size-fits-all treatment strategy such as person-centered psychotherapy will not do. As Lartey (2003) points out, "[Pastoral care as currently practiced] must not be assumed to be [of great value] for all in multicultural societies ... comprising diverse groups of people" (p. 165).

Let us turn to each of the four attachment patterns and describe their corresponding prototypes based on these nine interpersonal markers so that the reader can refer back to them during each chapter that follows.

Securely Attached Person

The securely attached person feels comfortable with proximity and physical contact with others. They find meaning in interactions with others. They generally trust others (unless given a reason not to) and hold positive expectations of others. The securely attached person is open to seeking help from others when they cannot do something by themselves. They express their emotions in a balanced manner; their self-image is generally positive, yet realistic and nuanced; consequently, they generally have positive self-esteem. The securely attached person makes appropriate self-disclosures, neither oversharing nor being secretive about their personal self. They can depend on others for emotional support in committed relationships but can balance this tendency with self-reliance and autonomy. They can formulate creative solutions to interpersonal conflict. Relatedly, the securely attached person demonstrates empathy with and care for others as well as themselves (Daniel, 2015).

Westen and his colleagues (2006) developed the Adolescent Attachment Prototype Questionnaire (AAPQ) as an alternative method of assessing attachment patterns, creating a narrative prototype characterizing each attachment pattern. Here is their characterization of the securely attached prototype:

> Patients who match this prototype tend to expect that they can rely on the availability and sensitivity of the people they love. They are able to become emotionally close and express affection toward significant others. They tend to feel comfortable depending on others and having others depend on them, and they tend to feel calmed and comforted by contact and support they receive when distressed. They are generally sensitive to other people's "signals," tend to be empathic and emotionally "present," and are able to problem solve and think constructively when in emotionally difficult interpersonal situations. They tend to have balanced, realistic views of significant others and view themselves as lovable and worthy of care. Individuals who match this prototype are able to explore and talk openly about emotionally significant events, even when doing so is painful. They are generally able to tell coherent narratives about significant life events, answer comfortably when asked for details and examples, and reflect on their childhood and its effects on who they are today. (p. 1082)

This narrative provides some convergent validity with the narrative provided earlier based on Daniel's (2015) nine interpersonal markers characterizing a securely attached person.

Anxious-Avoidant Person

The anxious-avoidant person feels uncomfortable with proximity and physical contact with others. They tend to dismiss or devalue interactions with others and ignore or conceal feelings of insecurity related to possible rejection or ridicule. The anxious-avoidant person prefers to work independently, even when they need help. They tend to restrict their emotional expressions, especially negative emotions, and instead present a false positivity in most interactions. The anxious-avoidant person displays an exaggerated view of themselves to compensate for low self-esteem. They seem secretive regarding personal information and value autonomy over relationship. The anxious-avoidant person tends to avoid conflict because it makes them feel uncomfortable. Their capacity for empathy is limited, expressing an interpersonal coldness (Daniel, 2015).

Here is Westen and his colleagues' (2006) characterization of the anxious-avoidant prototype:

> Patients who match this prototype tend to minimize or dismiss the importance of close relationships. They are uncomfortable with emotional intimacy,

physical contact, etc. They tend to derive a sense of self-worth by being independent and self-sufficient and disparage sentimentality, tenderness, or discussion or expression of feelings. When distressed, they tend to withdraw or attempt to cope by themselves. They may overly idealize their parents or attachment figures, having trouble acknowledging their imperfections. Alternatively, they may disparage, contemptuously derogate, or belittle their parents or their role in their own development in an attempt to dismiss their importance. Patients who match this prototype have minimal access to specific memories from childhood and little interest in exploring or retrieving them. They tend to offer sparse narratives about interpersonal events and appear unwilling or unable to describe interpersonal experiences in detail or to provide specific examples. They often offer generalizations about their significant relationships that do not cohere with supporting details (e.g., they may describe their relationship with their mother as "loving" but, when pressed for specific examples, provide memories that seem distant or unpleasant). They tend to take an excessively pragmatic approach to language, having no use for "wasted words." (pp. 1082–1083)

This narrative seems to converge with the interpersonal markers of this attachment category articulated by Daniel (2015).

Anxious-Resistant Person

The anxious-resistant person tends to dissolve interpersonal boundaries, constantly seeking proximity and physical contact but feeling dissatisfied when achieved. They feel as though they are being abandoned or losing the attention of others and expect abandonment to occur at any moment. The anxious-resistant person often feels helpless, expressing a desire for help even on tasks that they could be reasonably expected to complete themselves. They express their emotions frequently and dramatically, especially negative emotions. The anxious-resistant person experiences low self-esteem and tries to compensate by seeking interpersonal validation. They make frequent self-disclosures that seem tangential and often irrelevant to the situation and also feel dependent on others, constantly seeking out relationships. They hold resentments and often escalate conflict. The anxious-resistant person is preoccupied by others' feelings and gets entangled, often attributing their own feelings to others, which severely limits their capacity for empathy (Daniel, 2015).

Here is Westen and his colleagues' (2006) characterization of the anxious-resistant prototype:

> Individuals who match this prototype seek intense emotional intimacy with others but constantly feel ambivalent about them. They tend to experience significant others (within and without the family) as less accessible or

> responsive than they want them to be, leading to distress, frustration, anger, anxiety, passive helplessness, etc. They may feel smothered by significant others at the same time as never quite given enough, taken care of well enough, etc. When distressed, they turn to significant others for comfort, but they chronically feel disappointed. They may protest that they want autonomy or distance from attachment figures while behaving in ways that keep them uncomfortably involved or overinvolved. Individuals who match this prototype tend to have trouble staying on topic when discussing significant interpersonal events or relationships, often offering excessively long descriptions of events, wandering from topic to topic, crying continuously while describing past events, etc. They tend to use vague, meaningless, or empty words when describing interpersonal events (e.g., may insert nonsense words such as "dadadada" into sentences, use psychobabble such as "she has a lot of material around that issue," etc.). (p. 1083)

Again, this narrative captures the same relatedness pattern characterized by Daniel's (2015) interpersonal markers.

Disorganized/Disoriented Person

The disorganized/disoriented person is afraid to seek proximity to others but also feels lost without that closeness. They strongly distrust others, fearing that others will violate their boundaries. Afraid to seek out help, they nevertheless feel utterly helpless. Their emotional expressions are often chaotic, and they do not have much ability to regulate them. The disorganized/disoriented person experiences low self-esteem and an incoherent self-image. They resist making self-disclosures, but involuntary idiosyncratic thoughts and feelings might break through in interpersonal exchanges. They also feel deeply conflicted between a desire for autonomy and a desire to be taken care of. The disorganized/disoriented person shows poor tolerance for interpersonal conflict, sometimes manifesting a total collapse of protective strategies and instead acting out their feelings by engaging in inappropriate behavior. Fear of interacting with others interferes with empathy or care for others (Daniel, 2015).

Here is Westen and his colleagues' (2006) characterization of the disorganized/disoriented prototype:

> Individuals who match this prototype have had trouble getting beyond, mastering, resolving, or making meaning of traumatic events (e.g., loss or abuse), so that they tend to respond in intimate relationships in ways that appear inconsistent, contradictory, or dissociative. They have difficulty trusting significant others and tend to manifest contradictory responses when distressed or in need of help (e.g., pushing the other away while demanding help or responding simultaneously with anger and help-seeking). They tend to be controlling

in close relationships, either through hostile, critical, or punitive responses, or through overinvolved, "enmeshed," or smothering caregiving. Individuals who match this prototype experience strong emotions that often disrupt or derail their narrative descriptions of interpersonal events, rendering these descriptions incoherent, difficult to follow, etc. When talking about traumatic events (e.g., loss or abuse), they tend to show signs of disorientation, disorganization, or dissociation; seem to lose the capacity to keep in mind the perspective of the listener; and show signs of illogical, childish, or peculiar reasoning (e.g., indicating that a dead person is still alive in the physical sense, or appearing convinced that their thoughts or feelings killed someone in childhood). They may lapse into prolonged silences, unfinished sentences, or stilted, "eulogistic" speech when describing traumatic events or losses.

Again, Westen et al.'s (2006) disorganized/disoriented prototype aptly resembles Daniel's (2015) interpersonal markers.

Toward Matching a Person With a Specific Attachment Pattern to a Specific Model of Spiritual Intervention

What do these four attachment patterns and their interpersonal markers have to do with giving care to people who are seeking spiritual solutions to their emotional or spiritual problems? Care receivers, or anyone seeking mental health or spiritual intervention, will respond to the caregiver (Slade, 1999)—and to a Higher Power (Granqvist, 2020)—depending on their attachment pattern formed during infancy and early childhood. Thus, a one-size-fits-all response such as that advocated by Stephen Ministry (see Chapter 2) might not fit some care receivers.

I want to emphasize that some models of spiritual intervention are better suited to care receivers who have a particular quality of attachment relationship than others. For example, in Chapter 2, I argue that care receivers in Stephen Ministry can benefit more from this model of spiritual intervention if they have a secure attachment pattern. Similarly, spiritual directees might appear more suitably adjusted to mindful meditation if they have an anxious-avoidant attachment pattern (see Chapter 3). As Kennedy (1995) readily points out, "There is a certain type of temperament which not only naturally inclines itself toward silent and reverent attention, but also longs for it" (p. 47). Unwittingly, Kennedy seems to be describing a person classified as anxious-avoidant—someone who prefers to be alone to avoid painful feelings of rejection. This person might excel at contemplative prayer and not be challenged to confront the anxiety that emerges in intimate relationships such as that between spiritual director and directee. Thus, before making a disposition, a caregiver must consider which model of spiritual intervention would most benefit the care receiver, keeping in mind the care receiver's quality of attachment relationships.

In the psychotherapy outcome research literature, matching patients to specific treatment models based on therapist and patient characteristics is a popular topic of investigation: what works for whom (Fonagy et al., 2002; Roth & Fonagy, 2005)? Two groups of psychotherapy outcome researchers (Beutler, 1979; Beutler & Harwood, 2000; Blatt & Felsen, 1993; Blatt & Ford, 1994; Blatt & Shahar, 2005) produced evidence that matching particular patients to particular treatment conditions produces effective treatment outcomes. In other words, different kinds of folks may need different kinds of strokes (Blatt & Felsen, 1993; for a summary of this literature, see Goodman, 2010). Clergy and nonclergy alike can engage in a similar matching process when considering a potential care receiver's disposition to a particular model of spiritual intervention, informally assessing the person's attachment pattern to determine which model of spiritual intervention would work best (see Chapter 8). Of course, other factors require careful assessment (e.g., the presence of an addiction; see Chapter 4); however, the attachment pattern always needs consideration.

One factor that caregivers must always consider is the racial and ethnic heritage of the caregiver and care receiver and its effect on the construction of the therapeutic relationship. Bowlby's (1977) imperative that the infant seek an attachment figure perceived as stronger and wiser becomes complicated when applied to the therapeutic relationship. The reason is that, by the time the care receiver first meets the caregiver, they have already had a series of socialization experiences in the wider world that shape their perceptions of caregivers—perceptions also situated in a particular race, gender, and class.

Can an African American caregiver provide a secure base for a white care receiver who has been chronically exposed to the pervasive injustices visited on African Americans living in this country? Certainly, African American caregivers *can* provide a secure base and safe haven for white care receivers, but, for some white care receivers, their socialization process into the dominant culture—where racism is still pervasive—might present challenges to perceiving a caregiver from a historically oppressed race or culture as stronger and wiser. The reaction of a white care receiver to a caregiver of color might also depend on that care receiver's attachment quality. An anxious-resistant care receiver's insecurity, or an anxious-avoidant care receiver's devaluing tendencies, might be elicited by such an arrangement. Conversely, a care receiver from a historically oppressed race or culture might have difficulty trusting a white caregiver, who belongs to a culture historically identified with wielding its authority to oppress rather than to help. This dynamic can be construed in different ways, depending on the care receiver's attachment quality. Thus, the process of matching caregivers and care receivers must include consideration of the cultural climate and the racial and ethnic heritage of the participants if genuine spiritual healing is to occur.

Naturally, this matching process must also include consideration of spiritual and religious differences. When applied to spiritual beliefs, the attachment relationship implies a monotheistic (or at least a theistic) concept of a Higher Power. A nontheist reading this book might conclude that the application of attachment theory to spirituality does not apply to them. As I argued earlier in this introduction, however, even persons who practice nontheistic religions sometimes view a Higher Power anthropomorphically and believe that they can establish and maintain a relationship to this Higher Power. Even young children raised in atheistic homes often believe in an anthropomorphic God (Barrett, 2012). Nevertheless, the attachment model that I use to evaluate the seven models of spiritual intervention fits monotheistic spirituality more adequately than nontheistic spirituality. Thus, the attachment model might not serve as the optimal lens with which to evaluate these seven models of spiritual intervention when a care receiver views their spirituality nontheistically.

Overview of the Seven Models of Intervention

As I mentioned at the outset of this introduction, I group the seven models into two categories, which I hope organizes this project. Readers can easily find a model of spiritual intervention based on whether lay ministers or licensed professionals are implementing it.

Each chapter also follows a structure. I begin by presenting a clinical illustration, almost exclusively from my own work. I then describe the model of spiritual intervention, followed by sharing its history. Then, I view this model of spiritual intervention in the context of attachment theory. I consider when this model is a good match for a potential care receiver, including which spiritual struggles it addresses and for whom this model might be ill suited. I also discuss the training requirements to practice this model of spiritual intervention. Finally, I summarize my findings and share what I have learned from practicing this model of spiritual intervention.

The reader might be wondering why I chose to discuss these seven models of spiritual intervention out of the multitude of spiritual interventions in use today. Except for Stephen Ministry (see Chapter 2) and Godly Play (see Chapter 5), which are based on the Christian faith tradition, I am evaluating models of spiritual intervention that apply to persons adhering to many faith traditions, notably Christian, Jewish, and Muslim. Persons adhering to other faith traditions such as Buddhism and Hinduism might also find common ground in reading about these models of spiritual intervention (especially in Chapter 3).

I focused on evaluating more broadly spiritual models of spiritual intervention. For example, my evaluation of 12-step programs (see Chapter 4) excludes Christian-based recovery programs such as Celebrate Recovery (https://celebraterecovery.com/about/) and Re:generation (www.regenerationrecovery.org/about). These programs were founded on the evangelical Christian faith tradition and, therefore, have limited appeal. Further, these Christianity-based recovery programs purport to treat all types of addiction; thus, a member might not feel uniquely understood by anyone else. One member might have a drug addiction, another might have a food addiction, while a third might have a gambling addiction. Is the gambling addict going to feel uniquely understood by the food addict? One appealing feature of 12-step programs is that each program focuses exclusively on one addiction only. For these reasons, I did not focus on Christianity-based recovery programs. If the care receiver is an evangelical Christian and wants to engage in recovery with other evangelical Christians, however, these alternative recovery programs are available.

Programs that function like Stephen Ministry (see Chapter 2) also exist, such as Equipping Laypeople for Ministry (Sunderland, 2024) and BeFriender Ministry (https://befrienderministry.org/about/). Stephen Ministry, however, is the most popular lay ministry program in the world. The astronomical success that Stephen Ministry has enjoyed over the past 50 years (almost 14,000 churches worldwide as of 2023; Stephen Ministries St. Louis, personal communication, September 22, 2023) suggests that this method of spiritual caring is clearly working for thousands of congregants seeking care for their problems. Thus, I evaluate Stephen Ministry as the exemplar of Christian lay ministry organizations.

Many methods of clergy–laity collaboration are available. I discuss a collaboration between a hospital chaplain and a clinical psychologist (see Chapter 6) in conducting an exploratory spirituality group for psychiatric inpatients diagnosed with borderline personality disorder, which features drawings of representations of God. This type of collaboration, however, can occur in many different settings with many different patient populations. The Solihten Institute (https://solihten.org/who-we-are/history/) accredits 34 counseling centers across 22 US states that promote such collaboration. For example, my church houses the Solihten-accredited Samaritan Counseling Center of Atlanta (SCCA), which is financially independent of the church and has its own board of directors, but its executive director is an associate pastor of the church. The SCCA promotes collaborative spirituality groups co-led by clergy and licensed mental health professionals such as social workers. I envision such collaborative spirituality groups taking place in all the settings occupied by chaplains, such as hospitals, prisons, Veterans Administration (VA) centers, unhoused shelters, and, of course, churches. I predict that these church–mental health partnerships will become increasingly common as mental health becomes less stigmatized in religious communities. My research lab at Emory University has recently studied this phenomenon (Marure et al., 2025). There is a hunger for mental well-being among congregants, and churches partnering with licensed mental health professionals are well positioned to deliver pastoral care to congregants and others seeking spiritual and emotional help.

I also chose these seven models of spiritual intervention because I have trained in all of them and, therefore, know them from the inside out—I personally practice all of them. Almost all the case illustrations come from my personal experience as a practitioner of each model (except for Chapter 5). I could have chosen other models but, with those, I would be simply regurgitating what I have read from others. I wanted this book to represent an authentic perspective from someone who practices each of these models. As I continue to learn additional models of spiritual intervention, I could write a Volume 2, which would also evaluate these additional models in the context of attachment theory. I am grateful that these seven models of spiritual intervention are available to spiritually grounded and spiritually curious persons. My 18-year-old self could have benefited from them if I had only known about them. I would like to introduce them to you so that you can learn to practice them or benefit from them yourself.

Overview of Remaining Chapters

Part I: Models of Spiritual Intervention Conducted by Lay Ministers

Chapter 2. Stephen Ministry: Carrying Each Other's Burdens

Founded in 1975 by Kenneth Haugk, Stephen Ministry is a popular nondenominational Christian caregiving model of spiritual intervention, training lay persons in church congregations to care for fellow congregants in a quasi-therapeutic context without formal licensure requirements. Stephen Ministers work with persons suffering from challenging circumstances in their lives—from divorce and loss to infertility and caring for an elderly parent. They use the principles of humanistic psychology to guide their interventions, which include using empathy, validation, and unconditional positive regard to help a person grow and thrive. Stephen Ministers focus on the process taking place in the moment between a caregiver and a care receiver. I argue that Stephen Ministry imposes a one-size-fits-all strategy for helping the client (i.e., all clients receive empathy, validation, encouragement, and spiritual tools such as prayer). Stephen Ministry's strengths and limitations in the context of attachment theory, as well as its applicability to individuals who display each of the four attachment relationship models, are discussed. These four models represent distinct modes of relating to God, and the spiritually aware caregiver must know how to work with persons manifesting each of these modes. A case illustration of a Stephen Ministry caregiving relationship is offered.

Chapter 3. Spiritual Direction: An Invitation to the Practice of Contemplation

Practiced by the early Desert Fathers and Mothers of the third century CE, Spiritual Direction has experienced a resurgence in the contemporary setting. Unlike Stephen Ministry, Spiritual Direction is an ecumenical model of spiritual intervention that encompasses both Western and Eastern religious practices. Spiritual

Direction is a practice of listening together to how the Holy Spirit—however conceptualized by the spiritual director and directee—might be moving in the directee's life in the present moment. The process often includes periods of meditation in which participants sometimes sit in silence, gently letting go of their mental states such as thoughts, feelings, beliefs, intentions, and ideas in anticipation of hearing the Holy Spirit's still small voice within. At other times, the spiritual director and directee pray aloud, using a shared language for the Holy Spirit. Through this process, the spiritual directee seeks to discern and carry out the Holy Spirit's will in their daily life. Together, the spiritual director and directee cultivate the directee's greater attentiveness to this still small voice, which often inspires a sense of awe, serenity, and connection to the universe. Spiritual Direction's strengths and limitations in the context of attachment theory are discussed. A case illustration is offered.

Chapter 4. Twelve-Step Programs: Surrendering to the God of Our Understanding

With his collaborator, Dr. Bob, Bill W. became the co-founder of Alcoholics Anonymous (AA) on June 10, 1935—the date when Dr. Bob took his last drink of alcohol and 6 months after Bill W. had taken his. In December of 1938—4 years after a dramatic conversion experience in which he committed himself to a Higher Power—Bill W. created the AA 12-step program of recovery, which became the blueprint for subsequent programs of addiction recovery. Wikipedia currently lists 43 12-step programs at least partially patterned after AA. The only requirement for membership is a desire to stop the addictive behavior. Members incorporate spirituality as understood by the individual member through prayer, meditation, reading recovery literature, working with a sponsor (a more experienced, sober member) to complete the 12 steps, and attending meetings, where members share their experience, strength, and hope in their recovery from addiction. In addition to achieving sobriety one day at a time through surrender to a Higher Power, the primary purpose of 12-step programs is to carry their message to the addict who still suffers. The strengths and limitations of 12-step programs in the context of attachment theory are discussed. A case illustration is offered.

Chapter 5. Godly Play: Suffer the Little Children to Come Unto Me

In 1960, Jerome Berryman, a student at Princeton Theological Seminary, noticed that children played no role in theological studies. Reminded that Jesus urged His followers to allow children unhindered access to life's spiritual dimension, Berryman developed a Montessori-based storytelling technique for giving children ages 3–12 the language to experience God's presence through Bible stories. He created four linguistic genres—sacred stories, parables, liturgical action lessons, and contemplative silence—told at appropriate times in the Christian calendar. The Godly Play storyteller uses props specific to each story to recite the story verbatim, followed by asking a series of "I wonder" questions to elicit reflective thinking about what the children have observed. Godly Play also focuses on creating optimal environmental conditions for children to absorb the story's meaning. Vocal delivery, body language, prop placement, and seating arrangement combine to maximize the story's emotional impact. After reflecting on the "I wonder" questions, children engage in response time, when they can access toys and arts and crafts to express their feelings related to the story. The strengths and limitations of Godly Play in the context of attachment theory are discussed. A case illustration and an alternative to Godly Play are offered.

Part II: Models of Spiritual Intervention Conducted by Licensed Professionals

Chapter 6. Using Drawing in a Spirituality Group to Discuss Mental Representations of God

In this case illustration, I present aspects of a voluntary 14-session, psychodynamically oriented, exploratory spirituality group for nine female psychiatric inpatients diagnosed with borderline personality disorder. A clinical psychologist and a hospital chaplain co-led these weekly 45-minute sessions. Through drawings and group process, the patients uncovered and elaborated on their representations of God. Two patterns of representations were identified: (1) representations of a punitive, judgmental, rigid God that seemed directly to reflect and correspond with parental representations and (2) representations of a depersonified, inanimate, abstract God entailing aspects of idealization that seemed to compensate for parental representations. Interestingly, the second pattern was associated with comorbid narcissistic features in the patients. Those patients who presented punitive God representations were able to begin the process of re-creating these representations toward more benign or benevolent images in the context of this group, while those participants who presented depersonified God representations seemed unable to do so. I suggest that a spirituality group can facilitate the re-creation of representations of both God and self among spiritually curious borderline patients, thus helping them to "earn" their attachment security. The strengths and limitations of this spirituality group in the context of attachment theory are discussed.

Chapter 7. Spiritually Integrated Psychotherapy: Introducing Spirituality and Working Through Spiritual Struggles

Based on the contributions of Kenneth Pargament, James Griffith, Russell Siler Jones, and others, SIP is a therapeutic attitude that consists of attending to the patient's spiritual strivings and struggles. Whenever the patient discusses any topic of ultimate importance, conveying a profound sense of transcendence, boundlessness, or the eternal, then the therapist's "spiritual radar" should be beeping, signaling that spirituality has entered the therapeutic relationship. Pargament suggests that three sacred qualities of the therapeutic relationship—grace, deep acceptance, and reassuring presence—can help to heal patients' spiritual struggles, which are often associated with psychiatric symptoms. Grace and deep acceptance suggest closely related interventions in the sense that the therapist demonstrates to the patient, through careful listening, a nonjudgmental attitude and, through nonreactivity, an unconditional acceptance of the patient's entire being. Reassuring presence suggests that the therapist will not avert their gaze or withdraw their acceptance but instead bear witness to the patient's pain, even when being with the patient might be challenging. A treatment goal of SIP would be to facilitate restoration of the patient's relationship to the Higher Power of their understanding. The strengths and limitations of SIP in the context of attachment theory are discussed. Two case illustrations are offered.

Chapter 8. Attachment-Informed Psychotherapy: Transforming Attachment Relationships to a Higher Power and to Parents

I present AIP, which addresses the quality of therapeutic attachment relationships and discusses these relationships as a representation of a patient's attachment relationship to their Higher Power. This treatment model takes the caregiver–infant attachment relationship as a metaphor for both the therapist–patient and God–patient attachment relationships. I address the advantages and disadvantages of using this metaphor. How does the patient's attachment relationship to the caregivers during childhood influence the therapist's understanding of their attachment relationship to the therapist and to their Higher Power? How does this metaphor prevent the examination of other forces that shape the patient's attachment relationship to their therapist and to their Higher Power? I explore the similarities and differences between these two relationships. I also summarize how to work with patients using four different attachment relationship models and how to address the correspondence and compensation pathways to the patient's experience of their attachment relationship to their Higher Power. Can faith in a Higher Power serve as a containment function in the patient's psychic economy outside the therapy office? In other words, can the patient transfer this containment function from the therapist to their Higher Power? A case illustration is offered.

Chapter 9. Final Reflections

I summarize the seven models of spiritual intervention presented in this book and highlight their similarities and differences. I also review the inclusion and exclusion criteria for each model as well as the training and credentialing requirements for practitioners of each model. Finally, I review the critiques of each model using attachment theory as the benchmark of evaluation. To what degree does each model promote or hinder the development and maintenance of secure attachment relationships to the practitioner, to fellow believers, to nonbelievers, and to their Higher Power? Crucially, I suggest that, ultimately, clergy, lay ministers, and licensed mental health professionals must follow their spiritual intuition in both listening and responding to the person's verbal and nonverbal communications, especially their emotional expressions, in making the referral to one of these seven models of spiritual intervention.

References

Ainsworth, M. D. S. (1967). *Infancy in Uganda: Infant care and the growth of love*. Johns Hopkins Press.

Ainsworth, M. D. S., Blehar, M. C., Waters, E., & Wall, S. (1978). *Patterns of attachment: A psychological study of the strange situation*. Erlbaum.

Ainsworth, M. D. S., & Eichberg, C. G. (1991). Effects on infant–mother attachment of mother's unresolved loss of an attachment figure, or other traumatic experience. In C. M. Parkes, J. Stevenson-Hinde, & P. Marris (Eds.), *Attachment across the life cycle* (pp. 160–183). Tavistock/Routledge.

Ainsworth, M. D. S., & Wittig, B. A. (1969). Attachment and exploratory behavior of one-year-olds in a strange situation. In B. M. Foss (Ed.), *Determinants of infant behaviour IV* (pp. 111–136). Methuen.

Barrett, J. L. (2012). *Born believers: The science of children's religious belief*. Free Press.

Beutler, L. E. (1979). Toward specific psychological therapies for specific conditions. *Journal of Consulting and Clinical Psychology, 47*, 882–897.

Beutler, L. E., & Harwood, T. M. (2000). *Prescriptive psychotherapy: A practical guide to systematic treatment selection*. Oxford University Press.

Blatt, S. J., & Felsen, I. (1993). Different kinds of folks may need different kinds of strokes: The effect of patients' characteristics on therapeutic process and outcome. *Psychotherapy Research, 3*, 245–259.

Blatt, S. J., & Ford, R. (1994). *Therapeutic change: An object relations perspective*. Plenum.

Blatt, S. J., & Shahar, G. (2005). Psychoanalysis—with whom, for what, and how? Comparisons with psychotherapy. *Journal of the American Psychoanalytic Association, 52*, 393–447.

Bowlby, J. (1958). The nature of the child's tie to his mother. *International Journal of Psycho-Analysis, 39*, 350–373.

Bowlby, J. (1977). The making and breaking of affectional bonds. I. Aetiology and psychopathology in the light of attachment theory. *British Journal of Psychiatry, 130*, 201–210.

Bowlby, J. (1980). *Attachment and loss: Vol. 3. Loss, sadness and depression*. Basic Books.

Bowlby, J. (1982). *Attachment and loss: Vol. 1. Attachment* (2nd ed.). Basic Books.

Bowlby, J. (1988). *A secure base: Parent–child attachment and healthy human development*. Basic Books.

Bretscher, J. P. (Ed.). (2020). *Stephen Minister training manual, volume 1*. Stephen Ministries.

Briggs, J. R. (2014). *Fail: Finding grace and hope in the midst of ministry failure*. InterVarsity Press Books.

Carlson, E. A. (1998). A prospective longitudinal study of attachment disorganization/disorientation. *Child Development, 69,* 1107–1128.

Carlson, V., Cicchetti, D., Barnett, D., & Braunwald, K. (1989a). Disorganized/disoriented attachment relationships in maltreated infants. *Developmental Psychology, 25,* 525–531.

Carlson, V., Cicchetti, D., Barnett, D., & Braunwald, K. G. (1989b). Finding order in disorganization: Lessons from research on maltreated infants' attachments to their caregivers. In D. Cicchetti & V. Carlson (Eds.), *Child maltreatment: Theory and research on the causes and consequences of child abuse and neglect* (pp. 494–528). Cambridge University Press.

Cooper-White, P. (2011). *Many voices: Pastoral psychotherapy in relational and theological perspective* (rev. ed.). Fortress Press.

Daniel, S. I. F. (2015). *Adult attachment patterns in a treatment context: Relationship and narrative.* Routledge.

Doehring, C. (2015). *The practice of pastoral care: A postmodern approach* (2nd ed.). Westminster John Knox Press.

Dykstra, R. C. (Ed.). (2005). *Images of pastoral care: Classic readings.* Chalice Press.

Fonagy, P., Target, M., Cottrell, D., Phillips, J., & Kurtz, Z. (2002). *What works for whom? A critical review of treatments for children and adolescents.* New York: Guilford Press.

Freud, S. (1912). The dynamics of transference. In J. Strachey (Ed. and Trans.), *The standard edition of the complete psychological works of Sigmund Freud (Vol. 12,* pp. 97–108). London: Hogarth Press.

George, C., Kaplan, N., & Main, M. (1996). *Adult attachment interview* (3rd ed.). Unpublished manuscript, University of California, Berkeley.

Goodman, G. (1991). Feeling our way into empathy: Carl Rogers, Heinz Kohut, and Jesus. *Journal of Religion and Health, 30,* 191–205.

Goodman, G. (2010). *Transforming the internal world and attachment: Theoretical and empirical perspectives* (Vol. 1). Jason Aronson.

Goodman, G. (2014). *The internal world and attachment* (paperback ed.). Routledge.

Goodman, G. (2025a). *Practical applications of transforming the attachment relationship to God: Using attachment-informed psychotherapy.* Routledge.

Goodman, G. (2025b). *Using psychoanalytic techniques to transform the attachment relationship to God: Our refuge and strength.* Routledge.

Granqvist, P. (2020). *Attachment in religion and spirituality: A wider view.* Guilford Press.

Griffith, J. L. (2010). *Religion that heals, religion that harms: A guide for clinical practice.* Guilford Press.

Harlow, H. F. (1958). The nature of love. *American Journal of Psychology, 13,* 673–685.

Haugk, K. C. (2020). *Christian caregiving: A way of life* (2nd ed.). Stephen Ministries.

Hesse, E., & Main, M. (1999). Second-generation effects of unresolved trauma in nonmaltreating parents: Dissociated, frightened, and threatening parental behavior. *Psychoanalytic Inquiry, 19,* 481–540.

Hesse, E., & Main, M. (2000). Disorganized infant, child, and adult attachment: Collapse in behavioral and attentional strategies. *Journal of the American Psychoanalytic Association, 48,* 1097–1127.

Jones, E. E. (2000). *Therapeutic action: A guide to psychoanalytic therapy.* Jason Aronson.

Jones, J. M. (2024, March 25). Church attendance has declined in most U.S. religious groups. Gallup. https://news.gallup.com/poll/642548/church-attendance-declined-religious-groups.aspx

Karen, R. (1998). *Becoming attached: First relationships and how they shape our capacity to love.* Oxford University Press.

Kennedy, R. E. (1995). *Zen spirit, Christian spirit: The place of Zen in Christian life.* Continuum.

Lartey, E. Y. (2003). *In living color: An intercultural approach to pastoral care and counseling* (rev. ed.). Jessica Kingsley.

Lartey, E. Y., & Moon, H. (Eds.). (2020). *Postcolonial images of spiritual care: Challenges of care in a neoliberal age*. Pickwick.

Lyons-Ruth, K., Bronfman, E., & Parsons, E. (1999). Maternal frightened, frightening, or atypical behavior and disorganized infant attachment patterns. In J. Vondra & D. Barnett (Eds.), *Atypical patterns of infant attachment: Theory, research and current directions*. Monographs of the Society for Research in Child Development (Vol. 64, pp. 67–96). Wiley.

Lyons-Ruth, K., Connell, D. B., Grunebaum, H., & Botein, S. (1990). Infants at social risk: Maternal depression and family support services as mediators of infant development and security of attachment. *Child Development, 61*, 85–98.

Lyons-Ruth, K., Connell, D. B., & Zoll, D. (1989). Patterns of maternal behavior among infants at risk for abuse: Relations with infant attachment behavior and infant development at 12 months of age. In D. Cicchetti & V. Carlson (Eds.), *Child maltreatment: Theory and research on the causes and consequences of child abuse and neglect* (pp. 464–493). Cambridge University Press.

Lyons-Ruth, K., Easterbrooks, M. A., & Cibelli, C. D. (1997). Infant attachment strategies, infant mental lag, and maternal depressive symptoms: Predictors of internalizing and externalizing problems at age 7. *Developmental Psychology, 33*, 681–692.

Lyons-Ruth, K., Zoll, D., Connell, D., & Grunebaum, H. U. (1986). The depressed mother and her one-year-old infant: Environment, interaction, attachment, and infant development. *New Directions for Child Development, 34*, 61–82.

Main, M., & Goldwyn, R. (1994). *Adult attachment scoring and classification systems* (6th ed.). Unpublished manuscript, University College, London.

Main, M., & Hesse, E. (1990). Parents' unresolved traumatic experiences are related to infant disorganized attachment status: Is frightened and/or frightening parental behavior the linking mechanism? In M. T. Greenberg, D. Cicchetti, & E. M. Cummings (Eds.), *Attachment in the preschool years: Theory, research, and intervention* (pp. 161–182). University of Chicago Press.

Main, M., Kaplan, N., & Cassidy, J. (1985). Security in infancy, childhood, and adulthood: A move to the level of representation. In I. Bretherton & E. Waters (Eds.), *Growing points in attachment theory and research*. Monographs of the Society for Research in Child Development (Vol. 50, No. 1–2, Serial No. 209, pp. 66–104). Wiley.

Main, M., & Solomon, J. (1990). Procedures for identifying infants as disorganized/disoriented during the Ainsworth Strange Situation. In M. T. Greenberg, D. Cicchetti, & E. M. Cummings (Eds.), *Attachment in the preschool years: Theory, research, and intervention* (pp. 121–160). University of Chicago Press.

Marure, C. C., Boyers, S., Li, C., Segal, A., Yang, E., Fannon, J., Haushalter, S., Scott, S., Topper, J., Zweig, R., & Goodman, G. (2025, August). *Understanding the effect of mental health stigma within a church congregation*. Paper presented at the meeting of the American Psychological Association, Denver, CO.

Mesman, J., van IJzendoorn, M. H., & Sagi-Schwartz, A. (2018). Cross-cultural patterns of attachment: Universal and contextual dimensions. In J. Cassidy & P. R. Shaver (Eds.), *Handbook of attachment: Theory, research, and clinical applications* (pp. 852–877). Guilford Press.

New International Version. (1978). *The Holy Bible, new international version*. Zondervan.

Pargament, K. I. (1999). The psychology of religion and spirituality? Yes and no. *International Journal for the Psychology of Religion, 9*, 3–16.

Pargament, K. I., & Exline, J. J. (2022). *Working with spiritual struggles in psychotherapy: From research to practice*. Guilford Press.

Patton, J. (1993). *Pastoral care in context: An introduction to pastoral care*. Westminster John Knox Press.

Ramsay, N. J. (2004). A time of ferment and redefinition. In N. J. Ramsay (Ed.), *Pastoral care and counseling: Redefining the paradigms* (pp. 1–43). Abingdon Press.

Roan, C. (2023). California [Song]. On *The rise and fall of a midwest princess*. Amusement; Island. https://www.youtube.com/watch?v=GcXlN7meclE

Rogers, C. R. (1957). The necessary and sufficient conditions of therapeutic personality change. *Journal of Consulting Psychology, 21*, 95–103.

Rogers, C. R. (1980). *A way of being*. Houghton-Mifflin.

Roth, A., & Fonagy, P. (2005). *What works for whom? A critical review of psychotherapy research* (2nd ed.). New York: Guilford Press.

Scheib, K. D. (2016). *Pastoral care: Telling the stories of our lives*. Abingdon Press.

Scheib, K. D. (2018). *Attend to stories: How to flourish in ministry*. Wesley's Foundery Books.

Schuengel, C., Bakermans-Kranenburg, M. J., & van IJzendoorn, M. H. (1999). Attachment and loss: Frightening maternal behavior linking unresolved loss and disorganized infant attachment. *Journal of Consulting and Clinical Psychology, 67*, 54–63.

Slade, A. (1999). Attachment theory and research: Implications for the theory and practice of individual psychotherapy with adults. In J. Cassidy & P. R. Shaver (Eds.), *Handbook of attachment: Theory, research, and clinical applications* (pp. 575–594). Guilford Press.

Sullivan, H. S. (1953). *Conceptions of modern psychiatry: The first William Alanson White Memorial Lectures*. Norton.

Sunderland, R. H. (2024). *Saying our stories: A guide for individuals who are storylisteners*. Page.

van IJzendoorn, M. H., Schuengel, C., & Bakermans-Kranenburg, M. J. (1999). Disorganized attachment in early childhood: Meta-analysis of precursors, concomitants, and sequelae. *Development and Psychopathology, 11*, 225–249.

Wallin, D. J. (2007). *Attachment in psychotherapy*. Guilford Press.

Waters, E., Merrick, S., Treboux, D., Crowell, J., & Albersheim, L. (2000). Attachment security in infancy and early adulthood: A twenty-year longitudinal study. *Child Development, 71*, 684–689.

Westen, D., Nakash, O., Thomas, C., & Bradley, R. (2006). Clinical assessment of attachment patterns and personality disorder in adolescents and adults. *Journal of Consulting and Clinical Psychology, 74*(6), 1065–1085.

Part I

Models of Spiritual Intervention Conducted by Lay Ministers

Chapter 2

Stephen Ministry
Carrying Each Other's Burdens

Stephen Ministry is a popular nondenominational Christian caregiving model offered by many congregations all over the world. The genius of this model is that it trains lay persons in church congregations to care for fellow congregants in a quasi-therapeutic context without any formal psychotherapy licensure requirements. Stephen Ministers, also known as "caregivers," provide "distinctively Christian caring" (Haugk, 2020, p. 11) to "care receivers"—typically congregants who have identified themselves (or have been identified by other congregants known as "lookouts"; Bretscher, 2020b, p. 475) as experiencing emotional or spiritual problems with which they would like help. Caregivers meet with their care receivers individually for an hour on a weekly basis and "come alongside" (Bretscher, 2020a, p. 127) them for a circumscribed period of time. These caring relationships can last up to 2 years or, in some cases, even longer. Caregivers are typically assigned only one care receiver at a time to prevent burnout. Stephen Ministry has not released any program outcome data, but, anecdotally, Stephen Ministers and Stephen Leaders (lay organizers of a congregation's Stephen Ministry program) have reported to me the emotional and spiritual benefits accrued by both the care receivers and the caregivers (see later in this chapter to read about my own experience as a Stephen Minister caring for a care receiver). Critically, as Stephen Ministers strive to "carry each other's burdens" (Galatians 6:2, New International Version [NIV]), they also carry some of the burdens of pastoral care borne by the pastor.

Delayed Grief in a Care Receiver

Over the past 2 years, I have worked as a Stephen Minister with a care receiver ("Pilgrim"), speaking with him over the phone for 60 minutes once a week through the first 11 months and once every other week for 12 months after that. Pilgrim is a Caucasian man in his late 20s who contacted my church because he was struggling in romantic relationships: he did not feel connected to women he had dated. Insightfully, he shared that these struggles might have something to do with his mother's tragic death from alcohol abuse and dependence while he was in college. Pilgrim wanted to find someone to talk to who could help him mourn the loss of his mother and help him to connect to God as a parent figure and as a source of support and guidance in his life.

Pilgrim described his family life as secure and generally happy when he was a child. He has two older sisters, whom he got along with during childhood. His mother began to lose control of her drinking while Pilgrim was in high school, and everyone in the family except Pilgrim began to pull away from her. Pilgrim tried rescuing her from her addiction, even arranging a rehab stay for her while he was in college, but all these efforts were in vain. The more effort he made, the more drinking she did.

After his mother's death, Pilgrim reported that his family never mentioned his mother or her death. She became invisible—a ghost. Pilgrim's father remarried not long afterward, and the older sisters began romantic relationships and moved out of the house. By the time Pilgrim entered Stephen Ministry as a care receiver, he was living in his childhood home with his father and stepmother. He described these relationships as strained. His father was unsupportive and at times devaluing of Pilgrim's adult status.

Pilgrim reported that his family was nominally Catholic—attending Christmas and Easter services but otherwise not having much contact with the church. He had recently read Norman Vincent Peale's (2003) *The Power of Positive Thinking* and wanted to explore a similar spiritual approach to his difficulties that could change his negative thinking about his romantic prospects. The experience of having read this book led him to contact Stephen Ministry for help.

In the early phase of our relationship, I learned that Pilgrim worked at a job that did not afford much exercise of his creativity. He was developing a side job as an online entrepreneur, selling products on his own website. He pursued this side job with remarkable enthusiasm despite sarcastic comments from his father, who seemed to think that Pilgrim was wasting his time. Pilgrim chose to ignore his father's comments and continue his passion despite expressing his anguish during sessions.

Within the first 5 months of our working together, Pilgrim made apparent progress: he had developed a romantic interest in a female coworker who was reciprocating his interest. Pilgrim seemed to have turned a corner in working through the barriers to seeking and maintaining a romantic connection with a woman. Pilgrim mentioned that this woman had a boyfriend who was living in another state owing to a temporary job relocation, but she seemed to be giving Pilgrim all the special attention that he had been craving. When Pilgrim eventually tried to kiss this woman, she gently rebuffed him, reminding him that she had a boyfriend but reassuring him that he had done nothing wrong in trying. Heartbroken, Pilgrim wondered what he should do next: stop being this woman's friend or continue to make himself emotionally available in the hope that she would get tired of waiting for her boyfriend to return home and break up with him, thus creating an opening for Pilgrim. As a Stephen Minister caregiver, I focused on the process and not the results:

> It's hard to wait for someone you love so much and trust that God knows what's best for you. It reminds me of something Jesus said during the Sermon on the Mount: "Look at the birds of the air; they do not sow or reap or store away in barns, and yet your heavenly Father feeds them. Are you not much more valuable than they?" [Matthew 6:26–27, NIV]. God promises to take care of all your needs, even though it doesn't always feel that way.

In this intervention, I used empathy ("it's hard to wait") and encouragement ("God knows what's best for you") to facilitate the process of our interaction. I did not focus on what I would perceive as the correct outcome, which would have sounded something like this:

> You're torturing yourself by continuing to hang out with her. She's using you as a temporary substitute for her boyfriend until he returns, then she'll stop showering you with attention, and you'll be worse off than when you began. It's better to make a clean break now and look for somebody else. You can use this time to draw closer to God. God is the only One who can satisfy your deep longings anyway.

This intervention tells Pilgrim exactly what to do, but it does not help him to understand why he was attracted to this woman in the first place, and it will not stop him from getting involved with another emotionally unavailable woman in the future. This intervention also implies that, if he does not break it off with this woman, he would be defying my advice and perhaps disappointing God as well. The awareness of disappointment on my part and God's could, in turn, cause him to withdraw and stop coming to sessions (or, worse, stop seeking God's presence).

If I were treating this young man as a patient in psychotherapy, informed by the principles of attachment theory, I might focus instead on the connection between the unmourned loss of his mother and the desire to attract emotionally unavailable women. As Pilgrim's mother fell more deeply into the spiral of alcohol addiction, Pilgrim redoubled his efforts to rescue her from herself and regain a secure attachment with her. When she died, Pilgrim possibly interpreted this tragic outcome as a personal failure, which he would try to overcome in his romantic relationships by first seeking out emotionally unavailable women and then rescuing them by trying to convince them that he is more fulfilling than the other man (or, in the case of his mother, more fulfilling than alcohol).

Freud (1920) labeled this phenomenon the "repetition compulsion" and believed a person tried to master an unresolved trauma by repeating the conditions under which the original trauma occurred, hoping for a different result. More recent work (e.g., van der Kolk, 2014) has suggested that a trauma repetition is a feeble attempt at restoring a sense of control to neutralize the traumatic sense of helplessness engendered by the original traumatic event. Over many sessions, I would make a series of interpretations that would link the feelings of helplessness and guilt engendered by Pilgrim's mother's demise with the compulsion to locate similar women to produce a different result the next time—one in which Pilgrim feels in control of the outcome rather than at its mercy. Of course, in a treatment that integrates spirituality into the psychotherapy process, I would also underscore Pilgrim's difficulty with trusting God's providence in his life, perhaps because of Pilgrim's difficulty in trusting his mother to provide a secure base for him during his late adolescence and young adulthood. Pilgrim's attachment relationships with these two persons—his mother and God (and, to a lesser extent, his father)—correspond to each other in Pilgrim's experience of both as highly desired for connection but ultimately unavailable.

Pilgrim eventually relinquished his desire to connect romantically with this woman. Eight and a half months into our relationship, he began dating and eventually moved into an apartment with a woman who this time was physically available but who was again emotionally unavailable by virtue of her diagnosis of high-functioning autism spectrum disorder. Pilgrim initially ignored the red flags. Again, as a Stephen Minister caregiver, I focused on the process and not the results:

> I'm hearing you say that you feel both disappointed and frustrated that she is on her phone while you're both having dinner or when you're trying to have a conversation with her. And it's hard for you to talk with her or pray with her about your feelings when you don't feel she would be receptive to what you need to say.

In this vignette, I empathize with Pilgrim's feelings ("you feel both disappointed and frustrated") and validate the challenge of talking to her ("it's hard ... when you don't feel she would be receptive"). While making suggestions (e.g., "you should confront her") is not among the process-oriented intervention tools sanctioned by Stephen Ministry because God is the "Curegiver" (Bretscher, 2020a; Haugk, 2020), I do smuggle into this conversation the idea of talking with his girlfriend and even praying with her. Pilgrim did follow through on a conversation with her, and, predictably, she was unreceptive to his desire for more connection. Eventually, he broke up with her, which proved doubly difficult for him because she moved out of their apartment in secret, taking with her the cat they shared. Thus, Pilgrim had to mourn the loss of this relationship as well as the loss of his beloved cat.

At various points in my work with Pilgrim, I felt as though I was working with one arm tied behind my back. How would this vignette have played out if I were treating this young man in psychotherapy informed by the principles of attachment theory? My first intervention would have been to point out the pattern that he was repeating with this girlfriend. She represents yet another significant attachment figure who was physically present yet emotionally unavailable to him. I would emphasize that we need to work through his mother's emotional unavailability to him, not only after her death but also throughout his late adolescence and college years. I would interpret this search for an emotionally available girlfriend that involved dating emotionally unavailable women and trying to persuade them to love him in a secure attachment relationship as a doomed attempt to master the maternal trauma and repeat the past with a different result. Additionally, this search for a romantic relationship with a woman who reminds him of the negative attributes of his mother also represents a solitary attempt to change the past to his liking, rather than letting go of his past and trusting God as his refuge in this time of trouble. I might also suggest that letting go of his mother's emotional abandonment would be so difficult because it might feel like a betrayal of his mother—a transgression against his loyalty toward his mother. Perhaps this loyalty is so powerful because it had guaranteed protection and comfort during childhood. Unfortunately, with his mother in the throes of alcohol addiction, Pilgrim's loyalty no longer guaranteed these priceless commodities.

These two vignettes illustrate Pilgrim's difficulties in establishing a secure attachment relationship with a romantic partner as well as uncovering the roots of these difficulties buried within the poisoned soil of Pilgrim's toxic relationship with his mother. As his therapist, I could review the progress Pilgrim made in his assertiveness with his father and their improving relationship or the increasing acceptance of living a single life and his search for a supportive community. We celebrated many positive moments during these 2 years together. The question I ask myself is whether Pilgrim could have avoided the agony of his second romantic breakup if he had been in an Attachment-Informed Psychotherapy (AIP; see Chapter 8) that focused on the connections between the traumatic event of his mother's emotional unavailability and the recapitulation of this same unresolved pattern in his romantic relationships. Would an approach where this past event and its connection to present relationships were thoroughly explored have made more of a difference in his life? Would he have noticed the red flags raised by the girlfriend diagnosed with autism early enough to have avoided this relationship? Pilgrim clearly made progress during our time together, but I wonder whether the progress would have been more thorough and enduring if he had been in AIP.

One final issue I have not addressed is Pilgrim's relationship with me. How was Pilgrim able to develop a secure attachment to me, trusting me with his grief, anger, and disappointment and not fearing rejection from me? Greenberg (1986) suggested that an effective treatment requires the patient to experience the therapist as both an old and a new object. In other words, a dialectic exists between the patient's experience of the therapist as an object of the patient's transference (i.e., a childhood parental figure) and the experience of the therapist as someone who behaves differently from this figure. At the beginning of our work together, Pilgrim demonstrated inconsistent behavior toward me (similar to the behavior he had experienced from his mother). Pilgrim often came 30–40 minutes late to sessions and occasionally missed sessions. Not knowing whether I was a trustworthy, steadfast, committed person, Pilgrim might have been filling in the blanks of his lack of experience with me with assumptions that I might treat him as his parents had treated him—as inconsistently available to him. To protect himself from potential rejection, Pilgrim came late or abandoned sessions altogether. In this manner, he became the one in charge of abandoning, not me. In his mind, I was the familiar parent to whom he was responding.

After 3 months, when he realized that I was not going to reject, abandon, or otherwise disappoint him like his parents, he began to trust me and show up to do the work of grieving the loss of his mother and expressing anger toward both his parents for not being the parents he wanted them to be. I gradually became a new object—a parental figure different from the parental figures of his past. I was safe enough for him to begin to internalize my caregiving behaviors and revise his expectations of others. He eventually adopted two new kittens and demonstrated his trustworthiness, steadfastness, and commitment to their care and well-being.

As Pilgrim continues to work through his tragic loss, his expectations of others' behavior will continue to change. He will one day be able to meet and fall in love with an emotionally available woman who demonstrates trustworthiness, steadfastness, and commitment to him, and he will be able to reciprocate this love to her.

Principles of Distinctively Christian Caring

Stephen Ministers are carefully vetted by their clergy and Stephen Leaders and must undergo a rigorous 50-hour training program designed to introduce them to the Christian caregiving model espoused by Stephen Ministry and to prepare them to serve in the role of Christian caregiver. The Stephen Ministry training materials emphasize specific qualities that a caregiver must have to provide effective care. First, the Stephen Minister must be compassionate—willing to help people who are suffering. Second, the Stephen Minister must be full of faith—possessing an "unshakable faith in Jesus" (Bretscher, 2020a, p. 4). Third, the caregiver must be completely competent at caregiving. Fourth, the caregiver must be trustworthy—providing reliable support for the care receiver. Finally, the Stephen Minister must be Christ-centered—always viewing Christ as the center of what he or she is doing. Stephen Ministry training seeks to cultivate these five qualities amid the other training that these lay persons complete.

Much of the Stephen Ministry training focuses on the development of competence. A Stephen Minister listens attentively and responds reflectively to the care receiver. Caregiving sessions emphasize the care receiver's feelings rather than thoughts, beliefs, or behaviors. The work consists of helping the care receiver achieve greater clarity about how they feel—about themselves, others, their situation, and God—so that they can eventually move past their problems and resume the typical rhythm of their lives.

The Christian caregiving model espoused by Stephen Ministry (Bretscher, 2020a, 2020b; Bretscher & Haugk, 2023) draws heavily on humanistic psychology, specifically, the writings of Carl Rogers (e.g., 1957), who underscored empathy, genuineness, and unconditional positive regard as the key ingredients of effective person-centered psychotherapy (see also Rogers, 1980). Making suggestions to a care receiver falls outside the scope of caregiving interventions because it invalidates the care receiver's subjective experience and puts the Stephen Minister in the role of "Curegiver," which is God's role (Bretscher, 2020a; Haugk, 2020). This theoretical model is an interesting choice to make for a Christian caregiving model because it implicitly uses the metaphor of the person as a plant that simply needs sunlight, water, and nutriments to grow and thrive (Goodman, 1991). In contrast, Christianity emphasizes a person's sinful nature and the need for salvation by supernatural means. Merely adding sunlight, water, and nutriments—empathy, genuineness, and unconditional positive regard in this context—would not be sufficient for a transformation to occur. Nevertheless, I believe that Kenneth Haugk, the founder of Stephen Ministry in 1975, selected the writings of humanistic psychology as the theoretical foundation of his model of Christian caregiving because the skills of empathy, attentive listening, reflective responding, and validation are easy to teach and do not require years of training to practice. A Stephen Minister can conduct a caregiving session without a therapist's license if they refrain from doing more than just encouraging, listening, and reflecting back to the care receiver whatever he or she is sharing.

What makes the Stephen Ministry Christian caregiving model different from person-centered psychotherapy is that the session content is often immersed in spirituality. Contrary to Rogers (1957), the caregiver can suggest explicitly spiritual forms of encouragement such as Bible reading or prayer that would specifically address the care receiver's problems. These interventions, however, could pull the care receiver toward conformity to the caregiver's perceived expectations to participate in these interventions and thus pull the care receiver away from their own authentic responses. Stephen Ministry alloys a person-centered approach to intervention with a more supportive approach (see, e.g., Rockland, 2003) that provides explicit encouragement to the patient in accordance with New Testament scripture (e.g., 1 Thessalonians 5:11, NIV). In this fashion, the caregiver risks invalidating the care receiver's experience by introducing something foreign to the care receiver's intrapersonal subjective experience. Nevertheless, this "distinctively Christian caring" must include interventions that directly address the spirituality offered by Christianity; otherwise, this form of caregiving would be indistinguishable from secular support. In my work with Pilgrim, I quoted New Testament scripture and mentioned praying with his girlfriend, which I would never do with a psychotherapy patient. If I had sensed that Pilgrim was not open to these explicitly spiritual interventions, I would not have used them.

Critique of the Stephen Ministry Program

Perhaps the most problematic aspect of the Stephen Ministry Christian caregiving model is that it adopts a one-size-fits-all approach to caregiving. Stephen Ministry (Bretscher, 2020a; Haugk, 2020) underscores the idea that God is the Curegiver and that caregivers must continue to provide empathy, validation, and encouragement and be patient, waiting on God for results to occur, however the care receiver might define "results." The Stephen Ministry training materials support this approach with a New Testament verse from 1 Corinthians 3:6 (NIV): "I planted the seed, Apollos watered it, but God made it grow." It is tempting to apply a person-centered psychotherapy to every conceivable problem: loss, anxiety, fertility challenges, moderate depression, crisis of faith, divorce, and job loss, just to name a few. If God is the Curegiver, why would a caregiver need to do anything differently than to keep loving the person by providing empathy, validation, and encouragement?

Despite the care that Haugk and Akers (2020) have taken to circumscribe the professional boundaries of Stephen Ministry caregiving, the resulting range of psychiatric symptoms and situational crises that Stephen Ministers are trained to address is nevertheless vast and complex (see below). Can a one-size-fits-all intervention strategy effectively address this range of human suffering? For example, the Stephen Ministry Leadership team at a church screens a 60-year-old man who is going through a divorce initiated by his spouse and wants help mourning the loss of his partner of 10 years. In fact, divorce is a bread-and-butter issue of Stephen Ministry; the issue is extensively covered in Module 23 of its training materials (Bretscher, 2020b, pp. 609–638). As the Stephen Minister begins working with this care receiver, they gradually learn that this is his fourth failed marriage, and all four spouses initiated divorce proceedings. Immediately, we observe a pattern here. Regardless of whether the caregiver observes this pattern, they must use the process principles that they learned during their Stephen Ministry training—using empathy, validation, and encouragement, along with any spiritual tools that they feel would be helpful such as prayer and Bible verses. Unfortunately, any exploration of the underlying pattern of failed marriages is forbidden. The caregiver could refer the care receiver for psychotherapy, but the care receiver has by this time developed an attachment to this caregiver, which might make it difficult for the care receiver to follow up with such a referral.

Although never explicitly evaluating him for the quality of his attachment pattern, I suspect that Pilgrim had a primary attachment pattern of disorganized/

disoriented (e.g., unresolved mourning of his mother's loss) and a secondary attachment pattern of anxious-resistant (e.g., working to rescue his mother while simultaneously feeling resentful about it; see Chapter 1). In the Stephen Ministry model of spiritual intervention, the Stephen Minister's tools of intervention would be identical, regardless of the attachment pattern.

Considering Attachment Patterns in Spiritual Intervention

What do the four attachment patterns and their interpersonal markers described in Chapter 1 have to do with giving care to people who are seeking spiritual solutions to their emotional or spiritual problems? Care receivers, or anyone seeking mental health or spiritual intervention, will respond to the caregiver (Slade, 2018)—and to a Higher Power (Granqvist, 2020)—differently, depending on their attachment pattern formed during infancy and early childhood. Thus, a one-size-fits-all response such as that advocated by Stephen Ministry might not fit some care receivers. Returning to the previous illustration of the man coming to Stephen Ministry on the eve of his fourth failed marriage, we do not know which attachment pattern he had formed during childhood; we know only the outcome—that he has experienced considerable upheaval in his intimate relationships. Given this tumultuous interpersonal history, we can probably rule out a secure attachment. We would not expect a securely attached person to manifest this degree of emotional upheaval. As Daniel (2015) pointed out, the securely attached person balances both positive and negative expressions of emotion and demonstrates empathy and care for others. Which of the other three attachment patterns might fit this man?

This man's "symptoms"—multiple failed marriages—might indicate that he did not develop a secure attachment in early childhood, but it does not necessarily tell us which insecure attachment he might have developed. Only targeted inquiry would give us the specific information we would need to make an educated guess about the type of insecure attachment that might be affecting the longevity of his marriages. Could this information make a difference in how we might approach this man during the caregiving phase of the intervention?

A Stephen Minister giving care to this man would have to respond with the same interventions—empathy, validation, encouragement, and spiritual tools—regardless of his insecure attachment status. A spiritually oriented therapist, however, might offer a wider range of interventions that take into account the prevailing attachment pattern. Following Dozier and Bates (2004), the therapist might offer a "gentle challenge" (p. 174) to the person's primary mode of relatedness. Inevitably, this man would begin to behave toward the therapist—and perhaps has already been behaving toward his Higher Power—in the same manner in which he had treated his previous marital partners.

Anxious-Avoidant Attachment Pattern in Spiritual Intervention

Considering the anxious-avoidant attachment pattern, we would have to inquire about this man's relationship history with his parents during the evaluation phase of the intervention, which is not part of the standard Stephen Ministry intake interview. In addition, we would have to explore the circumstances under which these marriages failed. Did this man's partners divorce him because he was cold and aloof? Did he try to keep his emotional distance in these relationships, which frustrated his partners' need for emotional closeness? Did he avoid conflict in these relationships? Was this man stingy in the personal experiences that he shared in these relationships, causing his partners to feel shut out of his life? Were his responses to his marital partners' frustrations lacking empathy and sensitivity? A caregiver trained to pay close attention to the effects of early insecure attachment on adult interpersonal relationships would listen to these interpersonal markers and draw the tentative conclusion that this man had formed an anxious-avoidant attachment pattern in early childhood and was manifesting the interpersonal aspects of this attachment pattern with his marital partners.

If the therapist speculates that the man formed an anxious-avoidant attachment pattern during early childhood, they might anticipate that the man would eventually treat the therapist in a cold, grandiose, and dismissing manner with little empathy for the therapist. Similarly, the man probably also treats his Higher Power with disdain, holding a superficial belief that God could never reject him and concealing a deeper anxiety about the potential for divine abandonment. The therapist would need to challenge this primary mode of relatedness by surfacing the underlying fears of abandonment, rejection, resentment, and self-blame that sabotage his relationships to significant others and to his Higher Power and then working through them.

Anxious-Resistant Attachment Pattern in Spiritual Intervention

Considering the anxious-resistant attachment pattern, we would again take a careful relationship history during the intake interview and explore the circumstances under which these marriages failed. Did this man's marital partners divorce him because he was intrusive in all aspects of their daily lives? Did he manifest strong expressions of emotion that would escalate conflict in these marriages? Did this man rely too much on his marital partners for help with things that he could have done himself? Did he often misattribute motives to his partners that reflected his own motives for behavior, thus impeding his capacity to empathize with them? Did he have trouble staying on topic when discussing significant interpersonal events or relationships with his partners, frustrating them in the process? In this scenario, the caregiver would listen to these interpersonal markers and draw the tentative conclusion that this man had formed an anxious-resistant attachment pattern in early childhood and was manifesting the interpersonal aspects of this attachment pattern with his marital partners.

If the therapist speculates that the man formed an anxious-resistant attachment pattern during early childhood, they might anticipate that the man would eventually form a helpless, dependent relationship with the therapist, never feeling satisfied with the care that he was receiving. Similarly, he would express anger toward God for constantly failing him and not following through on God's promises of security and contentment. In contrast to the previous scenario, this man's fears of abandonment are more visible, and his grievances over past slights associated with inconsistent attentiveness to his needs are more available for discussion. The therapist would need to challenge this primary mode of relatedness by maintaining strict boundaries and not surrender to the temptation to rescue him from the inevitable frustrations that will arise—for example, when he learns that the therapist will not respond to text messages after the end of the workday. Gradually, the man will develop a tolerance and trust that the therapist, as well as his Higher Power, has his best interests in mind, even when the therapist is not available to him or when God does not answer his prayers immediately.

Disorganized/Disoriented Attachment Pattern in Spiritual Intervention

Considering the disorganized/disoriented attachment pattern, we would rely on data collected from this man's intake interview regarding his relationship history and his early relationships with his caregivers to provide clues about his current difficulties with maintaining relationships. Did this man's marital partners divorce him because he walled himself off from becoming known by them, constructing impermeable boundaries that frustrated their attempts to reach him emotionally? Did he demonstrate occasional emotional breakdowns when conflicts arose in these marriages, perhaps frightening his marital partners? Did this man demonstrate an incoherent self-image that made his marital partners wonder whether they really knew him or whether he really knew himself? Did his helplessness and simultaneous fear of receiving help hinder his empathic responses to his marital partners? In this scenario, the caregiver might draw the tentative conclusion that this man had formed a disorganized/disoriented attachment pattern in early childhood and was displaying the interpersonal markers associated with this pattern with his marital partners.

If the therapist speculates that the man formed a disorganized/disoriented attachment pattern during early childhood, they might anticipate that the man would eventually form a profoundly fearful, mistrusting relationship with the therapist which might require an ongoing exploration of complex trauma that encompasses multiple spheres of development (e.g., Arvidson et al., 2011). Establishing a working alliance (Horvath & Greenberg, 1989) with this man will prove especially challenging because he lacks what is known as "epistemic trust" (Fonagy & Allison, 2014)—"trust in the authenticity and personal relevance of interpersonally transmitted information" (p. 372). This man will have difficulty trusting in the goodness and genuineness of the therapist's interventions. It is also quite possible that he is experiencing grave doubts about God's benevolence and trustworthiness as revealed in Scripture and the teachings of clergy. The therapist must work to establish a working alliance and epistemic trust so that this man can absorb the interpretations that might be helpful to him. Cultivating a sacred space where this man can verbalize his traumatic experiences, both past and present, and reframe his relationship to his Higher Power as a source of healing, not destruction, requires enormous patience and long-suffering. This work is not always successful. The point is that an uncomplicated diet of empathy, validation, encouragement, and spiritual tools—interventions offered by Stephen Ministers—might not be sufficient to help such persons heal from their complex trauma.

Stephen Ministry's person-centered interventions, while well-meaning and likely helpful for most care receivers, might be interpreted differently by care receivers with insecure attachment patterns. For example, an anxious-avoidant person might interpret validation as a pitiful expression of the therapist's weakness and desire to ingratiate themselves to this person. An anxious-resistant person might view validation as a gratification of the infantile dependent relationship that they are seeking with the therapist. A disorganized/disoriented person might perceive validation as an attempt at seducing the care receiver to let down their guard to gratify the therapist's needs. Without the therapist's requisite self-awareness, skill, and knowledge of the care receiver's attachment pattern, the person-centered interventions at the heart of the Stephen Ministry program might have unintended consequences that could exacerbate the care receiver's problems.

When Is This Model of Spiritual Intervention a Good Match?

Stephen Ministry is clear about the types of care receivers that a caregiver should not work with. Some examples include people exhibiting suicidal ideation, substance and behavioral addictions, personality disorders, and psychotic disorders. Haugk and Akers (2020) clearly define a continuum of care and locate Stephen Ministry along this continuum (p. 25). At the lowest level of the continuum, friends and family provide informal care and support, while, at the highest level of the continuum, mental health professionals provide licensed psychological care. Somewhere in the middle falls Stephen Ministry, identified as "one-to-one, ongoing, Christ-centered care and support" (p. 25). The authors identify Stephen Ministry caregiving as occupying an important gap between the informal, familial forms of care and the professional, licensed forms of care.

The continuum of care suggested by Haugk and Akers (2020) functions as a guardrail against assigning inappropriate care receivers to Stephen Ministers, but this design places a hefty burden on the Stephen Leadership team to carefully vet potential care receivers. Stephen Ministry works best with persons suffering from moderate depression, anxiety, and loss (e.g., death of a loved one, loss of health or job, divorce, crisis of faith). The astronomical success that Stephen Ministry has enjoyed over the past 50 years (almost 14,000 churches worldwide as of 2023; Stephen Ministries St. Louis, personal communication, September 22, 2023) suggests that this method of spiritual caring is clearly working for thousands of congregants seeking care for their problems. There is a subsample of persons for whom this method of spiritual caring would not succeed. My own experience of being a Stephen Minister suggests that, despite the limited types of interventions available to me, I was able to make a difference in the life of my care receiver (see above).

Training Requirements to Become a Stephen Minister and Stephen Leader

Stephen Ministers undergo a rigorous 50-hour training program taught by Stephen Leaders in their congregation. Stephen Ministries St. Louis provides all the training materials for prospective Stephen Ministers—congregants encouraged to take the training (although clergy can also complete the training). Lay church leaders can complete the Stephen Leader Training Course (SLTC) in St. Louis or on Zoom. Stephen Leader training consists of ten 2½-hour sessions totaling 25 hours, led by two Stephen Ministry St. Louis staff members. Typically, the lay church leader's church pays Stephen Ministries St. Louis for the lay church leader's training, but, in cases where the church is experiencing financial difficulty (as was the case when I completed the SLTC), the lay church leader must pay $1,687 (as of 2023). Although this training might seem costly, clergy and boards of deacons and trustees should view this cost as an investment in the expansion of the church's pastoral care ministry (Stephen Ministries, n.d.).

Stephen Ministries St. Louis not only trains lay church leaders in the theory and practice of spiritual care but also prepares them to cultivate and train Stephen Ministers and assign care receivers to Stephen Ministers within their own congregations—spiritually centered persons who have a proclivity to listening to persons struggling with spiritual and emotional problems. Thus, Stephen Leaders train Stephen Ministers locally at no cost to their church. My Stephen Minister training cost me $58 (as of 2021) to cover the cost of the training materials (a two-volume Stephen Ministry manual; Bretscher, 2020a, 2020b). Stephen Ministers receive 50 hours of intensive Stephen Leader–led training, which can take place either in person or on Zoom. Stephen Ministers also commit to ongoing biweekly supervision regarding their care receivers, typically led by Stephen Leaders or the pastor in charge of pastoral care. Finally, Stephen Ministers must commit to ongoing Stephen Leader–led continuing education to maintain and improve their skill set. Stephen Ministry training requires an extensive time commitment, both during training and ongoing after training. Stephen Ministers are permitted to take a break between care receivers (after finishing work with one care receiver and before beginning work with a new care receiver), but an extended break would require retraining before they began to work with care receivers again (Stephen Ministries, n.d.).

Although my training to become both a Stephen Minister and a Stephen Leader took place on Zoom, I developed a feeling of closeness with my fellow trainees. We were engaged in a process of learning how to provide care to our fellow Christians in trouble. I especially enjoyed going into breakout rooms in pairs or trios and engaging in role-plays of specific caregiving scenarios. Then, we would come together as a large group and discuss the challenges we faced role-playing the Stephen Minister or the care receiver. Often, the trainee who was assigned the role of care receiver would have the most profound insights into how the trainee who was assigned the role of Stephen Minister made them feel. Did the care receiver feel cared for or unheard? Did the care receiver feel validated or subtly judged? Did the care receiver have the space to share their innermost feelings, or did the Stephen Minister intervene too often? For me, these role-plays of specific scenarios, and the discussions that took place afterward, were the most effective and meaningful parts of my training experience.

Conclusions

In this chapter, I reviewed the essential principles of the Stephen Ministry program of care. Founded in 1975 by Kenneth Haugk, Stephen Ministry has helped thousands of persons suffering from challenging circumstances in their lives, from divorce and loss to infertility and caring for an elderly parent. Stephen Ministers rely on the principles of humanistic psychology—that, given the proper nutriments, a person will grow and thrive. Those nutriments—empathy, validation, unconditional positive regard—represent the interventions that Stephen Ministers use to focus on the process taking place in the moment between a caregiver and a care receiver. Stephen Ministers are trained not to strive for specific results but to trust God as the Curegiver, who will bring healing in God's time, not the caregiver's.

Based on an understanding of attachment theory and the four distinct individual patterns of relatedness associated with the quality of attachment relationships, I asked whether the Stephen Ministry approach to caregiving—which uses the same tools to intervene on behalf of every care receiver—might be most effective for persons classified as having a secure attachment who are simply needing temporary support. I suggested that care receivers might experience empathy, validation, and encouragement differently, depending on their attachment pattern. This additional knowledge can allow a caregiver to make connections between early caregiving patterns of significant attachment figures and current relationship patterns, including the relationship patterns observed between the caregiver and the care receiver.

In my case illustration, Pilgrim sought help with his challenges related to sustaining romantic relationships, which he believed had something to do with not mourning the tragic loss of his mother 9 years earlier. As his Stephen Minister caregiver, I used the tools of empathy, validation, encouragement, and prayer to facilitate acceptance of his loss and an openness to new experiences with emotionally available women. I outlined how I might have worked with Pilgrim differently had both my arms been free to make connections between his mother's emotional unavailability in his teenage and young adult years and his subsequent repetitive selection of emotionally unavailable women. I would have interpreted these choices as feeble attempts at mastering the unresolved loss of his mother, to re-establish a psychological equilibrium that replaced profound feelings of helplessness with a false sense of control and a lack of trust in his Higher Power to be present with him even if these women abandon him. In other areas of Pilgrim's life, the Stephen Ministry approach was successful: he became more assertive with his father (confronting him on belittling comments that he was making about Pilgrim in front of other family members) and began to search for a supportive peer community as well as a church with a strong outreach program.

The Stephen Ministry program helped this young man to thaw out and resume his spiritual and emotional growth. Still, I wonder about the permanence of his growth. Will he be able to consolidate the gains that he has made and avoid the relationship mistakes that he is prone to make? Or will he retreat from his pursuit of a long-term loving relationship and satisfy his needs for closeness with same-sex friendships such as the ones that he is making on his baseball team? Only by following up with Pilgrim longitudinally would we find answers to these questions.

Stephen Ministry has helped thousands of men and women get closer to God, to others, and to themselves through this simple program of caring. The training, though extensive, does not require a graduate degree or even a high school degree to complete. The program consists of caregiver volunteers; thus, the program is free of charge. The relatively small number of licensed mental health professionals would never be able to treat the sheer volume of care receivers who present for help at churches all over the world, and most care receivers would never be able to pay their fees.

This model of caring, which emphasizes volume, should be replicated in other settings such as mosques, temples, hospitals, military bases, prisons, and other community spaces where chaplains interact with people experiencing spiritual and emotional suffering. For more complex problems, however—especially problems that occur in the context of underlying insecure attachment patterns—it is advisable to work with a licensed mental health professional who can tailor the treatment to the client's primary mode of relatedness and situational distress (see the continuum of care; Haugk & Akers, 2020, p. 25). Stephen Ministry will always be available for persons who are experiencing temporary stresses brought on by unfortunate circumstances. Stephen Ministry is an exemplary model of the integration of emotional and spiritual care for persons who are suffering.

References

Arvidson, J., Kinniburgh, K., Howard, K., Spinazzola, J., Strothers, H., Evans, M., Andres, B., Cohen, C., & Blaustein, M. E. (2011). Treatment of complex trauma in young children: Developmental and cultural considerations in application of the ARC intervention model. *Journal of Child & Adolescent Trauma, 4*, 34–51.

Bretscher, J. P. (Ed.). (2020a). *Stephen Minister training manual, volume 1*. Stephen Ministries.

Bretscher, J. P. (Ed.). (2020b). *Stephen Minister training manual, volume 2*. Stephen Ministries.

Bretscher, J. P., & Haugk, K. C. (2023). *The gift of empathy: Helping others feel valued, cared for, and understood*. Stephen Ministries.

Daniel, S. I. F. (2015). *Adult attachment patterns in a treatment context: Relationship and narrative*. Routledge.

Dozier, M., & Bates, B. C. (2004). Attachment state of mind and the treatment relationship. In L. Atkinson & S. Goldberg (Eds.), *Attachment issues in psychopathology and intervention* (pp. 167–180). Erlbaum.

Fonagy, P., & Allison, E. (2014). The role of mentalizing and epistemic trust in the therapeutic relationship. *Psychotherapy, 31*, 372–380.

Freud, S. (1920). Beyond the pleasure principle. In J. Strachey (Ed. and Trans.), *The standard edition of the complete psychological works of Sigmund Freud* (Vol. 18, pp. 7–64). Hogarth, 1961.

Goodman, G. (1991). Feeling our way into empathy: Carl Rogers, Heinz Kohut, and Jesus. *Journal of Religion and Health, 30*, 191–205.

Granqvist, P. (2020). *Attachment in religion and spirituality: A wider view*. Guilford Press.

Greenberg, J. R. (1986). Theoretical models and the analyst's neutrality. *Contemporary Psychoanalysis, 22*, 89–106.

Haugk, K. C. (2020). *Christian caregiving: A way of life* (2nd ed.). Stephen Ministries.

Haugk, K. C., & Akers, I. B. (2020). *When and how to use mental health resources* (2nd ed.). Stephen Ministries.

Horvath, A., & Greenberg, L. (1989). Development and validation of the Working Alliance Inventory. *Journal of Counseling Psychology, 36*, 223–233.

New International Version. (1978). *The Holy Bible, new international version*. Grand Rapids, MI: Zondervan.

Peale, N. V. (2003). *The power of positive thinking*. Touchstone.

Rockland, R. H. (2003). *Supportive psychotherapy: A psychodynamic approach*. Basic Books.

Rogers, C. R. (1957). The necessary and sufficient conditions of therapeutic personality change. *Journal of Consulting Psychology, 21*, 95–103.

Rogers, C. R. (1980). *A way of being*. Houghton-Mifflin.

Slade, A. (2018). Attachment and adult psychotherapy: Theory, research, and practice. In J. Cassidy & P. R. Shaver (Eds.), *Handbook of attachment: Theory, research, and clinical applications* (3rd ed., pp. 759–779). Guilford Press.

Stephen Ministries (n.d.). www.stephenministries.org

van der Kolk, B. A. (2014). *The body keeps the score: Brain, mind, and body in the healing of trauma*. Penguin Books.

Chapter 3

Spiritual Direction

An Invitation to the Practice of Contemplation

To peel back the curtain of an actual Spiritual Direction session, I am presenting a case illustration from my Spiritual Direction practice, including a session dialogue recreated from session notes that I took immediately following this session. The directee wants to deepen her relationship to God but finds her surroundings not conducive to this search for depth. I repeatedly bring her back to her relationship to God, particularly her prayer life, and interpret the chatter in her mind and in her surroundings as avoidance of God's presence. She is gradually recognizing the barriers to this deeper relationship to God that she is seeking.

Julie: Case Illustration Introduction

Julie (her self-chosen pseudonym) is a 47-year-old Caucasian wife and the mother of a 7-year-old son. She works for the federal government and attends my church. Julie contacted me shortly after I made an announcement at my church that I wanted to work with someone in Spiritual Direction. Julie and her family live in a middle-income neighborhood in Atlanta. She feels resentful about her father's untimely death due to cancer and about being the sole breadwinner in her family. I am working with her in monthly sessions. In our initial session (December 23, 2024), Julie identified three areas of concern in her life: (1) the potential impact of the incoming Trump administration on her federal job—not knowing whether she would be receiving a pink slip; (2) her husband's and son's complete lack of interest in attending church with her; and (3) her desire to discern how God might want her to use her graduate degree in theological studies that she earned 10 years ago. In this initial session, she also shared that she has tried contemplative prayer in the past but always assumed that she was doing it incorrectly because she found it so difficult to "set aside my to-do list and the chatter in my mind." I excerpted the following session dialogue from our second Spiritual Direction session. After 5 minutes of silent prayer, I briefly prayed aloud that Julie and I would experience God's presence together in this session.

Session Excerpt (January 27, 2025)

Me: What's on your heart today?

Julie: I'm remembering a time when I strongly felt the presence of God in my life. It was before my husband and I got married. We were at my in-laws' house on the beach. I was by myself, looking at the sunset, and in that moment, God seemed to be saying to me, "Come enjoy the sunset with me." It was as if God just wanted me to spend time with Him, away from all the chaos around me. I would like to get that feeling back.

Me: You long for that connection to God you once had.

Julie: Yes! But I just feel frantic all the time [makes a frantic, stressed-out face with her hands raised and arms shaking]. The Trump administration has been firing federal workers. They have been targeting those of us who have been supportive of DEI [diversity, equity, and inclusion] efforts. That includes me.

Me: How do you feel toward God amid all this turmoil at your job?

Julie: I don't know—I guess I feel too frantic and worried to notice what I'm feeling toward God. I'm too enslaved to completing my to-do list to find out [laughs]. When my dad was alive, he used to tell me every morning, "Have a productive day, Julie." That Calvinist work ethic is so engrained in me.

Me: So being productive is important to you—to the point that it seems to be interfering with practicing meditation because meditation feels like doing nothing.

Julie: Exactly! I'm just sitting there—I need to be *doing* something. My dad never read novels because he felt they were a waste of time. The only reading he did was self-improvement because by reading those kinds of books, he was actually doing something to improve himself.

Me: Maybe you need to be productive because anything less would feel like a betrayal of your dad and what he stood for. Being unproductive would cause worry about not living up to expectations.

Julie: Yeah, that's true. I also became disenchanted with prayer because both my dad and I prayed for his recovery from cancer, but he died from cancer anyway—way too soon. Prayers of petition just don't work the way we want them to. I know that God doesn't have to answer any of our prayers because He is going to do what He thinks is best anyway, so why pray? After my dad died, I've felt deeply ambivalent about praying.

Me: I know about your frustration with unanswered prayer! That's why meditation—contemplative prayer—is so appealing to me. I'm not asking for anything. I'm just sitting in God's presence, enjoying God's company. You had that experience with God on the beach. It sounds as though you yearn for God's presence from your beach experience.

Julie: I know in our last session, you recommended just five minutes or even just one minute of silent prayer, but the chaos in my life just makes me so frantic that I just don't do it. My husband doesn't work—he basically sleeps all day, and many of the household chores are left to me to complete. And I'm certainly not getting any support at home for starting a regular silent prayer time.

Me: You sound resentful toward both Trump and your husband. Listening to you today, I'm wondering whether the Person you really feel resentful toward is God. He took away your dad way too soon and is leaving you feeling unprotected at work and unsupported at home. Is that how you see it?

Julie: It could be. I should be able to set aside five measly minutes in my day for silent prayer! It just needs to get on my to-do list [laughs]!

Me: Your angry feelings might also be getting in the way.

Julie: Yeah, I think I could tell God I'm angry with Him, though. I know that He loves me anyway.

Me: We have to stop now. Would you like to pray us out?

Julie: Sure [Julie prays for both of us to feel God's presence in our lives today and through the next month].

My Spiritual Direction Process With This Directee

I lay the groundwork for my sessions with Julie by praying for her every day. Specifically, I pray that she will draw closer to God in silent prayer. In this session, I make several interventions. Initially, I engage in reflective listening (e.g., "You long for that connection"). This empathy allows her to open up about her fear for her job, the resentment that she feels toward the Trump administration, and her feelings of isolation at home. When I bring it back to her relationship to God ("How do you feel toward God amid all this turmoil?"), she responds that she is unsure, but my question prompts a memory of her father telling her to be productive. I then make a series of interpretations: first, I suggest that her compulsive productivity might be defending against experiencing the direct presence of God; second, I suggest that trying not to be productive might feel like a betrayal of her beloved father's prime directive to be productive. Implicitly, Julie might also be transferring her father's expectations of productivity onto God; thus, being unproductive might feel like a betrayal not only of her father but also of God.

In psychodynamic language, I make an interpretation of her defense against God's presence, then move to an interpretation of the transference of her father's expectation of productivity onto God, and her worry that not living up to the expectation of these powerful males would feel like a betrayal of them. She responds by indirectly expressing her disappointment toward God for not having answered her prayers for her father's recovery, which causes her to give up on prayers of petition. I empathize with her feelings ("I know about your frustration") and I make a brief self-disclosure about the appeal of silent prayer for me because I am not asking for anything but rather just sitting in God's presence. Then I tie it back to her longing ("You yearn for God's presence"). She makes a commitment to silent prayer, but I emphasize her angry feelings toward the Trump administration and her husband and wonder whether she might be feeling angry toward God for abandoning her (letting her father die, leaving her feeling unprotected at work) and not supporting her (giving her a husband who neither works nor shares her spiritual beliefs). Julie tells me that she knows that she can express angry feelings toward God.

If we had had more time in this session, I might have challenged her to reflect on her knowledge of God's acceptance of all her feelings—including her angry feelings. Is her knowledge of God's acceptance of all her feelings purely an intellectual knowledge or does she know it deep in her heart? Can she trust God not to abandon her (as her father did) if she were to express these feelings to God?

In my responses to Julie, I primarily used Rogerian techniques such as unconditional positive regard, empathy, and genuineness (Rogers, 1957; see also Chapter 2). In contrast to Spiritually Integrated Psychotherapy (SIP; see Chapter 7) or Attachment-Informed Psychotherapy (AIP; see Chapter 8), I did not interpret Julie's transference feelings toward me or my countertransference feelings toward Julie. Transference feelings are patient/directee feelings that originate in our relationships with our earliest caregivers and that we attribute to people who occupy caregiving roles in our adult lives (such as romantic partners and therapists). Countertransference feelings are therapist/director feelings that can originate from the same early relationship sources or from direct interactions with the patient/directee (i.e., how a patient/directee makes the therapist/director feel). As the reader shall see below, the Spiritual Direction literature mentions transference and countertransference phenomena only infrequently (for a rare exception, see May, 1982, pp. 103–108). In this literature, spiritual directors seem to be laser-focused on keeping God at the center of the session, but I do wonder how spiritual directors process transference and countertransference feelings that inevitably arise in these encounters. In the session above, I felt warm and loving toward Julie. I could see parallels between her life and mine, which facilitated my feelings of empathy toward her. I hope that I conveyed these feelings toward her, not with my words but with my body language—leaning slightly forward in my chair, looking relaxed and attentive, manifesting a gentle tone of voice and a warm, caring look in my eyes. I also felt good about our session afterward because she seemed eager to engage in this Spiritual Direction process with me. I will refer back to this session to illustrate various points in this chapter.

Description of Spiritual Direction

Spiritual Direction is not a monolithic practice and, therefore, does not have one definition agreed upon by all practitioners. If we define "the Holy Spirit" as the Divine Presence in all religions, regardless of whether that Divine Presence exists inside the self, outside the self, or both inside and outside the self (see later discussion), then Edwards's (2001) definition suffices:

> The meeting of two or more people whose desire is to prayerfully listen for the movements of the Holy Spirit in all areas of a person's life (not just in their formal prayer life). It is a three-way relationship: among the true director who is the Holy Spirit ... and the human director (who listens for the directions of the Spirit with the directee), and the directee. (locations 70–72)

May (1982) defines Spiritual Direction as "attempting to remain attentive to God-in-the-moment and remaining as open to the Spirit and as surrendered to grace as one can be" (p. 73). Although part of an ancient tradition that stretches back thousands of years, contemporary Spiritual Direction seems to prefer using the term "spiritual companion" to describe what was traditionally known as the spiritual director. "Spiritual companion" has a more egalitarian connotation that emphasizes the mutual "not knowing" of both director and directee. For the purposes of this chapter, I will be using the traditional terms "spiritual director" and "spiritual directee" because these terms more clearly delineate the different roles of the two participants in the Spiritual Direction process.

Can Spiritual Direction really be as simple as paying attention to God? To what end do we learn to pay attention to God? Again, May (1982) writes, "In its purest form Spiritual Direction is a journey towards more freely and deeply choosing to surrender to God" (pp. 51–52). Thus, it seems that more deeply surrendering to God is a goal of Spiritual Direction. Laird (2011) underscores a different goal, "unquestionable accuracy of our self-knowledge," which he defines as "know[ing] the crucial distinction between any sort of interior weather and the mountain on which the weather comes and goes" (p. 78). He seems to be alluding not only to developing an understanding of which feelings belong to us and which feelings belong to others but also to developing an understanding between genuine feelings that originate from our true self and feelings artificially generated by our false self—what contemplative writers often refer to as the "ego." De Wit (2019) refers to Spiritual Direction as "the cultivation of inner flourishing" and views its goal as "a process of uncovering our humaneness by exposing and eliminating that which chokes it rather than directly cultivating the humaneness itself" (p. 15). Thus, a third goal might be the removal of thoughts, feelings, and behaviors that make us less than human. Finally, de Wit (2019) identifies a fourth goal of Spiritual Direction: "open-mindedness is the outcome or fruit of the disciplines of mindfulness" (p. 225). Presumably, the practice of continual surrender and removal of attitudes that spring forth from our ego makes us more open to experience, especially experience of God.

Based on my reading of the literature, I am identifying four goals of Spiritual Direction: (1) surrender to God, (2) the cultivation of self-knowledge or insight, (3) the letting go of attitudes and mental states that interfere with our surrender and cultivation of self-knowledge, and (4) ultimately, an open-mindedness to experience, especially experience of God.

I want to highlight two presuppositions of Spiritual Direction that seem to hold regardless of the type of Spiritual Direction (see below) or religious affiliation (e.g., Christian, Buddhist). The first presupposition is that spirituality is an innate quality of humanity. According to Edwards (2001), we are not human beings on a spiritual journey but rather spiritual beings on a human journey. This idea reminds me of the biblical phrase "strangers in a strange land" (Exodus 2:22, King James Version [KJV]), which is repeated in the New Testament in describing believers as "foreigners and strangers on earth" (Hebrews 11:13, New International Version [NIV]). "We are spirits in the material world," as Sting sings (Sting, 1981). Edwards (2001) emphasizes our innate spirituality: "We are spiritual (or we could say soul) beings intrinsically; this is not an imposed 'add-on' to our lives. We are embodied spirits, embodied souls, on a mysterious journey from, in, and to the Holy One" (locations 381–382). Presumably, some persons' inability to recognize their intrinsic spirituality is directly related to whatever is blocking this awareness. Some writers use the metaphor of God as light always shining upon us, but we often pull down the shade (Burtchaell, 1985). Spiritual Direction helps directors and directees to become aware of the shades that we pull down to block out God's love and tender care.

The second presupposition is that this blocked awareness of God's constant presence represents the Original Sin of humanity, as the contemplative literature defines "sin." Whereas the classical Judeo-Christian tradition views sin as disobedience to God (e.g., "through the disobedience of the one man the many were made sinners"; Romans 5:19, NIV), the contemplative literature defines the Original Sin of humanity as a "fall from awareness of and responsiveness to God's Spirit in our souls and in creation" (Edwards, 2001, location 384). Stated slightly differently, sin is belief in the illusion that God is not present inside us—that God is separated from us in some remote location with only intermittent access or no access at all. The apostle Paul's letter to the Romans supports God's enduring presence in the here and now:

> Who shall separate us from the love of Christ? ... Neither death nor life, neither angels nor demons, neither the present nor the future, nor any powers, neither height nor depth, nor anything else in all creation, will be able to separate us from the love of God that is in Christ Jesus our Lord. (Romans 8:35, 38–39, NIV)

The illusion of separation is the sin; in this view, disobedience is only a secondary consideration. The ego causes, or at least reinforces, our illusory belief and experience of separation from God.

The ego—or false self, as I will often be referring to it in this chapter—is supremely concerned with acquisition—food, shelter, sex, security, dominance, possessions—and unconcerned with grace—the humble acceptance of God's freely given, unearned gifts. Thus, the contemplative literature views clinging to these gifts as sin. In fact, some writers suggest that attachment to anything blocks our awareness of God's presence inside us and in the world—even cherished mental images of God. This definition of sin implies that Spiritual Direction facilitates the surrender of acquisition until all that is left is emptiness. In this vast empty space, medieval German Christian mystic Meister Eckhart proclaims that God "giv[es] birth to himself spiritually in the soul," which happens when God finds the soul empty and detached enough (Blakney, 1941, p. 129). According to May (1991), "Anyone who faces emptiness becomes contemplative in that very moment, for then the truth is seen—just as it is" (p. 105). Images of self and God merely clutter the mental landscape and prevent us from making direct contact with the Holy Mystery that is God. The ego thrives on attachment to these mental images, which disrupts the contemplative process. Laird (2011) translates into English early Christian mystic Saint Gregory of Nyssa's warning that any mental image or concept of God "becomes an idol of God and does not make God known" (p. 139). Therefore, God is ultimately ineffable.

In addition, contemplative writers define sin as lacking faith in the emptiness, the "cloud of unknowing" as an anonymous medieval Christian monk describes his direct experience of God (Anonymous, 2009). Ultimately, sin is having faith in the symbols and mental images to which the ego or false self clings, rather than having faith in the immanent and transcendent Higher Power. Letting go of these symbols and mental images forecasts the death of the ego or false self that stands in the way between me and the Holy. The Holy is always there, waiting for us to clear away the clutter so that we can enjoy God's presence. De Wit (2019) succinctly describes this process:

> The moment at which our internal commentary ceases and all conceptualizations, meaning conceptual frameworks within which we define ourselves and our reality, sink into nothingness [i.e., emptiness] is given many different names: nakedness, liberation, enlightenment, openness, truth, wholeness. From the perspective of ego, such moments are associated with its own death and destruction. (p. 90)

Perhaps Jesus is referring to this death of ego in these words from the Gospel of Matthew: "Whoever wants to be my disciple must deny themselves and take up their cross and follow me. For whoever wants to save their life will lose it, but whoever loses their life for me will find it" (Matthew 16:24–25, NIV; see also Luke 9:23–24). The apostle Paul also writes to the church at Corinth, "I die daily" (I Corinthians 15:31, KJV). Jesus seems to be using the word "life" here to mean the ego, the false self that clings to the finite—whether that be possessions, ideas, doctrines, or mental images.

Based on the foregoing discussion of (1) a universal spirituality innate in all humans and (2) contemplatives' view of Original Sin as blocked awareness of God's constant presence through attachments to the finite, what do the director and directee do in Spiritual Direction? Are people who enter Spiritual Direction signing up to learn how to "take up a cross" or "die daily" to their attachments to experience God's presence more intimately? Following these ideas, Edwards (2001) believes that Spiritual Direction facilitates "our willingness to let go what is being held onto that impedes [God's] radiation" (locations 373–374). Later, Edwards (2001) characterizes Spiritual Direction as "realizing the divine Presence in and around us all the time, praying for the empowerment to freely embrace that Presence as the very heart of our true soul identity, and living out of its movements" (locations 830–832). Toward this end, the spiritual director "bring[s the spiritual directee] to God in prayer and ... join[s] God's hope for them, beyond our understanding, as well as to protect a special time for them to listen deeply and embrace God's song in their song" (locations 1236–1237). There is no Spiritual Direction manual or cookbook for this process; joining in God's hope for the directee, listening deeply, and embracing God's song manifest differently for every directee.

In my session with Julie, I pray in silent meditation with her, then I listen for how God is moving in her life. I always address Julie's spirituality explicitly rather than implicitly, as SIP therapists also sometimes do (see Chapter 7). After she tells me about the purge taking place among federal employees, I ask her, "How do you feel toward God amid all this turmoil at your job?" I keep the focus always on God and God's presence. To use Edwards's (2001) phrasing, I am really asking, "Is this worry about your job impeding God's radiation in your life?" A spiritual director is intent on "exposing and eliminating that which chokes [our humaneness] rather than directly cultivating the humaneness itself" (de Wit, 2019, p. 15). I do not instruct Julie to forgive President Trump and his minions; I merely draw her attention back to God and her feelings toward God. Julie then begins to realize that her frantic reaction is blocking her from her awareness of God's constant presence, even in this potentially dire situation. I am helping Julie to re-establish contact with her innate spirituality—the Holy Spirit within her—that her frantic reaction is obstructing. This is my understanding of how Spiritual Direction works.

Practical Application of Spiritual Direction

Have you, the reader, ever tried meditation? Meditation is the daily homework that the spiritual directee completes between Spiritual Direction sessions. In my own first Spiritual Direction session, my director asked me to reserve 5 minutes every day to meditate. But what is meditation?

I first became aware of meditation from reading the psychotherapy literature almost 20 years ago with the explosion in popularity of the use of Dialectical

Behavior Therapy (DBT) and other so-called "third wave" cognitive-behavioral therapies (Hayes, 2002, 2004). These psychotherapy models are used to treat persons diagnosed with psychiatric disorders that are as varied as borderline personality disorder (BPD) and substance use disorders (SUDs). The psychotherapy literature refers to meditation as "mindfulness," which is at the center of all third wave psychotherapies.

The psychotherapy literature describes mindfulness as a process of "paying attention in a particular way: on purpose, in the present moment, and nonjudgmentally" (Kabat-Zinn, 1994, p. 4). For Kabat-Zinn (2003), mindfulness is a meditation practice, which is the vehicle, or delivery system, by which mindfulness is most skillfully practiced. Meditation practice represents the heart of mindfulness-based stress reduction (MBSR) intervention—a radical "nonattachment to outcome" (p. 148) that grounds the patient squarely in the here and now, in a state of attention to all internal and external stimuli, and facilitates "acceptance of the full gamut of emotional expression held in awareness" (p. 153). Further, Kabat-Zinn (2003) characterizes mindfulness as "an inherent human capacity" (p. 146) that varies across situations and across persons. Meditation cultivates and refines the capacity for mindfulness through the attentive observation of "the interconnectedness of apparently separate aspects of experience, many of which tend to hover beneath our ordinary level of awareness regarding both inner and outer experience" (p. 149). Another characteristic of mindfulness and the third wave treatments, therefore, is their emphasis on unconscious phenomena and their need for integration, which clearly resembles a psychoanalytic approach to treatment (e.g., Kernberg, 1975).

In 2004, Bishop and his colleagues (Bishop et al., 2004) responded to the need to publish an operational definition that could be used to construct empirical instruments to assess mindfulness. Their model of mindfulness consisted of two components: (1) the self-regulation of attention maintained on immediate experience in the present moment and (2) an orientation to immediate experience in the present moment characterized by curiosity, openness, and acceptance. The self-regulation of attention occurs when the person observes and monitors internal and external experiences, notes them, and lets them go. In classical psychoanalytic terms, the patient uses their self-observing ego (Freud, 1933; Sterba, 1934) to observe all mental phenomena that enter preconscious awareness (Freud, 1900). Going beyond mindfulness practice, patients in Psychodynamic Therapy (PDT) then associate freely to these phenomena during the session.

Hayes (2004) provides a striking illustration of the patient as a dispassionate observer of mental phenomena. Called the Soldiers in the Parade mindfulness exercise, the patient is instructed to imagine that little soldiers are marching out of his or her ear and then in front of him or her as though parading in front of a reviewing stand. Each soldier is carrying a sign with a thought or feeling printed on it in the form of words or pictures. The patient must try to let the parade go by without joining the parade. When the patient inevitably joins the parade and leaves the reviewing stand, he or she must see what happened right before the observation of the parade stopped.

Having been in my personal analysis for over 16 years, I nevertheless found this exercise extraordinarily difficult to accomplish on my own for more than a few minutes when I first tried it. The exercise is designed to teach the patient "how to look at thoughts as thoughts rather than looking at the world through thoughts, and to learn how to detect the difference" (Hayes, 2004, p. 20). Such an exercise can help to introduce a space between the patient's perception and response, which would permit the patient to respond to situations "more reflectively (as opposed to reflexively)" (Bishop et al., 2004, p. 232). One can imagine how mindfulness as practiced in DBT might help patients diagnosed with BPD or SUDs diminish their impulsivity, a common symptom of these two conditions.

How is mindfulness practice related to Spiritual Direction? Meditation as practiced by Christian mystics, contemplatives, and spiritual directors and directees constitutes a mindfulness practice. Noticing and then letting go thoughts, feelings, and narratives that come to mind are common to both secular and spiritual contexts. The intention is different, however. While psychotherapy patients intend to experience relief from their symptoms such as impulsivity and rigidity of thought, spiritual directors and directees intend to experience the presence of God directly rather than in a second-hand manner such as by reading the Bible or going to church and taking communion. In fact, some contemplative scholars (e.g., Edwards, 2001; de Wit, 2019; May, 1982) argue that the desire for symptom improvement and even the desire for experiencing the presence of God directly represent attachments that the person must surrender. Taking this idea even further, the spiritual director and directee must surrender the goal of purposelessness of meditation. There comes a time when letting go of all attachments produces the fear that "I will truly cease to exist" (May, 1982, p. 69), taking the form of fear of death, losing control, or being abandoned. Responding to Jesus's beckoning, his disciple Peter walked on water until "he saw the wind, he was afraid and [he began] to sink" (Matthew 14:30, NIV). Thus, no one can remain in a state of purposeless detachment forever; everyone returns to the illusion of the necessity of clinging sooner or later. Mindfulness in Spiritual Direction is the practice of being ready for the direct experience of the presence of God, whether it comes or not. Being ready is the open-minded observation of thought processes and then letting them go like soldiers in a parade.

In a Spiritual Direction session, the spiritual director inquires about the directee's experience of meditation between monthly sessions. Which thoughts or feelings appear most frequently? Which thoughts or feelings are most difficult to let go of? Some spiritual directors might also inquire about childhood experiences related to the "stickiest" thoughts and feelings. For example, in my own meditation practice, the thought and worry associated with writing this book occupy my mind and interfere with my meditation experience of being in the present moment. As a child, I knew that the only way to please my father was to excel in school, which I tried my best to do. Writing this book—indeed, all my scholarly pursuits—feels like an homage to my father, to receive love from him posthumously. On the surface, this motivation does not make sense—my father has been dead for almost 34 years and has, thus, been slow to give me affirmation—but, at a deeper level, he is still very much alive in my mind.

In my case illustration, Julie complains that, during meditation, visions of to-do lists dance in her head, which interfere with her ability to observe her thoughts and feelings and let them go. She associates these to-do lists with her desire to be productive, which she attributes to her father's routine counsel to "have a productive day" and his own modeling of productivity by refraining from any frivolous activity such as reading novels. A spiritual director can inquire about any associations from the directee that might come to mind in connection with these sticky thoughts and feelings. Unlike a SIP therapist (see Chapter 7), however, a spiritual director would usually refrain from interpreting these childhood experiences as spiritual distractions, instead trusting in the Holy Spirit to bring this awareness to the directee. Vidrine (2015) warns the spiritual director not to be "seduced into thinking that I know the answers and ... kidnapped by my desire to be helpful. My compassion turns into a desire to control rather than an intent to join" (p. 47). The spiritual director stance offered by Vidrine and other writers resembles the psychoanalyst's stance offered by British object relations theorist Donald Winnicott (1971), who viewed the analyst's role as facilitating the patient's expression of their own experience rather than interpreting their experience for them. For Winnicott, the patient needs to create their own meaning within the therapeutic relationship without the therapist's interpretive interference. Of course, for Freud (e.g., 1919), interpretation was "the pure gold of analysis" (p. 168), because humans' tendency toward self-deception through defense mechanisms such as repression of unconscious material makes interpretation necessary. Spiritual Direction seems to have more in common with object relations theory than with classical psychoanalytic theory.

The use of silence is another practical application of Spiritual Direction during a session. The spiritual director creates space for the Holy Spirit to "speak" to both the director and the directee. Generally, this silence takes place during meditation at the beginning or end of the session (see my case illustration), but it can also take place at other times. Both parties wait for the Holy Spirit's presence and direction to materialize. Silence used in meditation has a long history. Medieval Christian mystic St. John of the Cross (1991) suggests that "the language God best hears is the silent language of love" (p. 95). Contemporary Christian mystic Thomas Keating (1997) believes that "silence is God's first language; everything else is a poor translation" (p. 90). When we truly quiet our minds, we can begin to hear the "still small voice" within ourselves (see I Kings 19:12, KJV). According to Edwards (2001), "The director need not verbally speak during the entire session, and yet their soul-presence does speak, on a deeper level" (location 1030).

One can even find the privileging of silence in psychoanalysis. Winnicott (2016) writes, "I seldom make an interpretation and the analysis proceeds best on the basis of my saying nothing at all" (p. 517). Winnicott reasons that, for the analysis to proceed successfully, "it is essential to accept certain ideas about oneself which are untrue" (p. 515). Might meditation in Spiritual Direction serve the same purpose? Spiritual directors and directees must come to the realization that a Higher Power loves them despite their distortions of this Higher Power's nature through finite images and beliefs about this Higher Power. I can imagine, however, that some might interpret God's silence as a rejection and stop listening for God in silence. A spiritual director, however, would not make the interpretation that childhood experiences of rejection with attachment figures might be related to the directee's idiosyncratic interpretation of God's silence. In this situation, the spiritual director might instead refer the directee to a SIP therapist, who is trained to make such interpretations (see Chapters 7 and 8).

In Spiritual Direction, the process is always focused explicitly on the spiritual directee's relationship to God. The spiritual director treats nonspiritual issues (e.g., family, work, hobbies) as opportunities to help the directee to see how God might be working in the directee's life. When Julie tells me about what is happening at work, I reply, "How do you feel toward God amid all this turmoil at your job?" While SIP therapists work with a patient's spirituality implicitly or explicitly (see Chapter 7), spiritual directors always work with spirituality explicitly because the directee has consented to receive Spiritual Direction; working with the directee's spirituality is the *raison d'être* of Spiritual Direction.

Notably, spiritual directors do not engage in solving the directee's problems. A spiritual directee might find a solution to specific problems through Spiritual Direction, but spiritual directors do not suggest these solutions. In this sense, Spiritual Direction resembles Stephen Ministry (see Chapter 2) in recognizing that God, not the spiritual director, is the Curegiver (Bretscher, 2020; Haugk, 2020). On this matter, Edwards (2001) is unequivocal:

> It's important that the focus remain on probing what the Spirit seems to be up to in what is brought and how the directee is responding, rather than on human issues and problem solving in which one's desire for God has lost centrality. (locations 1170–1171)

Trying to solve the spiritual directee's problems places the director in the position of God, Who is waiting patiently for the directee to trust that all is as it should be. This nonproblem-solving stance can test the spiritual director's faith that God's grace is the fundamental principle of the universe. God's activity in the spiritual directee's life is a gift, freely given. No activity on our part is necessary to enact this gift.

Freud (1919) also viewed problem-solving as insufficient to help patients with their problems. He made the contrast between his treatment—"the pure gold of analysis"—and problem-solving, "the copper of direct suggestion" (p. 168). He believed that making suggestions to patients about how they should improve their lives was not helpful because suggestions do not help patients to understand the often-irrational motivations underlying their feelings, thoughts, and behaviors. Thus, there is also clinical evidence for refraining from problem-solving. Only God can help a spiritual directee to solve their problems.

Edwards (2001) discusses seven models of Spiritual Direction, which I will only briefly review here.

- *The master–disciple relationship*: the oldest model of Spiritual Direction is the master–disciple relationship. Obedience to the master/spiritual director facilitates the directee's surrender of their separate ego-will. This model's flaw, however, is that "unenlightened parts of the master's mind can go unrecognized, possibly causing exploitation of the disciple" (Edwards, 2001, location 1047).
- *Gifted Spiritual Direction*: gifted Spiritual Direction consists of spiritual directors who are called to this form of ministry but lack formal theological or spiritual training. These lay persons, however, sometimes suppress "even a gentle challenge to the directee that has come to them and might truly be of the Spirit" (Edwards, 2001, locations 1054–1055).
- *Counseling-inspired Spiritual Direction*: counseling-inspired Spiritual Direction is more formal than the gifted model because the spiritual director has received professional clinical or theological training. Thus, spiritual directees who have identifiable psychological problems might fare better participating in this model of Spiritual Direction. Because of my clinical psychology training and Spiritual Direction training and supervision, my Spiritual Direction with Julie would fit in this category. Edwards (2001), however, cautions these professional spiritual directors, who might be lured into turning away from "a simple, open presence to God and to become more dependent on the director's conditioned knowledge and images" (locations 1062–1063). In my case illustration, I tell Julie, "Maybe you need to be productive because anything less would feel like a betrayal of your dad and what he stood for." That is just a straight-up psychological interpretation that typically has no place in Spiritual Direction. In that moment, I veered away from an exclusive spiritual focus.
- *Eldering and discipling*: eldering and discipling are most prevalent in evangelical churches, which privilege scripturally grounded guidance provided by clergy and church elders or deacons. Unfortunately, this model does not leave much room for "deep listening to the mysterious and often surprising ways that the Spirit moves within a person's life" (Edwards, 2001, location 1070).
- *Informal relationships*: "informal relationships" (Edwards, 2001) include friendships among church congregants who pray for each other. These relationships tend to feature mutual sharing rather than one person directing

another. Edwards (2001) suggests that this model might have "a wandering focus, wherein one or both persons really need more centering time" (locations 1076–1077).

- *Mutual Spiritual Direction*: mutual Spiritual Direction consists of two persons who each serve as the other's spiritual director. Person A might be the spiritual director and Person B the directee during a session, with the roles reversed during the next session; thus, these roles are interchangeable across (but not within) sessions. Contemplative persons often refer to this model of Spiritual Direction as spiritual companioning to eliminate the hierarchical connotations associated with the word "direction." Edwards (2001) suggests that, because of the dual roles that such relationships imply (being both spiritual director and directee of the same person), the person enacting the spiritual director role might experience "a slightly lessened sense of freedom ... to fully listen to God for the other person or to feel fully free to challenge the other person ... because they are aware that they will be speaking about themselves in the [next session]" (locations 1087–1089).
- *Group Spiritual Direction*: in group Spiritual Direction, three to six persons "gather on a regular basis to listen for God in their lives" (Edwards, 2001, locations 1092–1093). Dougherty (1995) has written extensively about the Shalem Institute for Spiritual Formation's practice of group Spiritual Direction. I too have benefited from group Spiritual Direction under the auspices of the Shalem Institute. During a session, two group members take turns presenting their work with a spiritual directee. The other group members focus on the presenter's spiritual development as it relates to their work with the directee. This peer supervision challenges me to observe more closely certain aspects of my own relationship to God of which I would not otherwise have become aware. A disadvantage to group Spiritual Direction is that "there is less time for the sharing of one's own life" (location 1093).

The empirical evidence supporting the effectiveness of Spiritual Direction is almost nonexistent. In my investigation of the vast Spiritual Direction literature, there seems to be a strong bias against empiricism, presumably because spiritual directors and the contemplative literature more generally possess an iron-clad epistemology of knowing that God's presence is with the spiritual director and directee, moving the participants toward more love, more grace, and more surrender to the all-encompassing presence of God. Empiricists such as me are simply doubting Thomases who cannot accept the Truth of God's love manifested in Spiritual Direction relationships. No one is more unequivocal about this position than de Wit (2019), who proclaims that the empirical method of research "must leave out ... the field of one's own mental or inner life—because it is not directly accessible by other researchers" (p. 34). The mental field "is only directly accessible by the person involved, requiring research in the first person, or self-examination" (p. 35). De Wit (2019) contrasts the contemplative traditions to the scientific traditions, which collect "information *about* [emphasis added] human functioning" (p. 37) rather than having a direct, first-person experience of human functioning. In fact, de Wit (2019) regards secular psychologies as "profane or materialistic; they are based on a concept of humanity that allows no room for a spiritual or contemplative dimension as an authentic power" (p. 53).

Thus, any scientific methodology that seeks to investigate the effectiveness of Spiritual Direction must also be profane or materialistic if it questions whether participation in Spiritual Direction produces "effective charity and care [which] are the visible fruits of genuine insight as part of a flourishing within" (de Wit, 2019, p. 64). Even if it were true that researchers could never study a person's mind directly, could they not still investigate Spiritual Direction's effectiveness in cultivating these "visible fruits"? A researcher could randomly assign participants to Spiritual Direction and noncontemplative prayer conditions to determine whether the Spiritual Direction condition produces more of these "visible fruits" after 1 year of participation than the noncontemplative prayer condition. One of these visible fruits might be implicit and explicit emotional awareness, already reliably assessed in a study of Panic-Focused Psychodynamic Psychotherapy (PFPP; Beutel et al., 2013). With such studies, we would have a basis for affirming that Spiritual Direction possesses advantages over traditional prayer between friends.

In an intriguing article reviewing neuroimaging studies, both secular meditation and free association (a technique developed by Freud and used by patients in psychoanalysis) were associated with changes in the default mode network (DMN) and the executive network (EN; Novac & Blinder, 2021). Perhaps researchers can directly observe activity in a person's mind after all. I also found one qualitative research dissertation study (Maier, 2017) in which the author interviewed five spiritual directors and used interpretive phenomenological analysis (IPA) to identify six themes characterizing the meaning of the spiritual director's experience: (1) collaborative relational approach, (2) emergent perspective, (3) love, (4) ongoing personal and spiritual work, (5) mutual impact, and (6) activities working as a spiritual director. What is striking is not the study's findings but, rather, its uniqueness in its object of study—spiritual directors. If Spiritual Direction is so spiritually meaningful to both participants, would not the contemplative community want to demonstrate its "visible fruits" to the wider spiritual and even secular communities? Such research would help to dispel the prevailing idea that Spiritual Direction—indeed, the practice of Christian mysticism in general—is some esoteric spiritual practice reserved for monks and ascetics who live sequestered from the world in monasteries and cloisters, with no practical relevance to common folk like you and me. Some writers (e.g., Lanzetta, 2018; Thurman, 1996) argue that Christian contemplation has the power to transform the world. But, considering the current state of this violent, spiritually impoverished world in which we live and the nearly 2,000 years it has been around, Christian contemplation seems to be off to a slow start. Many more persons might be interested in Spiritual Direction if they were aware of evidence demonstrating its effectiveness in creating change. If God is the author of all things, then that would include the scientific method. Why not take advantage of this method to demonstrate empirically Spiritual Direction's power to transform both the self and the world?

History of Spiritual Direction

Spiritual Direction traces its lineage to the third century CE, when some early Christians left secular society and settled in the desert regions of Egypt, Palestine, and Syria to seek God's presence (de Dreuille, 1999; Merton, 1960). Anthony the Great was one of the earliest "Desert Fathers," having moved to the Egyptian desert from Koma. In the desert, Anthony lived an ascetic life, attracting thousands of monks and nuns to join him (Chryssavgis, 2008). Beginning in the desert, this practice of Christian monasticism influenced the development of Spiritual Direction as a form of discipleship among monks.

The New Testament provides a precedent for spiritual mentorship. Jesus mentored His 12 disciples to prepare them for their own ministry after His ascension (Acts 1:9, NIV). Likewise, Ananias mentored the apostle Paul (Acts 9:17–19, NIV), who in turn mentored Timothy (I and II Timothy, NIV) and Titus (Titus, NIV) among others. It was not until the fourth century CE, however, that John Cassian (1985) codified the practice of Spiritual Direction with a set of guidelines for Christian monasteries to follow. Older monks provided Spiritual Direction to younger monks, who in turn became older monks and provided Spiritual Direction to younger monks.

In recent years, Spiritual Direction has enjoyed a renewed interest among mostly Catholic, Eastern Orthodox, and Anglican and Episcopal Christians, but also Christians from other Protestant denominations (Edwards, 2001). Training centers such as the Shalem Institute for Spiritual Formation in Washington, DC, beginning its training program in 1978, have carried on the ancient tradition of Spiritual Direction by teaching it to a new audience, which now also includes lay persons, Jews, Buddhists, Hindus, and Sufis. For example, my peer supervision group at the Shalem Institute includes a female rabbi whom I greatly admire for her authentic spirituality. The Shalem Institute also practices inclusivity, training gay and lesbian spiritual directors. Anyone desiring to practice the presence of God in their life and help others practice this presence is welcome to train at the Shalem Institute (see below). Spiritual Direction training is proliferating because "there seems to be a growing hunger for [Spiritual Direction] in churches" (Edwards, 2001, location 1651). The Samaritan Counseling Center of Atlanta (SCCA) employs two spiritual directors on its staff. Spiritual Direction appears to represent one method of satisfying the ravenous spiritual hunger experienced in late-stage capitalism. What are most persons seeking in Spiritual Direction? They seek discernment.

Discernment in Spiritual Direction

Discernment in Spiritual Direction is so much more than clearing the mental chatter in the mind to be able to listen to the still small voice of the Holy Spirit (I Kings 9:12, KJV). Discernment is the increasing awareness of the spiritual dimension in every aspect of life. Discernment, therefore, is the sense of God's presence in and around me and in and around others, including my spiritual directee. Barry (2000) describes this activity of the spiritual director in Spiritual Direction as "helping directees to become more and more aware of this religious dimension, of the activity of God drawing them into divine union" (p. 27). For example, Julie wants to discern how God might use her graduate degree in theological studies to serve others.

Discernment is about sensing God's presence, not necessarily determining which choice God wants us to make. Dougherty (1998) wonders why God remains silent when she asks God what she should do. She eventually begins to wonder whether "God's seeming silence in these circumstances isn't [actually] a tacit act of God's trust in me, inviting me to claim what I already know" (p. 9). God truly does not care whether I order sea salt caramel or mint chocolate chip ice cream at Morelli's here in Atlanta. God trusts that I know which flavor I prefer, and, if I end up not liking that flavor, God is still present in my life.

On the other hand, I have often struggled with decisions that I knew were not God's will for me, yet I made them anyway. In these situations, I do not feel worthy of God's grace and love. I am thinking specifically of hitting rock bottom in my addictive behavior before finding a 12-step program (see Goodman, 2025, Chapter 1). Was I worthy of redemption? Burtchaell (1985) provides a thought-provoking interpretation of Jesus's parable of the Prodigal Son, one of the most famous passages in the New Testament from the gospel of Luke 15:11–32 (NIV). A man has two sons, one faithfully working for his father, the other wanting his inheritance now so that he can travel the world. After squandering his inheritance on debauchery, the prodigal son returns to his father's house, prepared to work as a servant in exchange for food and shelter. Instead of castigating this son, the father prepares a banquet to celebrate his return. The faithful son, however, expresses bitter resentment at the forgiveness that his father extends to the no-good son. Burtchaell suggests that neither son "can grasp that the father loves him not for what he has done, but for what he has always been: his own child" (p. 15). Each son could think that the father loves him, because he has always been a faithful worker or because he has eventually returned to his father. But their father does not set any conditions on his love for both sons. In applying the parable to humans' relationship to a Higher Power-Caregiver, Burtchaell writes, "The Lord demands no satisfaction, because it is not in him to turn away from us in the first place" (p. 15). As mentioned earlier, Burtchaell (1985) uses the metaphor of God as light to demonstrate God's constant love for us: "The sun is always there and shining; whenever the shade is raised, the light streams in"

(p. 21). Will we raise the shade to receive the sunlight? The songwriter Leonard Cohen (1992) expresses this sentiment differently: "There is a crack, a crack in everything. That's how the light gets in." This perspective reduces the burden of having to make the right decision to maintain God's love. It is always there, regardless of the right or wrong decisions that I make.

How does a spiritual director help a spiritual directee to have this realization? According to the Spiritual Direction literature, our Higher Power is always within us, waiting for us to return, just like the prodigal son. The spiritual director must be prepared to help the directee realize that "while he was still a long way off, his father saw him and was filled with compassion for him" (Luke 15:20, NIV). Our Higher Power wants us to recognize this ongoing loving attachment relationship, even when we are still a long way off from recognizing the reality of this attachment relationship. The spiritual director must be prepared to help the directee "ever more fully allow [the river] to carry [them]" (Rohr, 2016, p. 58). Julie wants to know whether she can connect to God, even though her to-do list seems to be standing in the way.

For me, the problem with discernment in Spiritual Direction is related to the concept of Original Sin presented in the contemplative literature discussed earlier. Some writers suggest that, through the process of contemplation, spiritual directors and directees can become divine. Dr. Tony Sundermeier, the senior pastor of First Presbyterian Church of Atlanta, is fond of saying from the pulpit, "God is God, and you're not." Jesus said, "The kingdom of God is within you" (Luke 17:21, NIV). He did not say, "The kingdom of God is you." The distinction matters because the self-perception of divinity can lead us to believe that we are always right. We need to maintain a sense of humility, a sense that, while we are living in the awareness of the Divine living within us, we can still make mistakes and pursue paths contrary to God's will.

One of the most outspoken proponents of the idea of human divinity is Maria Jaoudi (1998), who proclaims: "We as humans may become divinized by coming to embody the presence of Christ" (p. 16). Later, Jaoudi (1998) exclaims: "It is love and consciousness that deify us" (p. 34). Laird (2011) uses the metaphor of a sponge in the ocean to illustrate the utter lack of any distinction between the ocean (God) and the sponge (us): "The sponge ... is immersed in the ocean depth that fills its every membrane. When the sponge looks out, it sees only ocean; when it looks within, it sees only ocean" (p. 83). The author implies that we as persons simply dissolve into the vastness of God. Still other writers are careful to draw a distinction between God and humans. For example, Leech (1980) seems to share Jaoudi's view that human nature is actually divine: "The purpose of the Incarnation was to raise humanity to share the Divine life. ... We come to share in the divinity of Christ" (p. 13). Leech (1980), however, cautions the reader to remain aware of the distinction between the Divine and humanity: "This union [humanity with God] does not abolish the separate identities of divine and human" (p. 14). This statement then raises the question, how are we like God, and how are we not like God? As we have seen, not all writers maintain this distinction, instead veering off in the direction of pantheism. If you think that I am being hyperbolic, consider Christian contemplative theologian Beverly Lanzetta's (2018) definitive statement: "The world [which includes persons], in a very real sense, *is* [emphasis in original] the body of God" (p. 330).

For some writers, Original Sin (discussed earlier) seems to be doubting that we are God, rather than turning away from God and turning instead toward the self. Separation from God is, therefore, an illusion because one cannot be separated from oneself. This issue bears directly on discernment. Are we listening to ourselves or to God for guidance? In other words, are we listening to God whenever we listen to ourselves? Ego cannot be God. If ego is the false self, then that false self is still part of the totality of who we are. And, if this totality is God, then God must also be the false self. But how can this be? If the false self blocks awareness of God, then God must be blocking awareness of God. Thus, I think of myself as separate from God but containing God in the form of the Holy Spirit. I seek to discern God's will for my life because I am *not* God, not because I *am* God. I believe in a firm boundary between the Creator and the created. I am not an ocean-saturated sponge that dissolves in the ocean. Obviously, different contemplative writers hold different views on the essence of divinity. The reader must decide which view is true.

Spiritual Direction Viewed in the Context of Attachment Theory

Theoretical Problems With Detachment

As the foregoing discussion suggests, the practice of Spiritual Direction is intimately related to the concept of attachment. In fact, the goal of meditation, which is practiced in Spiritual Direction, is detachment from everything that blocks the participant's awareness of God. I mentioned earlier that Meister Eckhart believes that God must find the soul empty and detached (Blakney, 1941). Similarly, here is how de Wit (2019) describes the practice of contemplation:

> We plane ego down, knowingly if not willingly. That leads to what Meister Eckhart called *Gelassenheit*, a "detachment" that contains an element of freedom—we do not, like the idiots we have been, need to follow the impulsiveness of ego any longer. (p. 273)

We can presume that this "impulsiveness of ego" includes classic attachment behavior such as proximity-seeking and contact maintenance directed toward a safe haven and secure base (see Chapter 1). Bowlby (1982) states that the goal of the attachment system is the protection of offspring. If we become egoless, however, then we realize that there is no longer any need for protection. Thus, perhaps the goal of Spiritual Direction is to transcend attachment, even attachment to a Higher Power—or at least attachment to our images of a Higher Power.

According to de Wit (2019), humans have become separated from their true selves, having partially forgotten "the spaciousness and openness of our fundamental humanity" (p. 109). We feel this separateness because of the "impenetrability of ego" (p. 108). We simultaneously experience "the desire to undo this separation" (p. 110). Mired in this perceived separateness, we cannot even cling to the "calm and open-mindedness" (p. 228) produced by contemplation itself, because "clinging [i.e., attachment] and open-mindedness are incompatible" (p. 228). In fact, "spiritual growth [through contemplation] inevitably leads towards a lessening of attachment in general, and this includes most importantly a lessening of attachment to self-image" (May, 1982, p. 59). As I mentioned earlier, this "lessening of attachment" also includes our attachment to a particular mental representation of God, because, according to Saint Gregory of Nyssa, it "'becomes an idol of God and does not make God known'" (Laird, 2011, p. 139). The practice of contemplation in Spiritual Direction produces a

> "mind [that] has nothing it can grasp, neither place nor time, neither space nor any other thing which offers our mind something to grasp hold of, but, slips from all sides from what it fails to grasp, in dizziness and confusion." (Laird, 2011, pp. 139–140)

Singh (1998) argues that, in the process of dying, we are all confronted with a mind that eventually has nothing left to grasp:

> Our persona, our personal sense of history, our goals, our ideas about reality melt away as we lie dying. ... Without the integrity of the ego's structure, there are no effective defense mechanisms left in place. The power of the Ground of Being begins to assert itself, pouring through the cracks. (pp. 171, 177)

Thus, there seems to be no room for attachment in a mature spirituality.

I question this conclusion. Are these contemplatives clinging to the concept of nonattachment? Bowlby (1977) famously stated that attachment security remains a lifelong concern "from the cradle to the grave" (p. 203). Even Jesus commanded His followers to prioritize attachment to Himself over all earthly attachment figures: "If anyone comes to me and does not hate father and mother, wife and children, brothers and sisters—yes, even their own life—such a person cannot be my disciple" (Luke 14:26, NIV). Prioritizing our attachment relationship to our Higher Power becomes more real when we face our own mortality. When death is at hand, humans are more likely to communicate with an omnipotent attachment figure—a Higher Power—Who helps them to transition to the next plane of existence. There are no atheists in foxholes. Persons pray to a Higher Power especially during times of distress (Granqvist, 2020). Does it really matter whether our mental representation of a Higher Power is accurate? What matters is that this mental representation, however distorted by our own childhood experiences with our own caregivers during childhood, points to the Ultimate Reality of an all-loving Caregiver Who responds to our distress with comfort—just like an earthly attachment figure.

The Psalms are replete with examples of depending on God for just this purpose. The psalmist writes, "My soul, wait thou only upon God; for my expectation is from him" (Psalm 62:5, KJV) and "The Lord is my rock, and my fortress, and my deliverer; my God, my strength, in whom I will trust" (Psalm 18:2, KJV). If we dissolve into the ocean of God like a sponge, then there is no longer any attachment relationship, no depending on the other for protection or comfort. Every attachment relationship implies a boundary between two distinct selves. If this boundary dissolves, then we become God; there is no longer any attachment relationship because our self ceases to exist in this scenario. God declares, "'Let us make mankind in our image, in our likeness'" (Genesis 1:26, NIV), not "Let us make more of ourselves." Vincent van Gogh painted more than 43 self-portraits during his short life ("Vincent van Gogh," 2025), but these paintings have been slow to become Vincent van Gogh. Some contemplative writers seem to confuse the signifier with the signified. We bear witness to God, but we do not become God: "God is God, and you're not." To believe otherwise is to believe in pantheism.

Detachment—the letting-go of the tendency to cling—can fit into this understanding of Spiritual Direction viewed in the context of attachment theory, if we are detaching from those things that block us from having an attachment relationship to our Higher Power. For example, realizing that the rich young ruler is feeling blocked in his relationship to God, Jesus instructs him to "go, sell everything you have and give to the poor" (Mark 10:21, NIV; see also Matthew 19:21, NIV). Jesus identifies that this man is clinging to his wealth. By giving his wealth away, he would be practicing detachment, opening himself up to an unobstructed relationship to God. The practice of Spiritual Direction consists of identifying the ideas, emotions, persons, possessions, and even obsolete images of our Higher Power and letting them go to establish an unobstructed, secure attachment relationship to God. We cannot expect to merge into God through Spiritual Direction, however. The merging of two life forms into a single organism—known in microbiology as primary endosymbiosis (Cuthbertson, 2024)—does not occur between humans and God. We are not absorbed into God. My goal as a spiritual director and a directee is not to be absorbed into the ocean of God. If God is love (I John 4:8, NIV), then there must be something that is not God whom God is loving. There is always an object of one's love.

Anxious-Avoidant Attachment and the Practice of Contemplation

Spiritual Direction focuses on the directee's relationship to mental phenomena—observing these phenomena and letting them go. Mindfulness-based psychotherapy researchers study the outcome of self-regulation rather than interactive regulation. Consider the title of a key article on mindfulness: "Intentional Systemic Mindfulness: An Integrative Model for Self-Regulation and Health" (Shapiro & Schwartz, 1999). The idea that interdependence on others can serve to regulate emotional states is alien to mindfulness, considered "a form of *mental training* [emphasis in original] to reduce cognitive vulnerability to reactive modes of mind" (Bishop et al., 2004, p. 231). Persons who train their minds to become mindful develop relationships with their thoughts and feelings, not necessarily other persons. Consider the anthropomorphization of emotions in this Buddhist monk's description of a mindfulness exercise: "Look straight in the eye of the disturbing emotion and understand what it is and how it works. ... When one genuinely looks at it, it suddenly loses its strength" (Goleman, 2003, p. 81). One might draw the conclusion that, in this therapeutic model, one's relationships to one's emotions replace one's relationships to real persons.

How does Spiritual Direction, with its emphasis on contemplative practice, work for directees who feel disconnected from interpersonal relationships—those directees classified as having an anxious-avoidant attachment pattern (see Chapter 1)? Anxious-avoidant persons "limit the influence of attachment relationships and experiences in thought, in feeling, or in daily life" (Main & Goldwyn, 1994, p. 126). Even though spiritual directees work directly with directors once per month, the practice of meditation often lacks an interpersonal dimension that could provide the gentle challenge that anxious-avoidant persons need to resolve their fears of closeness and dependence on others. In fact, it seems plausible to suggest that the practice of meditation reinforces an anxious-avoidant or disorganized/disoriented attachment pattern, characterized by defensive exclusion (Bowlby, 1973) of attachment needs. Consider the words of one of its originators, the Buddha (Siddhartha Gautama): "He who loves 50 people has 50 woes; he who loves no one has no woes. ... Do not depend on others" ("Buddha quotes," 2006, pp. 2, 6). These words reflect the attitude of the prototypical anxious-avoidant person. Achieving distance between the self and the self's thoughts and feelings might prove beneficial for someone struggling with issues of separation and differentiation, such as persons classified as anxious-resistant, but this same approach might also strengthen the defenses of a person classified as anxious-avoidant, walled off from their needs for dependence and intimacy.

Kabat-Zinn (2003) has denied the importance of social support in his audiorecordings of mindfulness instruction; however, I would argue that the fantasy of a listening, nonjudgmental, supportive therapist ready to contain whatever unbearable material emerges is simultaneously alive in the patient's mind and empowering the patient to sustain a mindful state of consciousness. Psychodynamic Therapy presents an interpersonal component that might increase the effectiveness of Spiritual Direction. Specifically, PDT explicitly identifies the therapist–patient relationship as the fulcrum of therapeutic change.

The Psychoanalytic Treatment of Sam

Jeffrey Rubin (2017), a psychoanalyst who practices and teaches meditation, presents the case of Sam (a pseudonym), "an immensely talented and maverick Zen teacher who had trained closely with one of the great Buddhist teachers of the 20th century and embodied what he had learned over several decades of samurai Zen practice" (p. 19). Sam became one of Rubin's patients in psychoanalysis, lying on the couch multiple times per week and talking about whatever came into his mind (i.e., free association). Rubin could immediately tell that this man was experienced in the practice of meditation:

> I was immediately struck by how present he was. Nothing seemed to escape his attentive ears and watchful eyes. He listened deeply and was unusually open and disarmingly honest, down-to-earth, without pretense or guile. He displayed a non-defensiveness that many years later still deeply impresses me. I also admired his self-awareness and his capacity for self-reflection. (p. 19)

Despite many years of meditation practice and mentorship from a well-known Buddhist teacher, Sam was experiencing "intense anxiety and dread … feeling both alien and split in two … a 'screwed up person' who 'felt like a reject and a loser' … irremediably disconnected from the human race" (p. 19). How could someone so practiced in meditation feel so disconnected from himself and others?

Regarding the contemplative path, de Wit (2019) optimistically writes, "Growth in genuine insight is accompanied by growth in our dedication to our fellow human beings, and conversely, genuine caring is bound to give us insight. … We cannot practice one without the other" (pp. 62–63). Sam felt no dedication to his fellow human beings because he felt so alienated from them. I am suggesting not that Sam's meditation practice caused this alienation but rather that, since his childhood, Sam always felt alienated. His meditation practice did not help him with this feeling or with his self-esteem. Instead, by training him to focus exclusively on the present, his Zen Buddhist meditation practice could very well have reinforced his defensive exclusion of overwhelming attachment needs associated with painful childhood memories (Bowlby, 1973).

From Rubin (2017), we learn that Sam's parents were both alcoholics. His father was "completely uninvolved with him" (p. 19), which prompted Sam to harbor feelings of hatred toward him. When he was a baby, Sam's mother "used his skin as an ashtray and had beaten him with a brine-dipped switch" (p. 19), abandoning him at age 3. Sam's paternal grandparents raised him; however, they were completely self-involved—the grandfather in crafting miniature sailing ships in bottles and the grandmother in collecting dolls. According to Sam, his grandparents "'hated each other, and hardly spoke'" (p. 19). Against this pathetic backdrop of physical and emotional abuse and neglect, Sam led "an intensely solitary childhood" (p. 19). Thus, Sam was well acquainted with being alone long before he began practicing meditation. We can wonder, however, whether meditation appealed to Sam because it reminded him of the utter familiarity of this solitary childhood.

Sam began to practice Zen Buddhist meditation and, on his first retreat, he had an enlightenment experience in which he "felt one with everything" (p. 20). After hearing Sam teach a course on Buddhism, the great Japanese Zen Buddhist master Taizan Maezumi approached Sam to be his dharma heir, which Sam initially refused. Soen Nakagawa, perhaps the greatest Zen Buddhist master of the 20th century, also expressed interest in Sam's meditation practice and was considering Sam as a successor. Given his widely recognized skill in the teaching and practice of Zen Buddhist meditation, why did meditation not transform Sam, as we would expect? According to Singh (1998), "With letting go, self-forgiveness, and life resolution, changes in the being become apparent. *A new capacity for compassion arises, for others and for ourself* [emphasis in original]" (p. 202). Sam never seemed to let go of his worthless self-concept, calling himself "'weak and cowardly'" (Rubin, 2017, p. 26) for admitting to Rubin his fantasy of exhibiting himself in public. He was skilled at the Buddhist meditative practice of forgetting himself and foregoing self-consciousness to protect himself against further retraumatization. According to Rubin (2017), "If there was no self, then there was no one who had been forsaken" (p. 27). If he preemptively abandoned himself, then no one else could abandon him.

Reflections on the Psychoanalytic Treatment of Sam

I am suggesting that practicing detachment from mental states and mental representations of self and others, including God, might disproportionately attract persons classified as having anxious-avoidant or disorganized/disoriented attachment patterns. A Zen Buddhist teacher once instructed Sam to "'put aside all human feelings'" (Brown, 2009). The Zen Buddhist practice of no-self was for Sam "like a powerful form of immunity" (Brown, 2009). Sam explained to *The New York Times Magazine* that

> "the Zen experience of forgetting the self was very natural to me. ... I had already been engaged in forgetting and abandoning the self in my childhood. ... In therapy ... I began to realize this feeling of invisibility wasn't just a peculiar experience but was maybe the central theme of my life. It was connected

to my having 'ability' as a Zen student and to my being able to have a precocious enlightenment experience. In a sense it was as if Zen chose me rather than that I chose Zen." (Brown, 2009)

With the help of his psychoanalyst, Sam healed his traumatic past. This journey of healing, however, required him to explore his past, not remain perpetually in the here and now. A goal of PDT is to "help patients free themselves from the bonds of past experience in order to live more fully in the present" (Shedler, 2010, p. 99). Persons whose attachment patterns are classified as anxious-avoidant or disorganized/disoriented might defend against a childhood past of parental rejection or abuse or neglect by focusing exclusively on the present. Thus, meditation practice, even Spiritual Direction, can serve to maintain the repression of traumatic and painful childhood memories rather than resolve them. Freud (1915) recognized, however, that these repressed memories often return in disguised form as symptoms. Sam manifested exhibitionism—a symptom that exposed his wish to feel a connection to humanity, which he never felt while growing up. Instead, he felt utterly alienated from his surroundings and himself.
He explained,

> "What [PDT] has done is indicate that forgetting the self is not a constructive approach. What one needs to do from a psychoanalytic perspective is remember the self. … Without the therapy experience I might have died without having been reunited with my life! And in that sense, without having truly lived." (Brown, 2009)

In *The Lion King* (Allers & Minkoff, 1994), the wise mandrill shaman Rafiki raps self-exiled lion king Simba over the head with his staff. Annoyed, Simba asks him, "Geez, what was that for?" Rafiki sarcastically replies, "It doesn't matter. It's in the past!" Simba protests, "Yeah, but it still hurts." Rafiki then delivers this insight that motivates Simba to return to Pride Rock and challenge his evil uncle for the kingdom: "Oh, yes, the past can hurt. But the way I see it, you can either run from it or learn from it." Sam chooses to learn from his past attachment relationships to his caregivers during childhood and, in time, processes the trauma caused by these relationships to become a whole person. Meditation practice could not accomplish this outcome for him because it reinforced his defensive attachment pattern. Therefore, meditation practice could not provide the "gentle challenge" (Dozier & Bates, 2004, p. 174; see also Dozier, 2003, p. 254) needed to transform his attachment pattern from insecure to secure.

In summary, Spiritual Direction is not for everyone—and especially not for those with a traumatic or rejecting childhood past. These persons might fare better in AIP (see Chapter 8).

When Is Spiritual Direction a Good Match?

Spiritual Direction is a good match for persons who want to enhance their spirituality with a Higher Power. The spiritual director must evaluate whether the person wants to let go of attachments that interfere with their relationship to God. Does this person have a hunger and a thirst for deepening their spiritual connection? As discussed above, Spiritual Direction might not be a good match for someone with a traumatic or rejecting childhood past. In these situations, the spiritual director needs to make a referral to a SIP (see Chapter 7) or AIP (see Chapter 8) therapist who can walk with them on the journey of repairing their past. The past can hurt, but Spiritual Direction is not the place to expose and process this hurt.

Spiritual Direction is especially well suited for persons who consider themselves "spiritual but not religious." This model of spiritual intervention does not require membership in a church, temple, or mosque. Attendance at formal worship services is not necessary. The prospective spiritual directee must want to walk a spiritual path with a director as a facilitator of this journey. The person must also consent to discussing spirituality explicitly. In SIP (see Chapter 7), the therapist addresses spirituality only implicitly unless the patient consents to exploring their spirituality explicitly. In Spiritual Direction, spirituality is the main course.

Training Requirements to Practice Spiritual Direction

Unlike SIP and AIP, spiritual directors do not have to be licensed mental health professionals in their state (although they can be). Instead, spiritual directors complete a rigorous certificate training program. Anecdotally, some spiritual directors have seminary training, but many of us simply feel called to work with persons who want to deepen their relationship to their Higher Power.

Many institutions offer Spiritual Direction training, including the aforementioned Shalem Institute for Spiritual Formation in Washington, DC, and the Ignatian Spiritual Directive Institute in Baltimore, MD. Spiritual Directors International (SDI; www.sdicompanions.org) is an educational umbrella organization that serves over 6,000 members from 42 countries (SDI, 2018). Although SDI published its five principles of Spiritual Direction training programs (SDI, 2018), Spiritual Direction as a discipline has no accreditation process. Thus, there is no ability to control the quality of training offered by Spiritual Direction training programs. I chose the training program at the Shalem Institute exclusively based on its reputation among my colleagues. Most training programs are oriented to progressive spirituality; in other words, they support women in leadership positions, sexual diversity (i.e., LGBTQIA+), and all faith traditions, not just Christianity. In fact, we read Buddhist and Jewish contemplative literature in addition to Christian contemplative literature. Conservative members of faith traditions might find some of this exposure insulting to their religious sensibilities and, therefore, would not be a good match to train in this model of spiritual intervention.

Some writers in the field (e.g., Edwards, 2001) have expressed their concern about the proliferation of Spiritual Direction training programs in the absence of formal accreditation standards. SDI is ideally situated to implement an accreditation process, but it has thus far refrained from doing so. Without this quality control, "everybody can assume the title of spiritual director, as well as define what they do as spiritual directors in their own various ways, sometimes to the confusion and detriment of the directee" (Edwards, 2001, locations 2008–2010). Because of this lack of oversight, Spiritual Direction training programs "come from many theological, spiritual, and ecclesial standpoints and assumptions about the nature of Spiritual Direction, implicitly or explicitly" (locations 2022–2023). Thus, potential spiritual directees might not know what they are getting when they seek out a director. Unfortunately, it seems to be the Wild Wild West of the spiritual frontier.

Before selecting the certificate program for my spiritual director training, I did my due diligence, talking with the spiritual directors in my church's counseling center and googling training programs. In my certificate training program at the Shalem Institute, we trainees were required to be working with at least one spiritual directee as well as our own spiritual director. Spiritual Direction sessions are typically scheduled monthly and last for 45 minutes. We also completed thousands of pages of reading related to Spiritual Direction and neighboring disciplines, such as theology, scripture (from various faith traditions), psychology, and social contexts (i.e., practicing Spiritual Direction in a postmodern secular world). We also completed two residencies totaling 19 days at the Bon Secours Retreat and Conference Center in Marriottsville, MD. We also participated in four workshops called "Zoom intensives," each lasting 6 hours. We wrote four reflection papers of five to seven double-spaced pages each as well as a 12-page double-spaced final paper. Finally, we participated in 15 monthly 2-hour peer group supervision Zoom meetings in groups of six "associates"—the term used to describe trainees. The entire program lasted almost 2 years, costing $8,910.00 (not including airfares to and from Maryland for the two retreats). In short, the training is rigorous and time-consuming. After graduation, spiritual directors typically charge $50–125 for a Spiritual Direction session, but some charge nothing, applying their skill as a form of service to their Higher Power. Considering the massive investment in time and money and relative lack of meaning that this certificate has in the marketplace, the spiritual director must really want this training to learn how to work with enhancing directees' as well as their own personal relationship to their Higher Power.

Conclusions

Spiritual Direction is a monthly 45-minute spiritual intervention that seeks to help the spiritual directee draw closer to their Higher Power and directly experience that Higher Power's presence. Silent meditation—what the Christian mystics refer to as "contemplation" (de Wit, 2019)—is the primary vehicle for entering into and experiencing the presence of God. Spiritual Direction sessions are essentially check-ins to see how the spiritual directee's daily meditation practice is coming along. With certificate training, lay persons can become spiritual directors. My church's counseling center retains two spiritual directors on staff, but it is more common for spiritual directors to work independently, receiving referrals through word of mouth and sometimes not charging for their service.

Basic Spiritual Director Stance Toward Spiritual Direction

Historically, the three qualities that characterized a spiritual director were being a person (1) to whom others come to talk about their desire for God; (2) who feels a calling to tend to the spiritual needs of others, especially the desire to enter into and experience God's presence; and (3) who pursues their own union with God through silent meditation and meeting with their own spiritual directors (Edwards, 2001). Contemporary writers underscore qualities such as simplicity, humility, the ability to maintain confidentiality, recognition of the spiritual directee's innate spirituality, intuitiveness, mental clarity, openness, and maintaining a balance of strength and gentleness (Edwards, 2001). Summarizing the contemporary stance toward Spiritual Direction, Edwards (2001) underscores the spiritual director's

> willingness to be very simply present to God for the directee, with a mind of "unknowing," spacious and available for we don't know what, yet trusting God to show us whatever we need to see. Such a contemplatively oriented director need not try to do anything more. (locations 1026–1028)

Some therapists in the AIP literature (e.g., Bateman & Fonagy, 2013) also promote a stance of not knowing in their clinical work. Adopting a not-knowing stance

> is central to ensuring that the therapist maintains his [sic] curiosity about his patient's mental states. He must accept that both he and his patient experience things only impressionistically and that neither of them has primacy of knowledge about the other or about what occurs between them. (Bateman & Fonagy, 2013, p. 601)

Thus, a mind of "unknowing" seems like good psychotherapy practice as well as good Spiritual Direction practice.

What Have I Learned From My Spiritual Direction Certificate Program and From Writing This Chapter?

First, I learned that both the ancient and contemporary Spiritual Direction literature is vast. A person cannot master it in a few weeks or months. I will be working through this literature (and perhaps contributing to it) for the rest of my life. I might always feel like a novice in learning about Spiritual Direction and the practice of Christian contemplation. Perhaps this feeling of "unknowing" is inherently part of the practice (Anonymous, 2009)

Second, I learned that God is always waiting to connect with us; we just need to let God into our conscious awareness. Unfortunately, we often pull down the shade to block out God's love and tender care shining upon us (Burtchaell, 1985). Can my spiritual directees and I become aware of the shades that we pull down to block this love and tender care?

Third, some of the Christian contemplative literature gives the impression that, through the process of contemplation, we become one with God so that God and I become indistinguishable. Medieval Christian contemplative St. John of the Cross (1991) writes, "The soul thereby becomes divine, God through participation" (pp. 560–561). For someone who fervently believes that "God is God, and you're not," this pantheistic idea stirs opposition within me. Can contemplation as practiced in Spiritual Direction maintain a boundary between God and humanity, the Creator and the created, the Redeemer and the redeemed? I do not envision for a second that I become my own God, Creator, or Redeemer. Fortunately, I have also been exposed to contemporary writers who do not subscribe to this idea (e.g., Edwards, 2001; May, 1982). May (1982) emphatically writes, "The divine is certainly not to be found entirely within ourselves or within our race" (p. 64). The Holy Spirit might live within me, but contemplation does not transform me into the Holy Spirit.

Fourth, subtle differences exist between Spiritual Direction and SIP (see Chapter 7). While SIP addresses both explicit and implicit spirituality, Spiritual Direction focuses exclusively on cultivating the presence of God in the directee's life. Therefore, the spiritual directee comes to Spiritual Direction with a conscious intent to enhance their connection to a Higher Power. Spiritual directors would not use the therapeutic technique of interpretation to make connections between past and present experience. Only therapists are trained to make interpretations.

Some SIP therapists dismiss the boundary between these two models of spiritual intervention. I was consulting with a SIP therapist who once informed me that "psychotherapy is meditation for two" (Russell Siler Jones, personal communication, June 12, 2024), and that the boundary between SIP and Spiritual Direction is extremely permeable if not nonexistent. Notably, spiritual directors are not state-licensed therapists trained to treat psychiatric disorders. Because Spiritual Direction is not state-regulated, healthcare insurance does not cover it; thus, spiritual directors practice with little or no financial remuneration, or they work with persons who have the financial resources to pay out of pocket for this service. Without a licensure process, could Spiritual Direction go the way of pastoral counseling and be absorbed by SIP, which consists only of licensed therapists? So far, Spiritual Direction seems to have retained its unique identity and popularity.

Fifth, Spiritual Direction might not be a good match for everyone. Persons classified as having anxious-avoidant or disorganized/disoriented attachment patterns might welcome a meditation practice that includes turning inward and away from others, observing feelings instead of feeling them, and focusing on the present instead of the past. Detaching from interdependent relationships might facilitate "enlightenment" but it will not heal the hurts accumulated during childhood that the body continues to hold onto in adulthood (van der Kolk, 2014). Spiritual Direction might instead strengthen the tendency to employ the defensive exclusion of attachment needs (Bowlby, 1973) and thereby prevent the person from becoming spiritually whole. Such persons might benefit instead from SIP (see Chapter 7) or AIP (see Chapter 8).

Finally, Spiritual Direction seems to be meeting a profound spiritual need exacerbated by the exponential increase in distractions and the resulting troubling decrease in cognitive capacity attributed to smartphone technology and society's obsession with social media (e.g., Ward et al., 2017). Persons are scrambling for ways to calm their minds and listen to the still small voice within themselves—free from the enslavement of technology. Julie wants to stop paying attention to the many to-do lists floating around in her head long enough to listen to God's voice. How does God want Julie to use her theological training to serve both God and others? The practice of contemplation embodied in mindfulness techniques discussed in this chapter can quiet the mind's chatter and enable the person to hear God's beckoning voice like a tuning fork—constant and true, but often drowned out by the fluttering noise of distractions. I have tinnitus, so, when I meditate, I become aware of a literal tuning fork sound of which I am otherwise unaware. I sometimes focus on this constant sound to quiet my mind. Everyone has their own unique method of meditating. Spiritual Direction offers an opportunity to explore with another human being the spiritual terrain discovered by this intense listening and observing.

References

Allers, R., & Minkoff, R. (Directors). (1994). *The lion king* [Film]. Walt Disney Feature Animation.

Anonymous (2009). *The cloud of unknowing with the book of privy counsel* (C. A. Butcher, Trans.). Shambhala.

Barry, W. A. (2000). Overcoming the hermeneutic of suspicion. *Presence: The Journal of the Spiritual Directors International, 6*, 25–30.

Bateman, A., & Fonagy, P. (2013). Mentalization-based treatment. *Psychoanalytic Inquiry, 33*, 595–613.

Beutel, M. E., Scheurich, V., Knebel, A., Michal, M., Wiltink, J., Graf-Morgenstern, M., Tschan, R., Milrod, B., Wellek, S., & Subic-Wrana, C. (2013). Implementing panic-focused psychodynamic psychotherapy into clinical practice. *Canadian Journal of Psychiatry, 58*, 326–334.

Bishop, S. R., Lau, M., Shapiro, S., Carlson, L., Anderson, N. D., Carmody, J., Segal, Z. V., Abbey, S., Speca, M., Velting, D., & Devins, G. (2004). Mindfulness: A proposed operational definition. *Clinical Psychology: Science and Practice, 11*, 230–241.

Blakney, R. (1941). *Meister Eckhart: A modern translation.* Harper & Row.
Bowlby, J. (1973). *Attachment and loss: Vol. 2. Separation: Anxiety and anger.* New York: Basic Books.
Bowlby, J. (1977). The making and breaking of affectional bonds. I. Aetiology and psychopathology in the light of attachment theory. *British Journal of Psychiatry, 130,* 201–210.
Bowlby, J. (1982). *Attachment and loss: Vol. 1. Attachment* (2nd ed.). Basic Books.
Bretscher, J. P. (Ed.). (2020). *Stephen minister training manual, volume 1.* Stephen Ministries.
Brown, C. (2009, April 23). Enlightenment therapy. *The New York Times Magazine.* The New York Times Company. www.nytimes.com/2009/04/26/magazine/26zen-t.html?unlocked_article_code=1.x04.rmwO.CIC2_Y8dQ0ni&smid=em-share
Buddha quotes. (2006, June 30). In Brainy quote. www.brainyquote.com/quotes/authors/b/buddha.html
Burtchaell, J. T. (1985). An ancient gift, a thing of joy. *Notre Dame Magazine, Winter 1985–1986,* 14–22.
Cassian, J. (1985). *Conferences* (Colm Luibhéid, Trans.). Paulist Press.
Chryssavgis, J. (2008). *In the heart of the desert: The spirituality of the desert fathers and mothers* (rev. ed.). World Wisdom.
Cohen, L. (1992). Anthem [Song]. On *The future.* Columbia Records.
Cuthbertson, A. (2024, May 2). Two lifeforms merge into one organism for first time in a billion years. *The Independent* (US ed.). www.the-independent.com/news/science/algae-evolution-agriculture-plant-history-b2539453.html
de Dreuille, M. (1999). *From east to west: A history of monasticism.* Crossroad.
de Wit, H. F. (2019). *The great within: The transformative power and psychology of the spiritual faith* (Kindle ed.). Shambhala.
Dougherty, R. M. (1995). *Group Spiritual Direction: Community for discernment.* Paulist Press.
Dougherty, R. M. (1998, fall). Scenarios for decision-making. *Shalem News,* 9.
Dozier, M. (2003). Attachment-based treatment for vulnerable children. *Attachment and Human Development, 5,* 253–257.
Dozier, M., & Bates, B. C. (2004). Attachment state of mind and the treatment relationship. In L. Atkinson & S. Goldberg (Eds.), *Attachment issues in psychopathology and intervention* (pp. 167–180). Mahwah, NJ: Erlbaum.
Edwards, T. (2001). *Spiritual director, spiritual companion: Guide to tending the soul* (Kindle ed.). Paulist Press.
Freud, S. (1900). The interpretation of dreams. In J. Strachey (Ed. and Trans.), *The standard edition of the complete psychological works of Sigmund Freud* (Vols. 4–5, pp. 1–625). Hogarth Press.
Freud, S. (1915). Repression. In J. Strachey (Ed. and Trans.), *The standard edition of the complete psychological works of Sigmund Freud* (Vol. 14, pp. 141–158). Hogarth Press.
Freud, S. (1919). Lines of advance in psycho-analytic therapy. In J. Strachey (Ed. and Trans.), *The standard edition of the complete psychological works of Sigmund Freud* (Vol. 17, pp. 157–168). Hogarth Press.
Freud, S. (1933). New introductory lectures on psycho-analysis: Lecture XXXI: The dissection of the psychical personality. In J. Strachey (Ed. and Trans.), *The standard edition of the complete psychological works of Sigmund Freud* (Vol. 22, pp. 57–80). Hogarth Press.
Goleman, D. (2003). *Destructive emotions: A scientific dialogue with the Dalai Lama.* New York: Bantam.
Goodman, G. (2025). *Practical applications of transforming the attachment relationship to God: Using attachment-informed psychotherapy.* Routledge.

Granqvist, P. (2020). *Attachment in religion and spirituality: A wider view*. Guilford Press.
Haugk, K. C. (2020). *Christian caregiving: A way of life* (2nd ed.). Stephen Ministries.
Hayes, S. C. (2002). Acceptance, mindfulness, and science. *Clinical Psychology: Science and Practice, 9*, 101–106.
Hayes, S. C. (2004). Acceptance and commitment therapy and the new behavior therapies: Mindfulness, acceptance, and relationship. In S. C. Hayes, V. M. Follette, & M. M. Linehan (Eds.), *Mindfulness and acceptance: Expanding the cognitive-behavioral tradition* (pp. 1–29). Guilford Press.
Jaoudi, M. (1998). *Christian mysticism east and west: What the masters teach us*. Paulist Press.
John of the Cross (1991). *The collected works of St. John of the Cross* (rev. ed.; K Kavanaugh & O. Rodriguez, Trans.). Institute for Carmelite Studies.
Kabat-Zinn, J. (1994). *Wherever you go, there you are: Mindfulness meditation in everyday life*. Hyperion.
Kabat-Zinn, J. (2003). Mindfulness-based interventions in context: Past, present, and future. *Clinical Psychology: Science and Practice, 10*, 144–156.
Keating, T. (1997). *Invitation to love: The way of Christian contemplation*. Continuum.
Kernberg, O. F. (1975). *Borderline conditions and pathological narcissism*. Jason Aronson.
King James Version. (2017). *The Holy Bible, King James version*. Thomas Nelson.
Laird, M. (2011). *A sunlit absence: Silence, awareness, and contemplation*. Oxford University Press.
Lanzetta, B. (2018). *The monk within: Embracing a sacred way of life*. Blue Sapphire Books.
Leech, K. (1980). *True prayer: An invitation to Christian spirituality*. Harper & Row.
Maier, K. E. (2017). *Following the enlivening thread: The experience of providing Christian Spiritual Direction* [Unpublished doctoral dissertation]. University of British Columbia.
Main, M., & Goldwyn, R. (1994). *Adult attachment scoring and classification systems* (6th ed.). Unpublished manuscript, University College, London.
May, G. G. (1982). *Care of mind/care of spirit: Psychiatric dimensions of Spiritual Direction*. Harper & Row.
May, G. G. (1991). *The awakened heart: Living beyond addiction*. Harper San Francisco.
Merton, T. (1960). *The wisdom of the desert*. New Directions.
New International Version. (1978). *The Holy Bible, new international version*. Zondervan.
Novac, A., & Blinder, B. J. (2021). Free association in psychoanalysis and its links to neuroscience contributions. *Neuropsychoanalysis, 23*, 55–81.
Rogers, C. R. (1957). The necessary and sufficient conditions of therapeutic personality change. *Journal of Consulting Psychology, 21*, 95–103.
Rohr, R. (2016). *The divine dance: The trinity and your transformation*. Whitaker House.
Rubin, J. B. (2017). Healing the trauma of neglect in a Zen Buddhist master. *The American Psychoanalyst, 51*, 19–20, 26–28.
Shapiro, S. L., & Schwartz, G. E. R. (1999). Intentional systemic mindfulness: An integrative model for self-regulation and health. *Advances in Mind–Body Medicine, 15*, 128–134.
Shedler, J. (2010). The efficacy of psychodynamic psychotherapy. *American Psychologist, 65*, 98–109.
Singh, K. D. (1998). *The grace in dying: How we are transformed spiritually as we die*. Harper San Francisco.
Spiritual Directors International. (2018). Five principles of Spiritual Direction training programs. *Presence: An International Journal of Spiritual Direction, 24*, 34–38. www.sdicompanions.org/docs/portrait/five_principles_of_spiritual_direction_training_programs.pdf

Sterba, R. (1934). The fate of the ego in analytic therapy. *International Journal of Psycho-Analysis, 15*, 117–126.
Sting. (1981). Spirits in the material world [Song]. On *Ghost in the machine*. A&M.
Thurman, H. (1996). *Jesus and the disinherited* (paperback ed.). Beacon Press.
van der Kolk, B. A. (2014). *The body keeps the score: Brain, mind, and body in the healing of trauma*. Penguin Books.
Vidrine, A. (2015). Who knows? On nondualism and Spiritual Direction. *Presence: An International Journal of Spiritual Direction, 21*, 43–49.
van Gogh, Vincent. (2025, February 9). In *Wikipedia*. https://en.wikipedia.org/wiki/Vincent_van_Gogh
Ward, A. F., Duke, K., Gneezy, A., & Bos, M. W. (2017). Brain drain: The mere presence of one's own smartphone reduces available cognitive capacity. *Journal of the Association for Consumer Research, 2*, 140–154.
Winnicott, D. W. (1971). *Playing and reality*. Basic Books.
Winnicott, D. W. (2016). Two notes on the use of silence. In L. Caldwell & H. T. Robinson (Eds.), *The collected works of D. W. Winnicott: Volume 6, 1960–1963* (pp. 513–518). Oxford Academic.

Chapter 4

Twelve-Step Programs
Surrendering to the God of Our Understanding

As co-founder of Alcoholics Anonymous (AA; Anonymous, 2000) and co-founder of the self-help movement in the United States (Flora et al., 2010), Bill W. is arguably one of the most iconic figures in American history, yet one unfamiliar to most. Bill W. also pioneered the integration of psychological and spiritual principles into a practical—and effective—group and individual intervention for alcoholics. A recent meta-analysis (Kelly et al., 2020) concluded that AA groups were at least as effective as popular psychotherapy treatment models such as Cognitive-Behavioral Therapy (CBT). It is no wonder, then, that other fellowship programs espousing the AA model have proliferated and flourished. An avowed atheist for his first 39 years (Anonymous, 2000), how did Bill W. create one of the most successful ecumenical spiritual movements of the past 100 years?

Case Illustration From My Own Experience

To get a clearer picture of 12-step programs and how they work, I am presenting a fictitious conversation between a sponsor and a sponsee (a less experienced member who wants to work on the 12 steps). I am basing this conversation on my own experiences as both a sponsor and a sponsee in a 12-step program. Though not a trained mental health practitioner, the sponsor uses their experience with addiction, their strength in a Higher Power to help stay sober from the addiction, and their hope for a better future than the one that they had been envisioning without recovery. In this illustration, the sponsor and sponsee are working from a book titled, *A Gentle Path Through the Twelve Steps* (Carnes, 2012).

Sponsor: Thanks for meeting with me today. Working the first step in our program is critical to getting sober and staying sober.

Sponsee: That's what I heard in last night's meeting. It's acknowledging that I am powerless over my addiction and that my life has got out of control because of it.

Sponsor:	That's exactly right. Taking this first step in the program means that you're serious about stopping your addiction and eventually turning to a Higher Power—the God of your understanding—to help you, especially at times when you want to go back to your addiction.
Sponsee:	Yeah, I believe in a Higher Power, but I don't know how a Higher Power can help me. Isn't God way up in heaven? Doesn't God have more important things to worry about, like the war in the Middle East?
Sponsor:	Maybe you want to view God as being too busy to help you so that you can give yourself permission to keep doing what you've been doing—messing up your life and your family's life with your addiction.
Sponsee:	Okay, I see your point. A part of me does want to keep acting out and not stay sober—especially when my wife threatens to kick me out of the house if I act out again.
Sponsor:	Again, that's another rationalization to start acting out. "The Big Book" [Anonymous, 2010] tells us that resentment is a key motivation for acting out. It sounds as though you feel resentment toward your wife for threatening to evict you from your own home.
Sponsee:	Damn right! Who does she think she is?
Sponsor:	Didn't you piss away your entire bank account and show up to your daughter's birthday two hours late because you were acting out?
Sponsee:	Yeah, sure.
Sponsor:	Look—you'll never be able to control your wife's behavior. All you can do is ask for help from your Higher Power to control your own behavior. She has plenty of reasons to be angry with you. In the program, we say we're responsible only for keeping our side of the street clean.
Sponsee:	I know, I know.
Sponsor:	Let's look at some of the other rationalizations you might use to give yourself permission to act out. In *A Gentle Path* [Carnes, 2012] on p. 106, I asked you to complete the assignment on rationalizations. Did you complete it?
Sponsee:	Yeah, I have my answers right here. I think the #1 rationalization I have used in the past to excuse my acting out is telling myself, "I deserve a reward for my hard work." My #2 rationalization is that "it's only a momentary lapse—no big deal." My #3 rationalization is that "although my addiction costs me a lot of money, I definitely have the money to spend." My #4 rationalization is that "I'm not really hurting anyone—I do it in secret so no one will find out." My #5 rationalization is that "I want to return to my old acting-out locations—just to reconnect with my old friends still living that lifestyle." So those are the five rationalizations I wrote down in the book, but I know there are others.

Sponsor: Hey, that's great work! I can tell that you spent a lot of effort thinking about the lies your brain tells you to get you to act out. Isn't it amazing how our minds can convince us of almost anything? That reminds me of that famous statement in the "How It Works" chapter of "The Big Book" [*Alcoholics Anonymous*, Anonymous, 2010, Chapter 5]: "Remember that we deal with alcohol—cunning, baffling, powerful! Without help it is too much for us" (pp. 58–59). Actually, it's not the addiction that's cunning, baffling, and powerful, but our own minds! Self-deception is the sworn enemy of sobriety. But there's a solution in the next sentence of that chapter: "But there is One who has all power—that One is God" (p. 59). All you have to do in those situations when your mind is playing tricks on you is to call on your Higher Power for help.

Sponsee: That's always been hard for me—to call on my Higher Power for help. I end up ignoring God in those moments so that I can do what *I* want to do—which I always regret afterward.

Sponsor: When that happens, that's the perfect time to call me or another member. Even if you end up getting their voicemail, just the act of calling can break the spell of acting out. Making a connection with another member can take you away from your isolation, your resentment, and your self-sufficiency—whatever is going on with you in that moment—and make you feel connected to the human race again. I believe that our Higher Power uses people in our lives to help keep us from relapsing. Never underestimate the power of the phone call to stay sober. Personally, I hate making calls, but those calls have helped me stay sober during some dark moments.

Sponsee: That sounds great, but I think about all the days, weeks, months, and years that I have left to stay sober—basically the rest of my life. It just feels overwhelming—like it's a lost cause.

Sponsor: That's another rationalization to add to your list—it's just too hard to maintain sobriety. You've heard of the 12-step slogan, "One Day at a Time." We don't focus on next year, next month, next week, or even tomorrow. I've heard some folks modify this slogan to "One Minute at a Time" or even "One Second at a Time." You have a much better chance of success if you commit to staying sober just for today. Tomorrow, you might act out. You can't control what happens tomorrow. But with help from your Higher Power, you're just committing to staying sober today. We do our best to stay focused on the here and now.

Sponsee: Thanks for that. That feels a lot less overwhelming. What you seem to be saying is that maybe with God's help, I can stay sober just for today. I might act out tomorrow, but I'm just focusing all my effort on today.

Sponsor: Now, you've got it!

Case Illustration Commentary on the Process

In this case illustration, a sponsor in a 12-step program is working with a sponsee on Step 1: "We admitted we were powerless over alcohol—that our lives had become unmanageable" (Anonymous, 2010, p. 59). The wording of this first step comes from the AA Big Book (originally published in 1939), but other 12-step programs replace the word "alcohol" with the addiction that applies to that program. For example, Overeaters Anonymous replaces "alcohol" with "food" because its members feel powerless over food (Anonymous, 2014, p. 3). All these programs assume that addiction operates the same way among all sufferers: isolation, resentment, and extreme self-sufficiency drive the person to their "drug of choice," which can be gambling, sex, shopping, or food, in addition to drugs and alcohol. A therapist might focus on the etiological reasons why an addict chose their particular addiction, but 12-step programs focus instead on the final common pathway of all addictions—the powerlessness and unmanageability that all addicts experience—and the spiritual solution that Bill W. discovered, which is surrender to a Higher Power. This surrender can be dramatic, as in Bill W.'s experience (Anonymous, 2000), or gradual, as in my own experience (Goodman, 2025a). In AA, it is commonly understood that "the speed with which the spiritual awakening takes place is no criterion of either depth or permanence of cure" (Anonymous, 2012a, p. 312). Regardless of the process of surrender, 12-step programs focus their members on always relying on a Higher Power for help, because the addict cannot stay sober by their own willpower. This is the message that the sponsor in the case illustration is conveying to the sponsee.

It is common practice for a sponsor to be blunt in their assessment of a sponsee's rationalizations for continuing their acting-out behavior. Experience shows that being polite and delicate with sponsees does not work. In my own experience, sponsors squeamish about confronting their sponsees about feelings and thoughts that we know carry a high risk of relapse have sponsees who cannot stay sober for any appreciable length of time. Sponsors must care enough about their sponsees to confront them on their self-deceptions, as the sponsor in the case illustration demonstrates. At the same time, sponsors provide ample praise when a sponsee works hard on an assignment or reaches out for help when needed rather than stay isolated and disconnected from other members. Sponsors seek to help their sponsees stay out of this bubble of isolation and self-deception by confronting them when their sponsees are not being honest with themselves or their loved ones about the seriousness or consequences of their addictive behavior.

Built into 12-step sponsorship are numerous opportunities for the sponsee to reflect on their experiences working the steps with their sponsor. *A Gentle Path Through the Twelve Steps* (Carnes, 2012) offers sponsees the opportunity to write down their reflections after working each step. Here are one sponsee's reflections after having worked the first step:

> I have a lot of difficulty asking others, including God, for help. The Serenity Prayer is a petition for God's grace. Can I petition God? Am I worthy of

asking God for anything? Can I ask others for help? Will they respond, or will they reject or ignore me like my family? (response to first-step reflections prompt in Carnes, 2012, p. 109)

This sponsee wants to trust that a Higher Power will be available and help them to stay sober, but there is also doubt about this availability because of previous experiences of unavailability from family (for a detailed treatment of the correspondence between the relationship to a Higher Power and the relationship to the parents during childhood, see Goodman, 2025b, Chapter 3).

Description of 12-Step Programs as a Spiritual Intervention

Every 12-step program includes the assumption that addiction proliferates because addicts have cut themselves off from their relationship to a Higher Power and have instead installed themselves as their own Higher Power. Using an Eastern religious term, the addict's "ego" has assumed all the functions of a Higher Power, thus rendering a relationship to a Higher Power irrelevant for daily living. The AA Big Book (Anonymous, 2010) makes a blunt assessment of the addict's problem: "Selfishness—self-centeredness! That, we think, is the root of our troubles ... [which] are basically of our own making. ... There often seems no way of entirely getting rid of self [ego] without [God's] aid" (p. 62). The solution to self-centeredness, according to the Big Book, is "to quit playing God ... [and] decide that ... God was going to be our Director" (p. 62). In Appendix Eb of *Alcoholics Anonymous Comes of Age* (Anonymous, 2012a), psychiatrist and AA influencer Harry M. Tiebout characterizes the alcoholic as having

> a narcissistic egocentric core, dominated by feelings of omnipotence, intent on maintaining at all costs its inner integrity. While these characteristics are found in other maladjustments, they appear in relatively pure culture in alcoholic after alcoholic. ... Religion by its demand that the individual acknowledge the presence of a God challenges the very nature of the alcoholic. (p. 311)

Tiebout goes on to remark how the alcoholic's true acceptance of the presence of a Higher Power "modifies at least temporarily and possibly permanently his [sic] deepest inner structure and when he [sic] does so without resentment or struggle, then he [sic] is no longer typically alcoholic" (p. 311).

What does the contemporary scientific community have to say about the common features of addiction? All addictions seem to manifest a common set of criteria (e.g., Reed et al., 2022):

- Impaired control over the behavior (e.g., onset, frequency, intensity, duration, termination, context);
- The behavior has become a central focus in the person's life;

- Unsuccessful attempts to control or reduce the behavior;
- Engagement in the behavior despite adverse consequences (e.g., financial, legal, occupational, social);
- Engagement in the behavior despite gaining little or no satisfaction from it;
- Engagement in the behavior results in marked distress or significant impairment in important areas of functioning (e.g., social, occupational);
- Engagement in the behavior is not better accounted for by another mental disorder (e.g., bipolar disorder).

Two additional criteria are sometimes used to define addiction (American Psychiatric Association [APA], 2022):

- Tolerance—need for markedly increased amounts of the substance or behavior to achieve the desired effect or a markedly diminished effect with continued use of the same amount;
- Withdrawal—experience of physical, cognitive, or behavioral symptoms due to reducing or stopping the behavior.

AA and other 12-step programs view these criteria as symptoms of a profound spiritual deficit marked by isolation, resentment, and extreme self-sufficiency. These are the outcomes experienced by a person who allows their connection to spirituality to atrophy and wither away. Taking alcohol consumption as an example, some nonspiritual individuals can consume alcohol temperately, but those who cannot consume alcohol temperately must turn (or return) to spirituality to regain control over their consumption.

History of the 12-Step Movement

The history of the 12-step movement begins with the story of Bill W. and his titanic struggle with alcoholism, documented in horrific detail in his riveting autobiography (Anonymous, 2010). It took four hospitalizations at the Charles B. Towns Hospital for Drug and Alcohol Addictions in New York City before Bill W. became sober and remained sober for the rest of his life. During his final hospitalization, Bill W. describes his sudden spiritual conversion:

> This was the finish, the jumping-off place. The terrifying darkness had become complete. In agony of spirit, I again thought of the cancer of alcoholism which had now consumed me in mind and spirit, and soon the body. ... I remember saying to myself, "I'll do anything, anything at all. If there be a Great Physician, I'll call on him." Then, with neither faith nor hope I cried out, "If there be a God, let him show himself." The effect was instant, electric. Suddenly my room blazed with an indescribably white light. I was seized with an ecstasy beyond description. I have no words for this. (pp. 144–145)

Bill W.'s conversion experience, however, did not come out of thin air. Although Bill W.'s conversion experience took place on December 14, 1934, his childhood friend and former drinking associate Ebby T. had sobered up and paid Bill W. a visit sometime during the latter half of 1934 (Anonymous, 2013). This visit planted a seed in Bill W. When Bill W. asked Ebby how he accomplished sobriety, Ebby told him about his association with the Oxford Group. Founded in 1908 by Frank Buchman, a Lutheran minister who had also experienced a remarkable spiritual transformation, the Oxford Group consisted of Christians of all denominations, socioeconomic strata, and ethnicities coming together to practice what they believed was first-century Christianity. The four principles of the Oxford Group, laid out by Buchman, were absolute honesty, absolute purity, absolute unselfishness, and absolute love. Bill W. would later join the Oxford Group with his wife Lois and try to help other alcoholics through this organization.

Bill W.'s association with the Oxford Group did not last long, however, because the Oxford Group leadership became impatient with his feeble attempts to convert alcoholics. According to Bill W., "The Oxford Groupers had tried [to sober up alcoholics], had mostly failed, and were fed up. ... At the end of six months nobody sobered up. ... Naturally the Oxford Groupers became very cool indeed toward my drunk-fixing" (Anonymous, 2012a, pp. 64–65). Therefore, Bill W. set out on his own to create a program specifically designed to help alcoholics get sober and to keep them sober.

Five months after his final drink and his spiritual awakening in Towns Hospital, Bill W. went on a business trip to Akron, OH, and found himself alone at the bar of the Mayflower Hotel (Anonymous, 2012a). Desperate to remain sober, Bill W. called random phone numbers in a church directory in the hotel lobby until he found another alcoholic with whom he could converse. That person was Dr. Bob, the other co-founder of AA. About a month after their first meeting, Dr. Bob took his final drink on June 10, 1935, which is considered AA's founding date (Anonymous, 2013).

Dr. Bob and his wife Anne were also Oxford Group members, attempting to practice absolute honesty, absolute purity, absolute unselfishness, and absolute love (Anonymous, 2012a). Well known to Bill W. and Dr. Bob through their association with the Oxford Group, these four principles embedded themselves in the original AA philosophy, especially absolute honesty. The "How It Works" chapter of the Big Book (Anonymous, 2010, Chapter 5) describes the character of those who fail to recover in the AA program:

> people who cannot or will not completely give themselves to this simple program, usually men and women who are constitutionally incapable of being honest with themselves. ... They are naturally incapable of grasping and developing a manner of living which demands rigorous honesty. Their chances are less than average. (p. 58)

In his autobiography (Anonymous, 2000), Bill W. recalls that, in addition to the four principles, the Oxford Group

> thought people ought to confess their sins "one to another." Heavily emphasizing this wholesale sort of personal housecleaning, they called the process "sharing." Not only were things to be confessed; something was to be done about them. This something usually took the form of what they called restitution, the restoration of good personal relationships by making amends for harms done. (p. 127)

Bill W.'s fascination with these practices later permeated his ideas for the 12 steps, which he created 4 years after his spiritual awakening (see below). People confess their sins not only to God but also in front of other persons—an illustration of being open and self-disclosing to both God and people and enshrined in Step 5. Bill W. also adopted the Oxford Group's commitment to make amends for harms done, which is enshrined in Step 9.

In the case illustration at the beginning of this chapter, the sponsee is working on Step 1, which means that "confession of sins" and "making amends for harms done" are not part of his conversation with the sponsor. The sponsee is working on his urge to control his wife's behavior; he is not even close to ready to make amends to her. He first must acknowledge his own powerlessness to control his addictive behavior and his wife's behavior. Although the 12 steps do not have to be worked through in order, Bill W. skillfully placed them in this order because each one logically follows from the previous one. If this sponsee were working on making amends to his wife in Step 9 before working on internalizing the reality of his powerlessness in Step 1, he would most likely have given up recovery altogether.

Essential Ingredients of 12-Step Programs

Members of 12-step programs incorporate spirituality as understood by the individual member through prayer and meditation, reading recovery literature, working with a sponsor (a more experienced, sober member) to complete the 12 steps, and attending meetings, where members share their experience, strength, and hope in their recovery from addiction.

Prayer and Meditation

Since its inception, AA and other 12-step programs have emphasized the importance of prayer and meditation to a Higher Power—"as we understood" this Higher Power (Anonymous, 2010, p. 59). Here again, the Oxford Group influenced Bill W.'s belief that prayer and meditation are essential ingredients in recovery from alcoholism and, by extension, from all addictions. In his autobiography (Anonymous, 2000), Bill W. noted that the Oxford Group was

> most ardent, too, in their practice of meditation and prayer, at least one hour a day, and two hours would be better. They felt that when people ... devoted themselves to meditation and prayer, then God could enter and direct their lives. (p. 127)

In my own experience as a member of a 12-step program, the spiritual illness from which we suffer is disconnection from a spiritual Source. Prayer and meditation reconnect us to our Higher Power—whether that Higher Power is a monotheistic God or "A. A. itself" (Anonymous, 2012b, p. 27). Bill W. believed that these practices were so essential that he enshrined them in Step 11: "Sought through prayer and meditation to improve our conscious contact with God" (Anonymous, 2010, p. 59). The re-establishment of a connection to a spiritual Source is what gives addicts in recovery the power to turn away from their addiction and walk the path of recovery.

Reading Recovery Literature

Bill W. and Dr. Bob believed that alcoholics should have their own book describing how their 12-step program works, which would include stories of persons who tell what their life used to be like, what happened, and what they are like now in recovery (Anonymous, 2010, p. 58). Consequently, the Big Book (Anonymous, 2010) was born. Since then, every 12-step program has published its own equivalent of the Big Book, featuring each addiction's unique characteristics and application of the 12 steps to facilitate the recovery process. Even the AA 12 steps are strikingly similar across 12-step programs, often exchanging the terms "alcohol" and "alcoholics" in Steps 1 and 12 with their own terms, such as "food" and "compulsive overeaters" in the Overeaters Anonymous Big Book (Anonymous, 2014, p. 210).

Bill W. believed that reading recovery literature written specifically for persons suffering from addiction was essential to recovery. *Twelve Steps and Twelve Traditions* (Anonymous, 2012b) suggests, "After we have finished reading the book *Alcoholics Anonymous*, we usually want to sit down with some member of the family and readily admit the damage we have done by our drinking" (pp. 83–84). Not all literature is equally valuable in helping an addict during the recovery process, though. Literature published by each 12-step program must be "conference-approved" (e.g., Anonymous, 2012b, p. 4), which means that regional representatives serving on the board of directors of that particular 12-step program approved all the literature published for its members to serve their recovery. The consensus is that reading recovery literature, particularly if it is conference-approved, is an essential ingredient of 12-step programs.

Working on the 12 Steps With a Sponsor

Despite never having had an official sponsor, Bill W., the co-founder of AA, nevertheless believed that sponsorship—one alcoholic "carrying the message" (Anonymous, 2010, p. 155) to another—is an essential ingredient of 12-step programs. Although it is a well-known feature of 12-step programs, caricatured in movies and even hilariously lampooned in the television series *Seinfeld*, sponsorship is never clearly defined or formalized in the AA literature. Reading this literature, however, one develops the impression that a sponsor serves the role of the stronger, wiser, more experienced, sober member who helps the newcomer break through their denial and work on the 12 steps of recovery. For example, in *Twelve Steps and Twelve Traditions* (Anonymous, 2012b), "Our sponsors declared that we were the victims of a mental obsession so subtly powerful that no amount of human willpower could break it. ... Our sponsors pointed out our increasing sensitivity to alcohol—an allergy, they called it" (p. 22). Thus, sponsors engage in what psychotherapists would call "psychoeducation"—sharing with their sponsees the biological and psychological contours of their disease as they themselves have experienced it.

Though not using the term "sponsor," Chapter 7 of the Big Book (Anonymous, 2010), "Working With Others," provides additional tips for sponsors working with alcoholics new to recovery. There seem to be two core messages of this chapter: (1) alcoholics are uniquely qualified to help other alcoholics enter and maintain recovery, and (2) alcoholics helping other alcoholics are actually receiving more help than they are giving. These core messages are repeated in one form or another in all the 12-step literature that I have read. One sober addict working with another addict seeking sobriety, both having struggled in the same ways with the same addiction, provides the seeker with a powerful motivation to open their mind to the sober addict's experience and wisdom gathered during the recovery process. In so doing, the sober addict is maintaining their sobriety by focusing on another human being instead of themselves. Recent research summarized by DeSteno (2018) supports the idea that acts of compassion and altruism enhance self-control.

In summary, working with other addicts seeking recovery through sponsorship is such an essential ingredient to one's own recovery process that it is codified in Step 12: "Having had a spiritual awakening as the result of these steps, we tried to carry this message to alcoholics, and to practice these principles in all our affairs" (Anonymous, 2010, p. 60). The Big Book (Anonymous, 2010) articulates the importance of sponsorship to the sponsor most succinctly: "Practical experience shows that nothing will so much insure immunity from drinking as intensive work with other alcoholics" (p. 89). Presumably, this reorientation of focus from the self onto the other person loosens the grip of the narcissistic personality structure mentioned earlier (Anonymous, 2012a) and simultaneously loosens the grip of the addiction, which serves to prop up an enfeebled self structure (see also Kohut, 1994; Kohut & Wolf, 1978). Sponsorship is the *sine qua non* of recovery from addiction.

Attending 12-Step Meetings

All 12-step literature emphasizes attending 12-step meetings as an essential ingredient of recovery from addiction. A meeting provides an opportunity for members to share honestly about their struggles with their addictive behaviors as well as their experiences with surrendering to a Higher Power. In fact, every 12-step meeting "is an assurance that God will restore us to sanity if we rightly relate ourselves to [God]" (Anonymous, 2012b, p. 33). Just as sponsorship benefits the sponsor as much as the sponsee, attending meetings benefits the old-timer as much as the newcomer: "We sit in A. A. meetings and listen, not only to receive something ourselves, but to give the reassurance and support which our presence can bring" (Anonymous, 2012b, p. 110). Listening to members' stories of what life was like before recovery and what life is like now in recovery can reduce the shame surrounding the addictive behavior and inspire the addict to work through the 12 steps to achieve sobriety like other members. Meetings also provide an atmosphere of nonjudgment: "We let God be the final judge" (Anonymous, 2010, p. 70).

Despite this nonjudgmental quality of meetings, 12-step programs nevertheless prioritize attending meetings to achieve sobriety and make that known to newcomers. For example, in the story, "The Perpetual Quest" (Anonymous, 2010), an alcoholic describes an encounter with her sponsor:

> He kept phoning and bothering me about going to a meeting. When he told me he went to A. A. meetings three or four times a week, I thought, Poor man, he has nothing better to do. What a boring life it must be for him, running around to A. A. meetings with nothing to drink! Boring indeed: no bouncing off walls, no falling down stairs, no regular trips to hospital emergency rooms, no lost cars, and on and on. (p. 393)

Later in the story, this person describes the benefit that she gained by finally attending a meeting with an open mind: "[After the meeting] I went for coffee with those people and listened some more" (p. 394). She was developing connections to others facing the same struggle that she was facing. Meetings break the isolation that sustains the addiction by providing opportunities for connection with other persons.

In a famous randomized controlled study (Alexander et al., 1981), researchers investigated the effect of isolation on addictive behavior in rats. They randomly assigned rats to two conditions. In one condition, rats were isolated in their own individual cages with no interactions with other rats. In the other condition, rats were placed together in a "rat park," which included many opportunities for interactions with other rats. In both conditions, rats were provided with two water bottles—one filled with water and the other with morphine. The rats who lived in isolation quickly became addicted to the morphine, while the rats who lived in the rat park drank water and did not become addicted to the morphine. If rats were people, this experiment would demonstrate that human interaction can diminish the craving for addictive substances and behavior. Accordingly, attending 12-step meetings, where communities form and thrive, is an essential ingredient of recovery from addiction.

What happens when a person new to recovery puts all these essential ingredients together? Let me return to the story of "The Perpetual Quest" (Anonymous, 2010). After tasting the sobriety that AA could help her to achieve, she

> did everything that was suggested to me. I went to a meeting every day, read the books and literature, and got a sponsor who told me to have a quiet time every morning and try to pray and meditate or at least sit still for a few minutes, before racing off for the day. (p. 395)

This person soon became sober and, at the time of writing her story, had been sober for many years. When practiced together, these essential ingredients of 12-step programs can help a person to walk the spiritual path of recovery.

Twelve Steps of Recovery From Addiction and Secure Attachment to God

I mentioned in Chapter 1 that there are four attachment patterns—secure, anxious-avoidant, anxious-resistant, and disorganized/disoriented. Are certain attachment patterns associated specifically with addiction? The substance use disorder (SUD) literature suggests that anxious-avoidant (Allen et al., 1996; Rosenstein & Horowitz, 1996), anxious-resistant (Fonagy et al., 1996; Rosenstein & Horowitz, 1996), and disorganized/disoriented (Fonagy et al., 1996; Riggs & Jacobvitz, 2002) attachment patterns—but not secure attachment patterns—are associated with SUD. These three attachment patterns are collectively known as insecure attachment. Insecure attachment is associated with SUD, but is it also associated with behavioral addictions? We can select a behavioral addiction such as sex addiction to discover whether the type of addiction determines an association to one specific attachment pattern. In the only two studies of their kind, men diagnosed with sex addiction were more likely to have insecure attachment than men not so diagnosed. In one study (Zapf et al., 2008), 40% of men not diagnosed with sex addiction reported having a secure attachment style, while only 8% of men diagnosed with sex addiction reported having this style. In the other study, attachment-avoidant behavior predicted the classification of men into the out-of-control sexual behavior category (Crocker, 2015). Unfortunately, both studies relied on self-report measures of attachment, the validity of which has been repeatedly called into question (Goodman, 2010; Roisman et al., 2007).

Addiction does not seem to favor a specific attachment pattern in these studies of SUD or sex addiction, but insecure attachment (i.e., anxious-avoidant, anxious-resistant, disorganized/disoriented) does seem to be associated with addiction. Thus, it seems likely that insecure attachment does contribute to the development of addiction. A model of spiritual intervention for addiction, therefore, must be consistent with the principles of attachment theory. Furthermore, developing a secure attachment to a Higher Power should be a feature of any model of spiritual intervention for addiction. Do the 12 steps of recovery from addiction promote or hinder a secure attachment to a Higher Power?

As mentioned earlier, it was 4 years after his dramatic conversion experience that Bill W. created the 12 steps of AA (Anonymous, 2010, pp. 59–60), which became the blueprint for all subsequent self-help programs of addiction recovery. I want to highlight the features of these 12 steps that reflect a secure attachment relationship to a Higher Power. I will be using Daniel's (2015) nine interpersonal markers to demonstrate how these 12 steps reflect core features of a secure attachment relationship to God.

Daniel (2015; see Table 7.1, p. 115) identifies nine interpersonal markers that discriminate among the four attachment patterns. These nine interpersonal markers are (1) proximity/distance, (2) trust/expectations of others, (3) attitude to seeking and receiving help, (4) expression and regulation of emotions, (5) self-image/self-esteem, (6) openness and self-disclosure, (7) dependence/independence, (8) conflict management, and (9) empathy. Do the 12 steps of recovery from addiction reflect a secure attachment to a Higher Power when analyzed through the prism of Daniel's (2015) nine interpersonal markers? I discuss each step in turn.

Analysis of the 12 Steps

> Step 1. We admitted we were powerless over alcohol—that our lives had become unmanageable.

By admitting powerlessness, the person is breaking through their denial of the addiction and instead practicing openness and self-disclosure, perhaps for the first time. The person is disclosing to themselves that they have no control over their lives (Daniel, 2015, p. 115; marker #6). The person also admits to themselves that they are not independent of alcohol; in fact, they are highly dependent on alcohol. Valorizing their independence from alcohol and from people is over (marker #7). Finally, by acknowledging the unmanageability of a person's life, that person is breaking through a defensively "magnified" self-image and facing their true state of affairs, thus creating a pathway toward solid self-esteem (marker #5)

> Step 2. Came to believe that a Power greater than ourselves could restore us to sanity.

This step suggests that trust is necessary to the addiction recovery process and is also the foundation of a secure attachment relationship (Daniel, 2015, p. 115). The person trusts that a Higher Power can help them; they have positive expectations that help will be forthcoming. The reader will also note the similarity between trust in "a Power greater than ourselves" and Bowlby's (1988) description of an attachment figure as someone who is "stronger and/or wiser" (p. 120). Bill W. is suggesting that this Higher Power at least has the capacity to help the person overcome their suffering and conflict (marker #2).

> Step 3. Made a decision to turn our will and our lives over to the care of God *as we understood Him* [emphasis in original].

This step reflects the deliberate change in attitude that the person must make to surrender to and accept the care of a Higher Power (Daniel, 2015, p. 115). The person becomes open to seeking help from God and no longer prefers to handle things themselves (marker #3). The reader will note that Bill W. portrays God as "caring," which reflects one of the hallmarks of a secure attachment relationship.

> Step 4. Made a searching and fearless moral inventory of ourselves.

This step instructs the person to face their intrapersonal and interpersonal conflicts for the purpose of managing them more effectively or resolving them altogether (Daniel, 2015, p. 115). The securely attached person finds constructive strategies for handling conflicts, and this method of courageously reflecting on these conflicts is one such constructive strategy (marker #8).

> Step 5. Admitted to God, to ourselves, and to another human being the exact nature of our wrongs.

By opening up to God, themselves, and others, the person can break through the shame of the addiction and live a life connected to God and to others without the barrier of secrets (Daniel, 2015, p. 115). Sharing thoughts and feelings with God and with others strengthens the safe-haven facet of the attachment system: without the barrier of shame, the person can now approach God in times of distress (marker #6).

> Step 6. Were entirely ready to have God remove all these defects of character.

To become ready for a major life change, which often includes pain and loss, the person must entrust themselves to the instrument of this change—in this case, God (Daniel, 2015, p. 115). Preparing for this change requires trust in the other person and a positive expectation that a person's life will be better than it was (marker #2).

> Step 7. Humbly asked Him to remove our shortcomings.

To ask God for the removal of shortcomings is to ask for help. Bill W. instructs the alcoholic to ask for help from God. This step echoes Daniel's (2015, p. 115) interpersonal marker of being open to seeking and receiving help (marker #3). The alcoholic no longer prefers to handle problems themselves. The use of the word "humbly" also suggests deflating one's grandiose self-image, making it more "nuanced" according to Daniel (2015, p. 115). This change in self-image is more aligned with a secure attachment relationship (marker #5).

> Step 8. Made a list of all persons we had harmed and became willing to make amends to them all.

This step harkens back to Step 4: the alcoholic needs to move from a position of ignoring intrapersonal and interpersonal conflicts to tackling them directly. Bill W. borrowed this idea from the Oxford Group, whose members "told how their lives had been transformed by the confession of their sins and restitution for harms done" (Anonymous, 2000, p. 156). Conflict management (Daniel, 2015, p. 115) is best served by constructive strategies such as making amends for harms committed against others (marker #8).

> Step 9. Made direct amends to such people wherever possible, except when to do so would injure them or others.

By making direct amends, the person is practicing disclosing their most vulnerable thoughts and feelings to those whom they have harmed (Daniel, 2015, p. 115; marker #6) as well as engaging in a constructive strategy of managing conflict (marker #8). In addition, the qualification that Bill W. adds—"except when to do so would injure them or others"—also reflects an interest in the other person's welfare—in other words, showing empathy with and care for others (marker #9).

> Step 10. Continued to take personal inventory and, when we were wrong, promptly admitted it.

This step follows the same Oxford Group–inspired prescription for conflict management suggested in Steps 4 and 8. None would argue that the two-pronged approach of acute self-reflection and prompt acknowledgment of wrongdoing to others is not a constructive strategy for conflict management (Daniel, 2015, p. 115; marker #8).

> Step 11. Sought through prayer and meditation to improve our conscious contact with God *as we understood Him* [emphasis in original], praying only for knowledge of His will for us and the power to carry that out.

As many authors have suggested (e.g., Granqvist, 2020; Kirkpatrick, 2005; Pargament, 2011), prayer is the *sine qua non* of spiritual proximity-seeking (Daniel,

2015, p. 115). In this step, Bill W. suggests improving contact with God through prayer—communicating directly with a person's Higher Power. Ainsworth and her colleagues (1978) indicated that proximity-seeking and contact-maintenance are the hallmarks of attachment security in infancy, and Bill W. underscores their continuing importance for maintaining a secure attachment relationship to God (marker #1). This is the only step that directly urges proximity-seeking to God.

> Step 12. Having had a spiritual awakening as the result of these steps, we tried to carry this message to alcoholics, and to practice these principles in all our affairs.

This step reflects the expression of care and empathy toward fellow alcoholics who still suffer from the disease (Daniel, 2015, p. 115). Because God has awakened the person to a spiritual awareness that frees them from the bondage of alcoholism, this act of grace also awakens feelings of empathy for fellow sufferers, who need to be told about their encounter with a Higher Power and the 12 steps of recovery from addiction. Bill W. encourages the person to share the good news of recovery, which reflects caring for others (marker #9).

The only interpersonal marker not explicitly represented in the 12 steps is "expression and regulation of emotions" (Daniel, 2015, p. 115). I would suggest, however, that the self-reflective elements of the 12 steps (especially Steps 4 and 10) imply emotion regulation. Emotion regulation is sometimes considered a prerequisite for self-reflection, or "mentalization" (Midgley et al., 2017). Thus, even emotion regulation (marker #4) is at least implicitly represented among the 12 steps of AA.

Bill W. relinquished his use of alcohol as a surrogate attachment figure and instead began to trust a Higher Power as his attachment figure. Furthermore, the formulation of these 12 steps suggests that Bill W. developed a secure attachment relationship to this Higher Power and treated this Higher Power as both a safe haven (e.g., seeking proximity to and contact with God, especially when distressed by one's shortcomings, through prayer and meditation; see Steps 5, 7, and 11) and a secure base (e.g., confidently using God to look outside oneself and make amends to others as well as carry the AA message to other alcoholics; see Steps 9, 10, and 12). In *Twelve Steps and Twelve Traditions* (Anonymous, 2012b), Bill W. writes of Step 12: "Here we turn outward toward our fellow alcoholics who are still in distress" (p. 106). This turn outward resembles the infant leaving the secure base—the caregiver's arms—to explore the environment.

When Is This Model of Spiritual Intervention a Good Match?

A psychotherapist or clergy member would suggest a 12-step program to a patient or congregant who seems to be struggling with addictive behavior (see above for addiction criteria). The 12-step model of spiritual intervention can serve as an adjunct to other forms of spiritual intervention such as psychotherapy or pastoral counseling, and, in fact, many therapists and clergy will not treat persons struggling with addiction who are not actively attending 12-step meetings. Anecdotally, many 12-step members also avail themselves of psychotherapy and other forms of counseling. The consensus among mental health professionals and clergy is that addictive behavior is best addressed with an "all-hands-on-deck" approach that often includes multiple services such as rehab, halfway houses, pharmacological intervention, and even one-on-one, around-the-clock monitoring (in the early phase of recovery). Drug addiction, especially opioid addiction in the US, is at epidemic proportions, with nearly 108,000 persons fatally overdosing on drugs in 2022 (National Institute on Drug Abuse, 2024). In that same year, there were 42,514 motor vehicle traffic fatalities in the US (National Highway Traffic Safety Administration, 2024). Thus, a person in the US is over two-and-a-half times more likely to die from a drug overdose than from a traffic accident. Bill W.'s 12-step model has helped thousands to achieve long-term sobriety from addiction through surrender to a Higher Power of the person's understanding (Anonymous, 2010).

Just as therapists perceive 12-step programs as an adjunct to psychotherapy but not a replacement for it, so too can clergy members perceive 12-step programs as an adjunct to membership in a place of worship but not a replacement for it. In a speech given at an AA convention in 1955, Father Edward Dowling, a Jesuit priest who was an early advocate of AA and friend of Bill W., declared, "People need the church for personal stabilization and growth, but also because I think the church needs A. A. as a continuous spur to greater aliveness and expectation and power. They are meant to complement and supplement each other" (Anonymous, 2012a, p. 269). Father Dowling also envisioned that places of worship and AA would mutually influence each other:

> A. A. has derived its inspiration and impetus indirectly from the insights and beliefs of the church. Perhaps the time has come for the church to be reawakened and revitalized by the insights and practices found in A. A. I don't know any fields of human endeavor in which the Twelve Steps are not applicable and helpful. I believe A. A. may yet have a much wider effect upon the world of our day than it has already had. (p. 270)

Father Dowling views AA as a revival of a vital spirituality, which should be at the core of the church and other faith traditions. Although not a member of the Oxford Group, Father Dowling nevertheless believed that, like the Oxford Group, AA could bend the world's attention in the direction of spirituality. In other words, AA has something vital that not only the church but also the entire world is lacking.

Requirements to Become a 12-Step Member

In addition to the 12 steps of recovery, Bill W. also conceived and wrote the 12 traditions of recovery. These 12 traditions are oriented not to the individual alcoholic's recovery but to the establishment and functioning of the AA fellowship at the local, national, and international levels of organization. Thus, the goal of the 12 traditions is to provide "continuous effectiveness and permanent unity" within the organization (Anonymous, 2010, p. 561). Tradition 3 concerns itself with membership requirements: "The only requirement for A.A. membership is a desire to stop drinking" (p. 562). Every 12-step program has a version of Tradition 3. If someone shows up at a meeting and wants help with their addictive behavior, then they are automatically a member of the program. There are no dues, no attendance requirements, no initiation. Some persons come in and out of the program, attending meetings only when they are struggling. Others come religiously because they feel that regular attendance keeps them sober and gives their lives purpose through their sponsoring others in the program.

Of course, 12-step programs are realistic about whom their programs can benefit. As quoted earlier in the AA Big Book (Anonymous, 2010), persons who do not recover "are constitutionally incapable of being honest with themselves. ... They are naturally incapable of grasping and developing a manner of living which demands rigorous honesty. Their chances are less than average" (p. 58). Apart from this group, whose difficulties with honesty we might now label as consistent with the criteria of antisocial personality disorder (APA, 2022), even persons diagnosed with "grave emotional and mental disorders ... do recover if they have the capacity to be honest" (p. 58). Thus, AA and other 12-step programs cast an enormously large net in identifying persons whom their programs can benefit.

Requirements to Become a Sponsor

As mentioned earlier, the guidelines regarding the sponsor's responsibilities are not codified in the way that a Stephen Minister's responsibilities are codified (see Chapter 2). Similarly, the qualifications for becoming a sponsor are nebulous. From my own experience with 12-step meetings in two different geographical locations (i.e., New York and Georgia), sponsorship is reserved for someone who has experienced at least 30 days of sobriety and has finished working on at least Step 1 (i.e., acknowledging one's powerlessness and the unmanageability of one's life). A person need not have worked on or completed all 12 steps to become a sponsor. I have never observed a person who did not meet these qualifications volunteer to become a sponsor. Sponsorship requires a person's time and commitment to a potentially long-term relationship. I have worked with both my sponsees for over 10 years, and my sponsor has worked with me since

I joined my 12-step program. Typically, local 12-step meetings are always petitioning members to consider becoming sponsors because there is more demand than there is supply.

Absent any concrete guidelines about how to sponsor, new sponsors typically sponsor in the way in which their sponsors sponsored them. The case illustration (see earlier) featured *A Gentle Path Through the Twelve Steps* (Carnes, 2012) because my sponsor used that book with me, and I adopted the same book with my own sponsees. Of course, not every sponsor uses this book as a guide through the 12 steps, but the feelings-based exercises throughout the book help the newcomer working the steps to confront unpleasant feelings that the addictive behavior might be masking. This recovery wisdom has been transmitted from sponsor to sponsee through the generations, making members feel as though they are part of something larger than themselves, going all the way back to Bill W. and Dr. Bob. There are no formal training and no degree program to complete, yet I would suggest that a sponsor's knowledge of the addictive behavior, empathy toward the addict, and means to walk the path of recovery far exceed the knowledge, empathy, and means of any nonaddict therapist. A sponsor brings to bear this collective wisdom accumulated from almost 100 years of 12-step recovery.

Considering sponsorship from an attachment perspective, what is the nature of the sponsor–sponsee relationship? Based on the AA Big Book (Anonymous, 2010), it appears that a sponsor presents themselves as "stronger and/or wiser" (Bowlby, 1988, p. 120) than the newcomer. The sponsor is stronger because they have presumably surrendered to a Higher Power of their own understanding and have, therefore, tapped into that vast energy source; the sponsor is also wiser because they have presumably achieved some success with sobriety, perhaps even having experienced one or more relapses and returned to the program to continue their recovery. Thus, the sponsor–sponsee relationship is well suited for consideration as an attachment relationship.

Considering how the sponsor works with the sponsee, does the sponsor take advantage of the sponsee's attachment to the sponsor? In my experience, the sponsor is only dimly aware of the sponsee's attitude toward them. The sponsor is focused on breaking through the sponsee's denial of their addictive behavior and helping them to work on the 12 steps of the program, not on how the sponsee might perceive the sponsor as emotionally responsive, inconsistently responsive, or consistently unresponsive (i.e., the caregiver behavioral correlates of the three primary attachment patterns). In fact, in the Big Book (Anonymous, 2010), there is almost no focus on leveraging the sponsor–sponsee relationship dynamics for the purpose of establishing or maintaining sobriety. Neither is there a focus on the sponsee's attachment pattern and tailoring the sponsor's work with the sponsee to their specific attachment pattern (for a more detailed discussion, see Chapter 2; Goodman, 2025b).

In 12-step programs, is the sponsor supposed to be emotionally responsive to the sponsee? Such behavior could help to establish a healing secure attachment relationship to the sponsor. In the Big Book (Anonymous, 2010), the author of the story "Listening to the Wind" affirms that any person who wants to stop drinking can "'call Alcoholics Anonymous, 24 hours a day'" (p. 466). This author called a phone number that she had received weeks earlier from someone in a laundromat who observed that she was intoxicated, and "five minutes later [the author's future sponsor] pulled into my driveway" (p. 467). That sounds like emotional responsiveness *par excellence*. In the story "Building a New Life" (Anonymous, 2010), the author found a phone number of a local AA fellowship and called: "Two men came to my apartment and stayed with me, drinking coffee until after the bars closed. They kept coming, taking me to meetings for a month" (p. 480). What therapist, clergy member, Stephen Minister, or spiritual director is going to dedicate this much time and effort to helping an addict get sober and stay sober?

Despite not explicitly using the sponsee's attachment relationship to the sponsor as a tool of recovery, the sponsor–sponsee relationship, when executed as designed, is a paragon of emotional responsiveness and caring, above and beyond what mental health and religious professionals and even family members can provide. In this sense, the AA sponsor models the kind of love that Jesus taught and demonstrated:

> For I was hungry and you gave me something to eat, I was thirsty and you gave me something to drink, I was a stranger and you invited me in, I needed clothes and you clothed me, I was sick and you looked after me, I was in prison and you came to visit me. (Matthew 25:35–36, NIV)

The sponsor visits the sponsee in their prison of addiction and shows them the way out. This is the embodiment of Tradition 5: "Each group has but one primary purpose—to carry its message to the alcoholic who still suffers" (Anonymous, 2010, p. 562). No other model of spiritual intervention demonstrates such radical love.

Conclusions

Unlike the other models of spiritual intervention discussed in this book, 12-step programs are designed for a specific population—persons who suffer from addictive behavior. Many models of spiritual intervention are not designed to work with addicts. For example, Stephen Ministers are instructed not to work with persons suffering from addiction (Haugk & Akers, 2020, p. 72). Even many therapists will not work with patients active in addiction unless they are also attending 12-step meetings. The only requirement for membership is a desire to stop the addictive behavior (Anonymous, 2010, p. 562). Unless a person struggles with being honest with themselves and others, 12-step programs offer serenity to those who follow their steps. According to one member,

> "I'm kind of glad that I can feel there is a Supreme Being who can keep things going right. I guess maybe this is something like that spiritual feeling which they talk about. Whatever it is, I hope it stays because I never felt so peaceful in all my life." (Anonymous, 2012a, p. 316)

Some members experience an epiphany like Bill W., while others experience their spiritual awakening more gradually. Regardless of the path taken, however, "there seems no doubt that all end up with this feeling of peace and serenity" (Anonymous, 2012a, p. 316). The therapeutic value of 12-step programs seems to consist of their "use of religious or spiritual force to attack the fundamental narcissism" of the addict (Anonymous, 2012a, p. 317). Unlike some of the other models of spiritual intervention such as Stephen Ministry (see Chapter 2) or Godly Play (see Chapter 5) that specify the Christian God as the fulcrum of change, 12-step programs encourage surrendering to the God of one's own understanding. This universalist approach naturally widens the appeal of 12-step programs to virtually anyone willing to believe in a Power greater than themselves (Anonymous, 2010, p. 59). Some observers have even suggested that the 12-step movement, if practiced by societies wholesale, could bring about a universal spiritual awakening (e.g., Anonymous, 2012a, p. 270).

In my own experience of having been a long-standing member of a 12-step program, many places of worship refuse to rent out space to 12-step meetings. Clergy fear what they do not know. The prospect of staggering alcoholics or bug-eyed drug addicts loitering outside the church would not be good for business if tithing congregants acted on their own stereotypes and stopped attending. I hope that this chapter convinces skeptical clergy that 12-step programs are worthy of renting space in their basements for their meetings. All it takes is allowing a 12-step meeting to rent space for 60–90 minutes per week in their basement at a reasonable cost. Perhaps 12-step members do not worship the Baptist God or Lutheran God or Methodist God or Episcopalian God or Presbyterian God or Catholic God, but they worship a Power greater than themselves. They believe in the power of spirituality to change their lives. Perhaps some 12-step members would even consider joining the church where their 12-step meeting is held. Thus, offering space to a 12-step meeting could boost church attendance. Some churches do welcome 12-step meetings with open arms, just as Jesus welcomed little children to come to Him (Matthew 19:14, NIV). Places of worship can do much more, however, to welcome these spiritual seekers in their midst.

Mental health professionals and clergy members can make referrals to 12-step meetings by searching for these meetings on the internet. Most 12-step meetings are advertised online nowadays. This self-described "simple program" (Anonymous, 2010, p. 58) has helped many thousands recovering from addictive behavior by suggesting that members perform several essential tasks: prayer and meditation, reading recovery literature, working with a sponsor (a more experienced, sober member) to complete the 12 steps, and attending meetings, where members share their experience, strength, and hope in their recovery from addiction.

This peer-group model of spiritual intervention represents the most egalitarian approach to spiritual intervention found in this book. There are no hierarchies, no trained experts telling members what to do. In fact, the AA Big Book (Anonymous, 2010) guards against such authoritarianism in its Tradition 2: "For our group purpose there is but one ultimate authority—a loving God as He may express Himself in our group conscience. Our leaders are but trusted servants; they do not govern" (p. 562).

Even *Seinfeld*'s George Costanza—feeling resentful that his alcoholic friend Hanky never made Step 9 amends to him—tries to convince Hanky's AA sponsor to "drop him down to step 2!" (Crittenden & Ackerman, 1997). When the sponsor refuses, George indignantly replies, "Well, aren't you the boss of him?" (Crittenden & Ackerman, 1997). In reality, sponsors do not tell their sponsees what to do; instead, they share from their own experience what worked or did not work for them in getting sober. In the case illustration, the sponsor discloses that he hates making phone calls during moments of vulnerability, but he makes them anyway because he knows that those calls can help protect him from losing his sobriety. A committed sponsee wants to implement the parts of the program that work for their sponsor.

Even though sponsors are merely "trusted servants," I believe that they often also become attachment figures. As discussed earlier, sponsees perceive their sponsors as "stronger and/or wiser" (Bowlby, 1988, p. 120), a hallmark of an attachment relationship. Sponsees also use their sponsors as a safe haven in times of distress and temptation. Calling a sponsor, who pulls into the sponsee's driveway within 5 minutes, builds trust and the expectation that the sponsor will always be there during a crisis. Sponsors also provide a secure base as the sponsee meets other 12-step members at meetings or other 12-step gatherings and risks re-entry into the wider society (e.g., new job, new school, renewed family ties). Thus, sponsors do often become attachment figures who foster a secure attachment relationship with their sponsees. In this narrow sense, the sponsor–sponsee relationship is hierarchical because one person (the sponsee) is relying on another person (the sponsor) for comfort and protection from their addictive behavior. Because the boundaries can be more fluid in this relationship than in other relationships, such as the therapist–patient relationship (see Chapter 7), the opportunities to serve as a safe haven and secure base expand in a sponsor–sponsee relationship.

Furthermore, the sponsee's knowledge that their sponsor suffers from the same addiction, yet has managed to get sober and stay sober, provides additional motivation to identify with the sponsor and emulate their recovery process. Even though "anonymity is the spiritual foundation of all our Traditions" (Tradition 12; Anonymous, 2010, p. 562), I know much more about my sponsor's personal life than I do about my therapist's personal life—and I have worked with my therapist for a much longer time. I consider my sponsor a close friend; I consider my therapist a professional with whom I work. My sponsor helps me to stay sober, sometimes through confrontation of my rationalizations for acting out, as in the case illustration, at other times through empathy based on his own personal experience as well as through encouragement. My therapist provides me with insights into my underlying motivations for wanting to act out in the first place and connects these motivations to childhood wishes and fears in the context of my relationships to my parents. The therapist role and sponsor role are thus complementary and only partially overlapping. I always encourage sponsees to seek out psychotherapy, which they can consider as another tool of recovery.

The 12-step programs of recovery from addiction have stood the test of time, helping many thousands of addicts find and sustain long-term recovery through this "simple program" (Anonymous, 2010, p. 58). In fact, in the experience of the authors of the Big Book (Anonymous, 2010), "Rarely have we seen a person fail who has thoroughly followed our path" (p. 58). Mental health professionals and clergy members need to consider referring their patients and congregants to 12-step programs if they suspect addictive behavior. Supporting 12-step programs in other ways, such as renting space for meetings, could help many addicts find recovery in the community. Addiction is a pernicious mental health challenge: "Without help it is too much for us. But there is One who has all power—that One is God. May you find [God] now!" (Anonymous, 2010, p. 59).

References

Ainsworth, M. D. S., Blehar, M. C., Waters, E., & Wall, S. (1978). *Patterns of attachment: A psychological study of the strange situation*. Erlbaum.

Alexander, B. K., Beyerstein, B. L., Hadaway, B. F., & Coombs, R. B. (1981). Effect of early and later colony housing on oral ingestion of morphine in rats. *Pharmacology Biochemistry and Behavior, 15*, 571–576.

Allen, J. P., Hauser, S. T., & Borman-Spurrell, E. (1996). Attachment theory as a framework for understanding sequelae of severe adolescent psychopathology: An 11-year follow-up study. *Journal of Consulting and Clinical Psychology, 64*, 254–263.

American Psychiatric Association. (2022). *Diagnostic and statistical manual of mental disorders* (5th ed., text rev.). Author.

Anonymous. (2000). *Bill W. my first 40 years: An autobiography of the cofounder of Alcoholics Anonymous*. Hazelden.

Anonymous. (2010). *Alcoholics Anonymous* (4th ed.). Alcoholics Anonymous World Services.

Anonymous. (2012a). *Alcoholics Anonymous comes of age: A brief history of A. A.* Alcoholics Anonymous World Services.

Anonymous. (2012b). *Twelve steps and twelve traditions*. Alcoholics Anonymous World Services.

Anonymous. (2013). *"Pass it on": The story of Bill Wilson and how the A. A. message reached the world.* Alcoholics Anonymous World Services.
Anonymous. (2014). *Overeaters Anonymous* (3rd ed.). Overeaters Anonymous.
Bowlby, J. (1988). *A secure base: Parent–child attachment and healthy human development.* Basic Books.
Carnes, P. (2012). *A gentle path through the twelve steps: The classic guide for all people in the process of recovery* (rev. ed.). Hazelden.
Crittenden, J. (Writer), & Ackerman, A. (Director). (1997, December 11). The apology (Season 9, Episode 9) [TV series episode]. In J. Seinfeld, A. Berg, & J. Schaffer (Executive Producers), *Seinfeld*. West/Shapiro Productions; Castle Rock Entertainment.
Crocker, M. M. (2015). Out-of-control sexual behavior as a symptom of insecure attachment in men. *Journal of Social Work Practice in the Addictions, 15,* 373–393.
Daniel, S. I. F. (2015). *Adult attachment patterns in a treatment context: Relationship and narrative.* Routledge.
DeSteno, D. (2018). *Emotional success: The power of gratitude, compassion, and pride.* Houghton Mifflin Harcourt.
Flora, K., Raftopoulos, A., & Pontikes, T. (2010). A look at the evolution of the self-help movement. *Journal of Groups in Addiction and Recovery, 5,* 214–225.
Fonagy, P., Leigh, T., Steele, M., Steele, H., Kennedy, R., Mattoon, G., Target, M., & Gerber, A. (1996). The relation of attachment status, psychiatric classification, and response to psychotherapy. *Journal of Consulting and Clinical Psychology, 64,* 22–31.
Goodman, G. (2010). *Therapeutic attachment relationships: Interaction structures and the processes of therapeutic change.* Lanham, MD: Jason Aronson.
Goodman, G. (2025a). *Practical applications of transforming the attachment relationship to God: Using attachment-informed psychotherapy.* Routledge.
Goodman, G. (2025b). *Using psychoanalytic techniques to transform the attachment relationship to God: Our refuge and strength.* Routledge.
Granqvist, P. (2020). *Attachment in religion and spirituality: A wider view.* Guilford Press.
Haugk, K. C., & Akers, I. B. (2020). *When and how to use mental health resources* (2nd ed.). Stephen Ministries.
Kelly, J. F., Humphreys, K., & Ferri, M. (2020). Alcoholics Anonymous and other 12-step programs for alcohol use disorder. *Cochrane Database of Systematic Reviews, 3,* CD012880.
Kirkpatrick, L. A. (2005). *Attachment, evolution, and the psychology of religion.* Guilford Press.
Kohut, H. (1994). Self deficits and addiction. In J. D. Levin & R. H. Weiss (Eds.), *The dynamics and treatment of alcoholism: Essential papers* (pp. 344–346). Jason Aronson.
Kohut, H., & Wolf, E. (1978). The disorders of the self and their treatment: An outline. *International Journal of Psychoanalysis, 59,* 413–425.
Midgley, N., Ensink, K., Lindqvist, K., Malberg, N., & Muller, N. (2017). *Mentalization-based treatment for children: A time-limited approach.* American Psychological Association.
National Highway Traffic Safety Administration. (2024). *Traffic safety facts: Research note.* https://crashstats.nhtsa.dot.gov/Api/Public/ViewPublication/813560
National Institute on Drug Abuse. (2024). *Drug overdose deaths: Facts and figures.* https://nida.nih.gov/research-topics/trends-statistics/overdose-death-rates#Fig1
New International Version. (1978). *The Holy Bible, new international version.* Zondervan.
Pargament, K. I. (2011). *Spiritually integrated psychotherapy: Understanding and addressing the sacred.* Guilford Press.
Reed, G. M., First, M. B., Billieux, J., Cloitre, M., Briken, P., Achab, S., Brewin, C. R., King, D. L., Kraus, S. W., & Bryant, R. A. (2022). Emerging experience with selected

new categories in the ICD-11: Complex PTSD, prolonged grief disorder, gaming disorder, and compulsive sexual behaviour disorder. *World Psychiatry, 21*, 189–213.

Riggs, S. A., & Jacobvitz, D. (2002). Expectant parents' representations of early attachment relationships: Associations with mental health and family history. *Journal of Consulting and Clinical Psychology, 70*, 195–204.

Roisman, G. I., Holland, A., Fortuna, K., Fraley, R. C., Clausell, E., & Clarke, A. (2007). The Adult Attachment Interview and self-reports of attachment style: An empirical rapprochement. *Journal of Personality and Social Psychology, 92*, 678–697.

Rosenstein, D. S., & Horowitz, H. A. (1996). Adolescent attachment and psychopathology. *Journal of Consulting and Clinical Psychology, 64*, 244–253.

Zapf, J. L., Greiner, J., & Carroll, J. (2008). Attachment styles and male sex addiction. *Sexual Addiction and Compulsivity, 15*, 158–175.

Chapter 5

Godly Play
Suffer the Little Children to Come Unto Me

Because I did not receive permission from my church to audio-record a Godly Play session, the following case illustration comes from a transcribed Godly Play Foundation (2016b) YouTube video, in which the storyteller tells the children the Parable of the Mustard Seed.

Parable of the Mustard Seed

I wonder if this could be a parable? This box looks very old. Parables are very old. Parables were given to you before you were born. It's also the color gold. Things that are gold are usually very valuable, and parables are very valuable—maybe even more valuable than gold. It's a box, and it has a lid on it. Sometimes parables are hard to get into. You have to be ready to go inside a parable. I think we might be able to go inside in a little while. It also looks like a gift or a present. Parables are like a present. They were given to you before you were born—even before your parents were born—or even before your grandparents were born—but they're not the kind of gift you get for Christmas or on your birthday. I know—let's go inside and see if this is a parable. If at first you can't get inside, don't get discouraged. Always come back because someday the parable will let you in. I wonder what this could be? It's the color yellow. Yes, it could be a big lemon, or it could be the Sun, or maybe even a lemon drop, I wonder? I wonder if there are other things that could help us say more before we begin this story? No, there aren't, so let's begin.

Once, there was someone who did such amazing things and said such wonderful things that people began to follow him around, and they kept hearing him talk about a place called the kingdom, and they didn't know what the kingdom was. They didn't know anyone who knew what the kingdom was. And they had never been to this kingdom, so they couldn't help it. They just had to ask him, "What is the kingdom of heaven?" And he said, "It's like a person who takes the tiniest of seeds—a seed so small that if it was on my finger, you would not be able to see it—and he plants the seed. And it grows.

It grows into a big bush or a big tree, and the birds begin to fly to the tree, and some build their nests in the tree."

Here is the series of "I wonder" questions:

Now, I wonder what this man was doing when this tree was growing? I wonder if the man who planted the tiny seed has a name? I wonder if he was happy when the birds started coming to the tree? I wonder if the birds were happy to find this tree? I wonder if you have ever come close to a tree like this? I wonder what this tree could really be? I wonder what these nests could really be? I wonder what this whole thing could really be? So we have the birds. and we have the nests, and we have the tree, and the man who planted the tiny, tiny seed. Now, I wonder what you would like to do for your work today?

Description of Godly Play

Definition

Godly Play is a method of introducing children ages 3–12 to Bible stories and liturgical events on the Christian church calendar that facilitates children's own understanding of their innate spirituality through these stories and events. According to founder Jerome Berryman (2009), children are "encouraged to construct their own meaning about God by the playful interaction of their experience with Christian language" (p. 15). What makes Godly Play "godly" is that the play focuses on children's knowing God for themselves.

The Christian language system used in Godly Play is derived from both the Old and New Testaments of the Bible. The storyteller introduces this Christian language system through four linguistic genres: (1) sacred stories, (2) parables, (3) liturgical action lessons, and (4) contemplative silence. Sacred stories are the great Bible stories that people think of when they think of the Bible—the Creation Story, Daniel and the Lion's Den, the Prophet Jonah, and the Birth of Jesus, to name a few. These stories serve the function of "identity making" (Berryman, 2009, p. 14). Parables are brief stories that illustrate spiritual truths, told exclusively by Jesus. These stories serve the function of "stimulating exploration of Christian meaning" (p. 14). Liturgical action lessons are stories about the Christian church calendar, organized in a circle: Advent, Christmas, Lent, Easter, and Pentecost. These stories serve the function of "making redemption available to the community" (p. 14). Contemplative silence is not a story but an experience within the Godly Play time that occurs when everyone is silently praying or working on their responses to the stories. In contemplative silence, Godly Play serves the function of "opening the way to experience the presence of the mystery of God directly" (p. 15). All Godly Play stories are contained in eight volumes (Berryman et al., 2024).

One distinctive feature of Godly Play is the storyteller's use of story props that assist the storytelling. In the Parable of the Mustard Seed (see above), the storyteller lays down a large oval piece of yellow felt and then adds various story props on top, including a seed planter, a slowly unfolding green felt mustard tree with many branches, small cardboard nests perched on these branches, and small cardboard birds flying to the tree and sitting on top of these nests and branches. These story props help to hold the children's attention and enable them to visualize the story. After the storyteller tells the story with these props, the storyteller makes a series of "I wonder" statements crafted to pique the children's curiosity about the possible meaning of the story. The storyteller concludes with a final "I wonder" statement: "I wonder what your work will be today?"

The children then disperse into the room to select an expressive arts medium to play with. Media include painting, drawing, clay modeling, and working directly with the story props from the story just told or another Godly Play story. The purpose of this "response time" is "the integration of each child's body, mind, and spirit with the creative process to learn the art of how to use Christian language to cope with their existential issues and discover the presence of God in their lives" (Berryman, 2009, p. 68).

At the end of the response time, the children gather back to their circle for a "feast," which includes juice and crackers or cookies and begins with going around the circle and allowing each child to say a brief prayer or silent prayer. The feast represents "an indirect preparation for their participation in Holy Communion in the church" (Berryman, 2009, p. 93). The goodbye ritual includes the storyteller's calling each child by name when they show that they are ready to leave and personally saying "goodbye" to each one. The entire Godly Play activity lasts between 45 and 60 minutes (Berryman, 2009).

The only other adult in the Godly Play room is the door person (Berryman, 2009). The door person serves multiple functions, including acting as gatekeeper (keeping children in and parents out), assisting children during the response time (helping them help themselves), helping children prepare and distribute the feast, announcing the names of children who appear ready to say goodbye and leave, and providing a brief explanation of the Godly Play session to inquisitive parents waiting to pick up their child. According to Berryman (2009), having more than two adults in the room has the unfortunate disadvantage of making the children feel outnumbered, which "undermines the community of children" (p. 28) and thus hinders their ownership of the process.

Godly Play emphasizes not only the verbal dimensions of sacred stories, parables, and liturgical action lessons but also the nonverbal dimensions of the storytelling that invite each child to enter the story and ponder it. These nonverbal dimensions include the storyteller's vocal delivery and body language, story prop placement, and seating arrangement in a circle. Storytellers pay careful attention to each of these dimensions to maximize the meaningfulness of the story being told. Based on extensive research, Mehrabian (1981) concluded that, when feelings are communicated, 55% of the meaning comes from facial expressions, 38% from vocal tone, and only 7% from the words themselves. Thus, Godly Play's emphasis on these nonverbal cues has support in the psychology literature.

Purpose

The Godly Play program is considered a spiritual intervention because Berryman (2009) wanted to discover and implement a playful way to intervene in the spiritual lives of children. According to Berryman (2009), there are four existential limits that all human beings must grapple with: death, the need for meaning, the threat of freedom, and aloneness. The four linguistic genres of Godly Play provide children with a language—the Christian language—that they then internalize and carry with them throughout life to help them confront these existential limits. For example, one of the sacred stories—the resurrection of Jesus—demonstrates that Jesus has overcome death through faith in Him. The "I wonder" questions include, "I wonder how sadness and happiness can come together to make joy?" "I wonder where joy comes from?" "I wonder how do we know when joy is here?" (Godly Play Foundation, 2016a). Christianity teaches that life in Jesus overcomes the sting of death (I Corinthians 15:55, New International Version [NIV]). The four linguistic genres of Godly Play apply a specific language—the Christian language—to help children to cope with all four existential limits.

What is the purpose of Godly Play? Why should clergy carve out a line in their budgets to train Sunday school teachers to implement Godly Play on Sunday mornings? Berryman (2009) suggests that Godly Play teaches

> the art of how to use the Christian language system to cope with our existential limits. The goal is for children to have an internal working model of this language system by the time they enter adolescence. Guiding children through early, middle and late childhood is like learning Christian as a second language. (p. 137)

To help children to develop their own meaning in response to these four linguistic genres, Godly Play includes three opportunities for children to reflect on the story. The "I wonder" questions provide a space for children to consider different facets of the story. The response time, which follows the "I wonder" questions, allows children to develop their own meaning of the story through their artwork and play. Finally, the feast provides an opportunity for communal reflection and celebration of the story and of each other. Considering the story of the resurrection of Jesus, the child can wonder with the teacher about the story's meaning, develop their own meaning through their artwork and play (e.g., drawing a picture of Jesus walking out of the tomb holding the child's hand), and consume the juice and crackers, pretending that it is communion in which they are symbolically taking Jesus inside them.

The Godly Play curriculum and methodology presuppose that "children already know God as a non-specific experience of relationship and that they participate in a kind of generic Godly play that permeates God's creation" (Berryman, 2009, p. 117). Godly Play relies on the theory of relational consciousness espoused by Rebecca Nye (2009) and David Hay (2006) that children have evolved the innate capacity for an awareness of a connection to spirituality—a "natural, playful knowledge of God" (Berryman, 2009, p. 117). Just as a person can deny their innate spirituality and thus experience a spiritual struggle (see Spiritually Integrated Psychotherapy [SIP], Chapter 7), so too do some children "discard relational consciousness altogether as they encounter cultural pressures that devalue it" (Minor & Grant, 2014, p. 214). Godly Play facilitates the restoration of this natural, playful knowledge of God and seeks to deepen this knowledge using the Christian language system.

Berryman (2009) considers play to be the royal road to a child's innate spirituality. He spends considerable time discussing Garvey's (1990) five criteria of play and demonstrating how Godly Play meets these five criteria. The five criteria include the following: (1) play is pleasurable; (2) play is done for itself; (3) play is voluntary; (4) play involves deep concentration; and (5) play has links to the creative process, problem-solving, the learning of languages, and social roles. Berryman (2009) argues that Godly Play is inherently playful because it meets these five criteria. As a Godly Play practitioner, I consider the response time portion of a Godly Play session to be most closely aligned with these five criteria. During this free time, children gain unfettered access to their conscious and unconscious wishes, fears, thoughts, and feelings.

Empirical Evidence Supporting the Effectiveness of Godly Play

One of the purposes of this chapter is to provide a contemporary summary of Godly Play. Unfortunately, the empirical evidence supporting the effectiveness of Godly Play is sparse. Like Freud (1933, p. 152; see also Rosenzweig, 1997), Berryman (2009) believes that the effectiveness of Godly Play is self-evident—beyond the collection of empirical evidence:

> Were we going to research what was going on in the classroom by objectifying and controlling it or remain participants in the process to become more effective teachers? The decision was made to stop researching Godly Play with a formal, quantitative approach and to only keep records that would help us become better teachers as the method and teaching materials developed. By this time we were no longer very much interested in whether Godly Play "worked" or not. It did. (p. 142)

This attitude, I believe, has prevented others from using the sophisticated tools of research methodology to determine whether Godly Play actually does work.

How would we know whether Godly Play works? As children age out of Godly Play (i.e., age 13), researchers could administer a multiple-choice questionnaire to determine their knowledge content of sacred stories, parables, and liturgical action lessons as a function of the number of Godly Play sessions attended throughout their childhood. Beyond assessing the internalization of the stories themselves, however, we might consider methods of assessing the children's spiritual development, which might include development of moral character, reliance on God to endure suffering or tragedy, and demonstrations of Christian love as manifested in service or behavior toward others. In other words, we might want to assess the apostle Paul's "fruit of the Spirit"—"love, joy, peace, forbearance, kindness, goodness, faithfulness, gentleness and self-control" (Galatians 5:22–23, NIV). Perhaps researchers could administer an instrument to detect qualities of spiritual well-being in children (see below). Researchers might also create new ways of measuring progress along the path of spiritual development. Considering the problems inherent in measuring Godly Play outcomes, as a developmental researcher myself, I can appreciate the difficulties that Berryman encountered as he considered whether to spend precious time on developing outcome measures that would do justice to the purpose of the Godly Play method of Christian education. Instead, he focused on cultivating "better teachers so [Godly Play] could work better" (Berryman, 2009, p. 142).

Minor and her colleagues (Minor & Grant, 2014) published a quantitative research study of Godly Play. Inspired by Hay's (2006) concept of relational consciousness (see earlier discussion), Minor and Grant (2014) assessed the spiritual well-being of 183 children participating in Godly Play using the Feeling Good, Living Life Questionnaire, which Fisher (2004) developed as a 16-item, 5-point Likert-type scale assessment of different facets of spiritual well-being in children ages 5–12. This instrument assesses both spiritual ideals (feeling good) and lived experiences (living life) in four domains of spiritual well-being: the quality of relationships with the self, the family, the environment, and God. The authors found that the length of time since the conclusion of Godly Play participation predicted spiritual well-being; in other words, children's spiritual well-being continued to increase after their exposure to Godly Play concluded. Psychotherapy researchers call this phenomenon the "sleeper effect"—changes that can occur long after treatment has ended (e.g., Fonagy, 2003; Muratori et al., 2003). Unfortunately, there was no control group of children who were participating in a parallel, traditional Sunday school curriculum, and so it is not known whether the increase in spiritual well-being is attributable to Godly Play or some other exposure such as confirmation or first communion.

Hyde (2010) used a qualitative methodology to study one Godly Play classroom. He discovered that Godly Play teachers nurture four dimensions of children's spirituality—the felt sense, integrating awareness, weaving the threads of meaning, and spiritual questing. We can contrast this model of religious education with the traditional model in which "children still sit at desks or around tables listening to a teacher, reading the Bible and/or a textbook, answering questions, and doing pencil-and-paper activities" (Roberto & Pfiffner, 2007, p. 1). Godly Play "provides an environment that allows children to encounter the living God directly" (Roberto & Pfiffner, 2007, p. 4).

Based on this brief review of studies, more research is obviously needed to establish the effectiveness of Godly Play to enhance children's spiritual well-being as well as other desirable outcomes mentioned earlier. Evaluating the Godly Play process—the ingredients of Godly Play that predict these outcomes—might also help to identify which ingredients are most significant to the development of these desirable outcomes. Godly Play teachers could then enhance these specific ingredients to maximize these desirable outcomes. Organizations such as the John Templeton Foundation and the Lilly Endowment are interested in funding research projects related to nurturing and deepening the Christian faith of children. I expect more rigorous research studies to be published in the coming decade.

History of Godly Play

Godly Play experienced a long germination period before it became widely available to Sunday schools across the US and the world. Jerome Berryman and Thea Schoonyoung were graduate students at Princeton Theological Seminary in 1960 when they met and began to discuss what they believed to be missing from children's Christian education. Specifically, Sunday school teachers instructed children in the stories and traditions of Christianity without giving any thought to how the children might be experiencing this teaching. After Jerome and Thea got married in 1961, they decided that children's Christian education needed revitalization, starting with incorporating children's opportunity to make their own meaning of Sunday school lessons through the medium of play. The Berrymans turned to Italy and the groundbreaking work of Maria Montessori. In 1971 and 1972, the Berrymans moved to Bergamo, Italy, to study at the Center for Advanced Montessori Studies. They learned that Montessori and some of her followers, especially Sofia Cavalletti, had already been experimenting with the application of the Montessori method to children's religious education. Even though Montessori paved the way, Jerome Berryman (1995) still took another 20 years before publishing the first edition of *Godly Play* in 1995.

In the early 1970s in the US, applying the Montessori method to children's Christian education was a radical idea. So why did the Berrymans spend so much time studying the Montessori method? Their goal was nothing less than revolutionizing children's Christian education. Montessori believed that "education should no longer consist only of imparting knowledge, but must instead take a new path seeking the release of human potentialities" (Montessori World Educational Institute, n.d., p. 2). Berryman (2009) understood children's spirituality to be one of these human potentialities that need cultivation to thrive. According to Berryman (2009), the Montessori method was "the best way to connect the child's intuition of God with the language of the church. Children could be encouraged to construct their own meaning about God by the playful interaction of their experience with Christian language" (p. 15). Thus, a playful Sunday school learning experience was born.

The distinctive qualities of a Montessori education include teaching individuals rather than groups, emphasizing the practice of tasks rather than listening and memorizing, adopting a holistic approach to education (including socioemotional and motoric development), cultivating responsibility for one's own self-regulation, maintaining a visually appealing classroom that includes developmentally appropriate toys, modeling positive values, considering developmental phases within the curriculum, nurturing self-reliance and freedom of choice, and respecting children's intrinsic motivation toward growth (Montessori World Educational Institute, n.d., pp. 2–3). At the time that the Berrymans were studying in Bergamo, Christian education for children in the US relied on listening to Bible lessons, memorization, and looking up Bible verses (codified in Bible verse memory contests and "sword drills"; see below).

The genius of the Berrymans' approach consists of their absolute trust in children's innate spirituality (as well as their absolute trust in the invisible hand of the indwelling Holy Spirit) to construct their own spiritual meaning through direct experience. Play therapists refer to childhood as "a distinct culture" that privileges play as the coin of the realm (Mullen, 2008, p. 69). The Berrymans contrast their radical approach to the emphasis on proper adult-centric doctrinal instruction prevalent in that era. Berryman (2009) viewed his role as introducing children to a common language of spirituality that they could use to construct meaning out of the four existential limits that all humans must face in this life. According to Berryman (2009), "Guiding children through early, middle and late childhood is like learning Christian as a second language" (p. 137)—with their first language being the unique, unverbalized spiritual experiences commonly revealed during childhood. The psychoanalyst Rizzuto (1979) wrote, "No child arrives at 'the house of God' without his pet God under his arm" (p. 8). At age 5, Berryman (2009) recalls lying in bed in the dark in his grandmother's bedroom and crying out, "'I don't want to die!'" (p. 16). His grandmother helped him to "get in touch with a larger presence, a Power without a name that I could *feel*" (p. 16; emphasis in original). Godly Play places these powerful nonverbal experiences within a Christian framework of linguistic understanding.

Godly Play Viewed in the Context of Attachment Theory

In evaluating whether a spiritual intervention is consistent with the principles of attachment theory, we always start with the basics: does the spiritual intervention create a safe haven and a secure base for the participants? From my point of view, Godly Play does cultivate a safe space for children to explore their own minds and the four existential limits discussed earlier. In discussing Montessori's insights into children's play, Berryman (2009) suggests that felt security is a necessary condition for children's ability to express "a love of learning, the ability for self-direction and a deeply spiritual nature" (p. 23). The Godly Play teachers cultivate this felt security by offering a balance between exhibiting a nonjudgmental attitude toward the meanings that children ascribe to the stories and response time play activities, and setting appropriate limits on children's behaviors that disrupt the storytelling and response time processes. According to Berryman (2009), "Children need limits to feel safe and the creative process does not work well when people do not feel safe" (p. 40).

The twin concepts of attachment and exploration are intertwined in attachment theory founder John Bowlby's (1982) writings. According to Bowlby (1982), both felt security and novelty activate the exploratory system. Infants and children explore the novelty in their environments only when a background of safety (Sandler, 1960) exists. This background of safety ensures that the child can explore and learn free from danger. When the caregiver becomes unavailable or a stranger or threatening stimulus enters the sensory field, however, the exploratory system is deactivated, and the fear system becomes activated, which in turn activates the attachment system, triggering proximity-seeking and contact maintenance. Exploration stops.

Montessori knew about this relationship between felt security and exploration and strove to create a school curriculum that would maximize children's feelings of safety so that their exploratory systems would almost always be activated. Thus, safety enables learning to take place through play in which "a child always behaves beyond his average age, above his daily behavior; in play it is as though he were a head taller than himself" (Vygotsky, 1978, p. 102). If the attachment system were to be activated (e.g., stranger entering the room, disruptive peers), however, play would immediately come to a screeching halt, and the children would focus exclusively on maximizing their felt security through seeking proximity to a teacher or any familiar adult whom they perceive to be "older and/or wiser" (Bowlby, 1988, p. 120). Play goes to die in the pit of anxiety; play thrives in the meadow of safety.

The exploratory system is most likely to be activated during the Godly Play response time, when the storyteller invites the children to explore the play materials or the Godly Play props. In the presence of the secure base (i.e., the Godly Play storyteller), the children are free to explore their mental states as well as the existential limits posed by the story that they have just heard. Response time allows the children to "generate meaning from the interplay between their life experience and the sacred story, the parable, the liturgical action or the contemplative silence involved in the presentation" (Berryman, 2009, p. 42); however, this interplay could not occur without the activation of the exploratory system produced by the deactivation of the attachment system.

Consistent with attachment theory, Godly Play features a storyteller who "does not tell [the children] how to think and feel about the lesson because that would take away their chance to have their own feelings and make their own meaning" (Berryman, 2009, p. 44). A prescriptive pedagogy might make a child feel rejected, especially when their idiosyncratic story meaning differs from the Sunday school teacher's orthodox story meaning. Rejection of the child by the attachment figure produces attachment anxiety and a feeling of a lack of safety (Ainsworth et al., 1978). Based on the earlier discussion, anxiety interferes with exploration; thus, under these conditions, less learning takes place. The nonprescriptive Godly Play pedagogy facilitates a background of safety because of its nonjudgmental quality. Play flourishes when children feel secure in the knowledge that all their meanings and mental states are acceptable. And, when play takes off, learning soars. In Godly Play, the storyteller is the quintessential spiritually responsive caregiver. I will be discussing another nonprescriptive pedagogical alternative to Godly Play later in this chapter.

When Is Godly Play a Good Match?

Godly Play is a good match when parents want their child to understand and use the Christian language system to make meaning of their existence and discover their purpose in life. It is not a good match for parents who want their child to participate in a traditional Sunday school pedagogy. As a child who grew up in a conservative Baptist church in rural Pennsylvania, I memorized Bible verses and participated in "sword drills." Sword drills are contests in which children must "draw your swords"—lift their Bibles above their shoulders—as the teacher announces the reference of a Bible verse (e.g., John 3:16), then says, "Go!" The first person to find the verse in their Bible must stand up and read the verse. That child is declared the winner. I was particularly good at sword drills, having memorized all 66 books of the Bible in order. My sister Mae Lynn excelled at Bible verse memorization. In Bible verse memorization contests, the teacher announces the reference of a Bible verse, and the child must be the first to stand up and recite the verse verbatim (King James Version only, please).

I grew up knowing my way around the Bible, but what did these competitive exercises teach me? They taught me that I am faster than the other children at looking up verses. Digital Bibles with powerful search engines have made this talent obsolete. Sword drills did not teach me how to use parables to make sense out of my existence in the world. I could have been making meaning out of Bible stories; instead, I was learning that my Sunday school teachers and parents valued my beating the other children in sword drills. Thus, for competitive parents who value Bible speed or rote memorization rather than critical thinking skills and a personal encounter with the divine Presence, Godly Play is probably not the appropriate spiritual pedagogy for their children.

Although Godly Play obviously teaches the language system of a specific religion—Christianity—might this curriculum appeal to parents and children from other faiths? In Berryman's (2009) extensive experience as the principal developer of Godly Play, "children from Jewish, Bahai [sic], and Sikh families ... chose to participate, as they said, because the class was 'spiritually healthy,' despite their different religious orientations" (pp. 141–142). Perhaps the symbols of the Christian language system differ from those of a different religion, but all children, regardless of religious orientation, must face the four existential limits (see earlier discussion). I think that this is what Berryman means by using the phrase "spiritually healthy." Parents from other faith traditions might want their children to seek spiritual solutions to these existential limits.

Godly Play provides a way of speaking about these existential limits that facilitates spiritual seeking. Jesus said, "Seek and you will find" (Matthew 7:7; Luke 11:9, NIV). Godly Play emphasizes the seeking of solutions rather than the solutions themselves, because only in seeking do children find the solutions to their existential limits. Thus, open-minded parents of other faith traditions might find Godly Play appealing for their children. Perhaps other faith traditions could adapt the Godly Play pedagogy to tell the sacred stories of these traditions to their children. For example, Guru Nanak's disappearance while bathing in a river, reappearing after 3 days to enlighten his followers that Hinduism and Islam are false divisions because we are all one in God (Sarna, 2005), could become a sacred story told in a Sikh version of Godly Play. In this manner, modified versions of Godly Play could teach the language systems of other faith traditions to children whose families practice those traditions. The content would change, but the methodology would remain the same.

Godly Play maintains specific age criteria for participants, which are ages 3–12. Because 3-year-olds occupy a different developmental phase than 12-year-olds, Berryman (2009) suggests that Godly Play classes should be divided into three age groups: 3–6-year-olds, 6–9-year-olds, and 9–12-year-olds, while nevertheless also noting that "each person goes through the stages uniquely and on his or her own timetable" (p. 125). Developmental phases are not static (e.g., Wang et al., 2024); thus, these age groups might need adjustment in the future to account for biological, cognitive, and emotional acceleration.

The storyteller can adapt the "I wonder" questions to the level of cognitive maturity of each age group. For example, in the case illustration at the beginning of this chapter, the storyteller is working with 3–6-year-olds. She asks, "I wonder if the man who planted the tiny seed has a name?" which corresponds to these children's concrete thinking. Working with 9–12-year-olds, the same storyteller might ask, "I wonder how the birds found the mustard tree? I wonder how the birds knew that they were welcome to make their nests in this tree?" These "I wonder" questions correspond to these children's more abstract thinking. Godly Play is sensitive to cognitive changes during childhood, allowing for modifications to the script to suit each age group.

Training Requirements to Practice Godly Play

Anyone who loves children and has access to the childlike part of themselves can become a Godly Play practitioner. Unlike Spiritually Integrated Psychotherapy (see Chapter 7), Godly Play does not require a state license to practice it; unlike 12-step sponsorship (see Chapter 4), however, it does require formal training. The Godly Play Foundation (www.godlyplayfoundation.org) sponsors all Godly Play training. Two Godly Play trainers lead in-person or online workshops or retreats to teach the Godly Play method. Completion of the core training module qualifies a person to become a Godly Play practitioner. The core training module takes 18 hours to complete and cost $350 when I completed it in summer 2024. These 18 hours are offered as an intensive weekend retreat or six weekly 3-hour sessions. The Godly Play Foundation also offers specialized training modules for Godly Play practiced in school settings and in clinical settings, each taking 90 minutes to complete and each costing $35.

Godly Play trainees must present one Godly Play story to the training group during the 18-hour training. Both trainers and fellow trainees provide feedback on the trainee's storytelling. At the end of the training, the Godly Play Foundation sends a certificate of training that verifies that the trainee has learned about the spirituality of the child, setting up a Godly Play environment, and supporting the circle of children in Godly Play. The only institution that provides Godly Play training is the Godly Play Foundation, located in Ashland, KS. Fortunately, online training and training in various regions of the US are regularly offered.

Storytelling/Story-Acting Play Intervention: An Alternative to Godly Play

The Storytelling/Story-Acting play intervention (STSA) is a low-cost play-based intervention that I believe can improve preschool children's school readiness skills. The US Department of State granted my colleague Valeda Dent and me Fulbright scholarships to travel to two villages in rural Uganda to study the effectiveness of STSA in two impoverished rural communities, Mpigi and Kabubbu. During my 6-month stay, I collected 497 stories from preschool children who lived in these two villages. Valeda and I conducted STSA in two community libraries in these villages, training the librarians to conduct this play intervention (Goodman & Dent, 2019). I also adapted STSA for young adolescent middle school students with positive results (Goodman et al., 2023).

The following two stories, told by two children living in rural Uganda, illustrate STSA's potential for cultivating verbal and dramatic self-expression:

> Some children went to school. One of the children took rice. When others asked her to give them some, she refused, and then one child slapped her. She went back home crying. There was a party, and her friends attended, but she did not attend because she was dirty. (Jauharah, age 5, from Mpigi, Uganda)

> A man and his wife produced a child, and at some point, they left the child in the house by herself. When they went away, a monster came and knocked on the door and asked the child to open, pretending to be the father of the child. The monster convinced the child that it had brought her millet [grain] to eat. When the child opened, the monster ate the child. (Olivia, age 5, from Kabubbu, Uganda)

I believe that STSA can be adapted to accommodate the telling and acting out of Bible stories like Godly Play. Instead of only telling the stories, the children would also act them out. What advantage does acting out Bible stories confer on the children? In her book *Praying with Body and Soul*, Vennard (1998) explores the ways in which our bodies teach us to pray. I credit her with giving me the idea of applying STSA to a Godly Play pedagogy. She suggests that adults can learn more about a Bible story by acting it out, alone or in a group. She calls this exercise "reading the Bible inside out" (p. 13). With our physical participation, "we learn more than we would if we were simply to observe the action. It is hard to learn to swim without getting in the water! So it is with Bible stories" (p. 13). According to Vennard, "When we move inside a Bible story with our imaginations and our bodies ... we have new and different knowledge to bring to our exploration" (p. 15). Thus, applying STSA to Godly Play storytelling adds an experiential dimension that might introduce new understandings to the children as their bodies move through space to portray the biblical characters.

History and Process of STSA in Uganda

While many preschool interventions have been effective at improving school readiness skills (e.g., Barnett et al., 2008; Weiland & Yoshikawa, 2013; Zigler et al., 2004), Valeda and I selected STSA because it has been shown to be effective, requires few materials, and is easy to conduct. Developed by Paley (1990), a Chicago educator, STSA capitalizes on oral storytelling (which has a venerable tradition in sub-Saharan African culture) to enhance children's cognitive and linguistic development. STSA consists of two phases: (1) young children's dictation of spontaneously generated stories (storytelling phase) and (2) young children's acting out these stories on a makeshift stage (story-acting phase). During a period of unstructured time for children in the library, a child can approach the librarian with a story. The librarian then writes down the story verbatim, with minimal intervention, and reads it back to the child to ensure accuracy. The librarian also underlines all the characters in the story, and the child author assigns child actors to all the characters. After three or four stories have been collected, the librarian assembles all the children around a large makeshift rectangle on the floor, instructing them to sit behind the lines. The librarian then calls up the first child author, who selects from the group those child actors who will be acting out the story characters. The librarian reads the story first to acquaint the children with it, then reads it again with the child actors acting it out. Each child author's story is read and acted out in the same fashion.

Paley's (1990) STSA play intervention combines narrative and play that can be deeply engaging to children and, in the process, helps them to develop strong oral language skills. Paley discusses this play intervention and some of its effects, usually in conjunction with other aspects of her classroom environment, producing rich, vivid, and engrossing ethnographic studies during the period in which she taught at the Chicago Laboratory School (e.g., Paley, 1990). Nicolopoulou and her research team implemented and evaluated this play intervention in classroom settings both similar to and different from Paley's (e.g., Nicolopoulou, 2002). While a strong ethnographic dimension was always included, principles of evidence-based research involving quantitative measures of intervention outcomes also guided their efforts. In an effort to promote an evidence base for this powerful educational intervention that includes principles of play, Nicolopoulou and her research team conducted five iterative studies in the US building on Paley's research: (1) a 2-year study of two middle-income preschool classrooms; (2) a 3-year study of two middle-income preschool classrooms in a different setting; (3) a 1-year study of a Head Start classroom, using another classroom for comparison; (4) a 2-year study of four Head Start classrooms in a large urban center, using two other classrooms as comparisons; and (5) a 2-year study where a total of seven experimental and seven control classrooms, serving low-income families, were studied. Each of these studies yielded significant results that validate the effectiveness of STSA in promoting school readiness skills (for a summary of findings, see Nicolopoulou, 2019; Nicolopoulou & Cole, 2010; Nicolopoulou et al., 2015).

Our goal in studying preschool children from Uganda was to determine whether 6 months of participation in STSA could improve children's school readiness skills. A significant finding would support the idea that this play intervention could make preschool children more prepared to enter the school environment. We wanted to demonstrate that this finding holds true even when caregivers are not providing optimal learning environments at home, such as infrequent patterns of reading with their children, or optimal supports because of a poor quality of life. In other words, can STSA buffer these children from their emotionally and materially impoverished home environments and facilitate the development of school readiness skills? We learned that STSA did just that (Goodman & Dent, 2019). In fact, two STSA groups are still active in Kabubbu, led by the community librarian, Nalugwa Ritah.

Applying STSA to Godly Play Storytelling

To provide children with the opportunity to embody Bible stories, STSA would need to become a more structured activity. Instead of providing children unstructured time to tell stories to an adult from their own imaginations, the Godly Play storyteller would be telling a Bible story. After the story ends, and before the response time begins, the children would decide among themselves (with the storyteller's assistance) who would play the various characters in the story. Then, the Godly Play storyteller would slowly tell the story again, allowing the child actors to play their roles. As Vennard (1998) points out, "[The children] can put [them]selves physically into the biblical descriptions: standing up, moving forward, shouting, reaching out, kneeling, begging, praising God" (p. 16)—whatever the story calls for. I would imagine that this acting out portion would enrich the children's response time, which would take place immediately afterward. Embodied understanding would ground the children's intellectual understanding, making an encounter with the Holy One more immanent.

Conclusions

Godly Play is a play-informed curriculum for children ages 3–12 that teaches children how to cope with four existential limits using the Christian language system. Godly Play helps children to develop an internal working model of this language system that they can carry with them into adolescence and adulthood. It differs from traditional Sunday school curricula because it engages children's deepest spiritual yearnings through the medium of play. Play appears to be the royal road to children's innate spirituality, allowing them to develop their own meanings in relation to Bible stories. This meaning development occurs primarily during the response time, when children select an expressive arts medium through which to express their impressions of the story that they just experienced. Empirical support for Godly Play is limited, but the extant literature looks promising.

I suggested that Godly Play intuitively uses the principles of attachment theory to facilitate experiential learning among the children who participate. A key concept in the attachment literature is the secure base. Children use a secure base from which they explore their environments. Threatening or unfamiliar stimuli in the environment signal the activation of the fear system and attachment system, which in turn triggers proximity to a secure base. When the threat has passed, proximity to the secure base produces a feeling of security and the resulting deactivation of the attachment system, permitting the exploratory system to be activated. The exploratory system permits children's curiosity about the world around them to be gratified. When the environment signals danger again, the exploratory system immediately becomes deactivated, and the fear system and attachment system become activated, making the learning process nearly impossible. Montessori and, later, Berryman understood this dynamic in the classroom setting; thus, they implemented a play-informed pedagogy that would prioritize felt security among the children who participate. Only when children feel safe in their environment are they ready to learn. Berryman stressed the minimization of all threats to this felt security, including strangers wandering in and out of the room as well as peer disruptions. In accordance with the principles of attachment theory, the Godly Play storyteller and the door person are jointly responsible for creating the most favorable conditions for children's learning how to use the Christian language system, which they need to grapple with the four existential limits.

Godly Play is for any child whose parents value the importance of play and their child's innate spirituality. Any adult who is connected to their innate playfulness and spirituality can become a Godly Play practitioner by taking an 18-hour core training module sponsored by the Godly Play Foundation. A Godly Play practitioner must approach their intention prayerfully, as Godly Play is designed to make a lasting impression on children through the development of their internal working model of the Christian language system.

The STSA play intervention is an alternative method of helping children to internalize the Christian language system. In its modified form, which replaces spontaneous storytelling by the child with biblical storytelling by an adult, the children can encode the Bible stories not only in their minds but also in their bodies. Acting out a Bible story among a group of children gives them the freedom to explore Bible characters from the inside out. How does it feel to act out the role of a blind man who approaches Jesus for healing? How does it feel to act out the role of a physically disabled woman who has been bent over for 18 years and then, suddenly, is free to stretch upward and walk upright? How does it feel to act out the role of Jesus, who shows mercy and heals the blind man and the physically disabled woman? How does it feel to act out the role of a bystander in these two stories? STSA has the power to enrich the children's response time by giving them added insight through the kinesthetic experience of acting out characters in the Bible stories.

Godly Play nurtures a genuine connection to the sacred through the medium of play. I encourage Sunday school superintendents to consider implementing Godly Play in their curricula. Children deserve to engage their playful natures to seek answers to our temporary existence on this Earth and to nurture their innate spirituality, which is God's gift to us all.

References

Ainsworth, M. D. S., Blehar, M. C., Waters, E., & Wall, S. (1978). *Patterns of attachment: A psychological study of the strange situation*. Erlbaum.

Barnett, W. S., Jung, K., Yarosz, D. J., Thomas, J., Hornbeck, A., Stechuk, R., & Burns, S. (2008). Educational effects of the Tools of the Mind curriculum: A randomized trial. *Early Childhood Research Quarterly, 23*, 299–313.

Berryman, J. W. (1995). *Godly Play: An imaginative approach to religious education*. Fortress Press.

Berryman, J. W. (2009). *Teaching Godly Play: How to mentor the spiritual development of children* (2nd ed.). Church Publishing. Kindle edition.

Berryman, J. W., Beales, R., & Minor, C. V. (2024). *The complete guide to Godly Play* (Vols. 1–8). Church Publishing. https://store.godlyplayfoundation.org/products/gp110-disc

Bowlby, J. (1982). *Attachment and loss: Vol. 1. Attachment* (2nd ed.). Basic Books.

Bowlby, J. (1988). *A secure base: Parent–child attachment and healthy human development*. Basic Books.

Fisher, J. W. (2004). Feeling good, living life: A spiritual health measure for young children. *Journal of Beliefs and Values, 25*, 307–315.

Fonagy, P. (2003). The research agenda: The vital need for empirical research in child psychotherapy. *Journal of Child Psychotherapy, 29*, 129–136.

Freud, S. (1933). New introductory lectures on psycho-analysis. In J. Strachey (Ed. and Trans.), *The standard edition of the complete psychological works of Sigmund Freud* (Vol. 22, pp. 1–182). Hogarth Press.

Garvey, C. (1990). *Play: The developing child* (2nd ed.). Harvard University Press.

Godly Play Foundation. (2016a). *Godly Play story: The mystery of Easter*. Retrieved on December 16, 2024. www.youtube.com/watch?v=ivkLTqkiWjc

Godly Play Foundation. (2016b). *Godly Play story: The parable of the mustard seed*. Retrieved on December 14, 2024. www.youtube.com/watch?v=qlLiRsDKk7g&t=287s

Goodman, G., Blum, B., Rentrop, C., Malberg, N., & Agrawal, P. (2023). The efficacy of two group interventions on mental representations, attachment security, and trauma symptoms in ethnically and socioeconomically minoritized young adolescents in an urban middle school. *International Journal of Environmental Research and Public Health, 20*, 5789.

Goodman, G., & Dent, V. F. (2019). A story grows in rural Uganda: Studying the effectiveness of the Storytelling/Story-Acting (STSA) play intervention on Ugandan preschoolers' school readiness skills. *Journal of Infant, Child, and Adolescent Psychotherapy, 18*, 288–306.

Hay, D. (2006). *The spirit of the child* (2nd ed.). Jessica Kingsley.

Hyde, B. (2010). Godly Play nourishing children's spirituality: A case study. *Religious Education, 105*, 504–518.

Mehrabian, A. (1981). *Silent messages: Implicit communication of emotions and attitudes* (2nd ed.). Wadsworth.

Minor, C. V., & Grant, B. (2014). Promoting spiritual well-being: A quasi-experimental test of an element of Hay and Nye's theory of children's spirituality. *International Journal of Children's Spirituality, 19*, 213–227.

Montessori World Educational Institute (n.d.). *The Montessori method of education* (pp. 1–8). Author. https://montessoriworld.org/MontessoriMethod.pdf

Mullen, J. A. (2008). Through a cross-cultural lens: How viewing childhood as a distinct culture impacts supervision. In A. A. Drewes & J. A. Mullen (Eds.), *Supervision can be playful: Techniques for child and play therapist supervisors* (pp. 69–90). Jason Aronson.

Muratori, F., Picchi, L., Bruni, G., Patarnello, M., & Romagnoli, G. (2003). A two-year follow-up of psychodynamic psychotherapy for internalizing disorders in children. *Journal of the American Academy of Child & Adolescent Psychiatry, 42*, 331–339.

New International Version. (1978). *The Holy Bible, new international version.* Zondervan.

Nicolopoulou, A. (2002). Peer-group culture and narrative development. In S. Blum-Kulka & C. E. Snow (Eds.), *Talking to adults: The contribution of multiparty discourse to language acquisition* (pp. 117–152). Lawrence Erlbaum.

Nicolopoulou, A. (2019). Using a storytelling/story-acting practice to promote narrative and other decontextualized language skills in disadvantaged children. In E. Veneziano & A. Nicolopoulou (Eds.), *Narrative, literacy and other skills: Studies in intervention* (pp. 263–284). John Benjamins.

Nicolopoulou, A., & Cole, M. (2010). Design experimentation as a theoretical and empirical tool for developmental pedagogical research. *Pedagogies: An International Journal, 5*, 61–71.

Nicolopoulou, A., Schnabel Cortina, K., Ilgaz, H., Brockmeyer Cates, C., & de Sá, A. B. (2015). Using narrative- and play-based activity to promote low-income preschoolers' oral language, emergent literacy, and social competence. *Early Childhood Research Quarterly, 31*, 147–162.

Nye, R. (2009). *Children's spirituality: What it is and why it matters.* Church House.

Paley, V. G. (1990). *The boy who would be a helicopter: The uses of storytelling in the classroom.* Harvard University Press.

Rizzuto, A.-M. (1979). *The birth of the living God: A psychoanalytic study.* University of Chicago Press.

Roberto, J., & Pfiffner, K. (2007, Fall/Winter). Best practices in children's faith formation. *Lifelong Faith*, 1–13. Lifelong Faith.

Rosenzweig, S. (1997). Letters by Freud on experimental psychodynamics. *American Psychologist, 52*, 571.

Sandler, J. (1960). The background of safety. *International Journal of Psychoanalysis, 41*, 352–356.

Sarna, N. (2005). *The book of Nanak.* Penguin Global.

Vennard, J. E. (1998). *Praying with body and soul: A way to intimacy with God.* Augsburg.

Vygotsky, L. S. (1978). *Mind in society: The development of higher psychological processes* (2nd ed.). Harvard University Press.

Wang, Z., Asokan, G., Onnela, J.-P., Baird, D. D., Jukic, A. M. Z., Wilcox, A. J., Curry, C. L., Fischer-Colbrie, T., Williams, M. A., Hauser, R., Coull, B. A., & Mahalingaiah, S. (2024). Menarche and time to cycle regularity among individuals born between 1950 and 2005 in the US. *Journal of the American Medical Association Network Open, 7*, e2412854.

Weiland, C., & Yoshikawa, H. (2013). Impacts of a pre kindergarten program on children's mathematics, language, literacy, executive function, and emotional skills. *Child Development, 84*, 2112–2130.

Zigler, E. F., Singer, D. G., & Bishop-Josef, S. J. (Eds.) (2004). *Children's play: The roots of reading.* Washington, DC: Zero to Three Press.

Part II

Models of Spiritual Intervention Conducted by Licensed Professionals

Chapter 6

Using Drawing in a Spirituality Group to Discuss Mental Representations of God

In the early years of life, the child develops a range of self- and object representations that soothe the child when alone, aid in the delay of instinctual gratification, and warn of potential danger situations in external reality. One of these early object representations is the representation of God. Winnicott (1971, pp. 1–25) traced the origins of the God representation to the young child's world of transitional objects created in the intermediate area of experience (potential space), where illusion and reality simultaneously dwell. This intermediate area of experience, "unchallenged in respect of its belonging to inner or external (shared) reality, constitutes the greater part of the infant's experience, and throughout life is retained in the intense experiencing that belongs to the arts and to religion" (p. 14).

The psychoanalyst Rizzuto (1979) conducted a meticulous study of object representations and God representations among four psychiatric inpatients, hypothesizing that such an investigation might "provide an unsuspected projective test of childhood object relations which the patient has unknowingly transformed into his God image" (p. 8). Based on her findings, Rizzuto posited that the representation of God is constructed out of a range of representational materials:

> Like the transitional object, God is heavily loaded with parental traits (those objects the child finds). But as a creation of the child [God] has other traits that suit the child's needs in relating to his parents and maintaining his sense of worth and safety. (pp. 208–209)

By comparing responses to two separate questionnaires regarding one's parents and God, Rizzuto was able to identify patients' specific parental representational materials that corresponded with their representation of God.

Similarly, Granqvist and his colleagues (Nkara et al., 2018, cited in Granqvist, 2020) used the unpublished Religious Attachment Interview (RAI) to support the correspondence hypothesis. Coherent descriptions of parents were correlated with coherent descriptions and the benevolence of God. In addition, Cassibba and colleagues (2008) reported that a highly religious group of Catholics in Italy (i.e., priests, nuns, seminary students) were coded as having more loving experiences with their mothers as well as more coherent discourse on the Adult Attachment Interview (AAI) than a group of lay Catholics. Furthermore, in both groups, securely attached participants reported having a more loving image of God than insecurely attached participants. In summary, ample evidence supports the correspondence pathway.

While Rizzuto's (1979) case studies were able to demonstrate a correspondence between the structure and content of parental and self-representations and those of the God representation, Rizzuto did not address whether a therapeutic exploration of the person's representation of God could provide insight into or integration of one's unmodulated parental or self-representations and lead to greater self-understanding and self-acceptance. Kirkpatrick (1999), however, does raise this possibility: "In cases [of] religious change ... does one's orientation toward interpersonal attachments then change concomitantly? If so, this knowledge might provide a useful basis for the development of therapeutic strategies for dealing with relationship-based difficulties, particularly in religious populations" (p. 819). Could an exploration of one's representation of God produce global therapeutic benefits in some clinical populations?

Kirkpatrick (1999) further suggests that representations of God might not always correspond with the parental representations established in early childhood, at least in a direct way. In addition to the correspondence hypothesis, God representations might be formed to compensate for insecure or otherwise deficient parental representations—the compensation hypothesis. Thus, under highly stressful circumstances, the quality of God representations "might be expected to correlate *inversely* with contemporaneous outcome measures" (p. 818) as well as with the quality of parental representations. Kirkpatrick (1999) concludes:

> For people who seek and value close relationships, but who have difficulty developing and maintaining them due to fears of being unloved and/or abandoned, it is easy to see how God's unconditional (or easily earned) love may be perceived as immensely attractive, and how the experience of finding such a relationship may be emotionally powerful and deeply rewarding. (p. 816)

Kirkpatrick seems to be suggesting that the quality of the God representation could be modified beyond the preschool years and used to defend against perceived disappointments inherent in the parental representations established during early childhood.

Consistent with this idea, Granqvist and his colleagues (2007) established support for a link between sudden religious changes and assessments of parents' perceived insensitivity on the AAI, with ratings of parents during childhood as less loving and less sensitive correlated with their ratings of intense increases in religiousness. In a follow-up study, Granqvist and his colleagues (2014) observed that the intense increases in religiousness reflected "an unorthodox blend of theistic religiosity *and* New Age spirituality" (Granqvist, 2020, p. 167; emphasis in original). Granqvist (2020) summarizes these research findings: "Experiences of parental insensitivity and current attachment insecurity predispose a person to 'desperate searching', in which the person grabs on to whatever religious/spiritual means are available to regulate distress" (p. 167). Granqvist (2020) further suggests that, when unbearably stressful conditions predominate, secondary strategies of emotion regulation (i.e., insecure attachment patterns) are insufficient. Thus, the person tries out the primary strategy of emotion regulation (i.e., secure attachment pattern) in their encounter with a Higher Power Who can never disappoint them (see the case illustration of Hudson below; for a more detailed discussion, see Goodman, 2025b, Chapter 3).

Clearly, more work is needed (1) to sort out what might be complicated relationships between parental and God representations and (2) to identify under what conditions the compensation versus correspondence processes operate. In the context of a process-oriented spirituality group, I pursued these ideas clinically by soliciting the representations of God held by psychiatric inpatients diagnosed with borderline personality disorder (BPD) as well as their relationships to their parental representations. I was also interested in exploring whether changes could occur in these mental representations in the context of the potentially safe space of the group. I present the organization of this psychodynamically oriented, exploratory spirituality group and a sampling of the drawings of the God representation made by the participants. I also describe a portion of the group process reflecting the openness to change in these mental representations, at least by some participants, over the course of the group sessions.

The Spirituality Group

The 14-session exploratory spirituality group (loosely based on a model presented in Gallagher et al., 1994) was co-led by a male clinical psychologist and a female hospital chaplain on a long-term, psychodynamically oriented psychiatric unit dedicated to the treatment of inpatients diagnosed with BPD. These inpatients were admitted to this unit because they satisfied diagnostic criteria (American Psychiatric Association [APA], 2022) and because they posed a danger either to themselves or others. The group was advertised on the unit as an opportunity to talk about participants' images of God, what God means to each participant, and how these images influence their lives. Nine out of 25 female inpatients agreed to participate in weekly 45-minute sessions. Because group participants were inpatients and thus a "captive audience," all of them regularly attended sessions. Only one participant dropped out prior to the completion of the 14 sessions. This model of spiritual group intervention is one of many such models identified collectively as "arts-based spiritual care" (ABSC; Rieger et al., 2023). A scoping review of ABSC in healthcare settings concluded that ABSC provides "a transformative presence in care encounters" (Rieger et al., 2023, p. 1).

Participants were informed that the group's purposes were threefold: (1) to increase awareness of spirituality—particularly conscious and unconscious images of God—held by each participant; (2) to place these images and associated feelings and beliefs in the context of their current and past life situations and psychiatric symptoms; and (3) to provide an opportunity for participants to explore and discuss each other's image or images of God, thus potentially facilitating a re-creation and modification to a more integrated and benevolent image. I had hoped that the participants would also begin to develop attachment relationships with my co-leader and me and that these relationships would provide the participants with a secure base (Bowlby, 1982) from which to explore these images of God (see Goodman, 2025b, Chapter 4). The resulting sense of safety would permit them to confront unintegrated, frightening images of God that would otherwise produce a sense of discomfort and avoidance in other contexts.

In the initial session, participants were asked to spend 10 minutes making a drawing depicting their image of God as they believe God to be. Each participant then elaborated on her drawing in the group, an exercise designed to stimulate group discussion. I was struck by how the drawings seemed to fall into two broad categories: (1) a punitive, judgmental, rigid God who shows love only to those who follow God's rules and refuse to question God's authority; and (2) an abstract and nebulous, impersonal or depersonified life force that serves as a positive energy source in the universe. Five participants drew pictures depicting a punitive God, while the other four drew pictures depicting a depersonified, formless God. These two categories were unrelated to participants' specific religious backgrounds; all nine participants came from traditional Judeo-Christian religious backgrounds.

To illustrate these two categories, the drawing made by Jasmine (all names used are pseudonyms) depicts yellow rays of sunlight emanating from a pleasant-looking blue cloud at the top. Pointy orange and yellow flames of fire rage at the bottom. Black stairs descend from the blue cloud in the upper left-hand corner to the top of the flames in the lower right-hand corner. On the bottom stair, just above the flames, is a stick figure lying down. Separating the stick figure from the heavenly blue cloud and rays of sunlight above is a sheet of black (see Figure 6.1). When asked by the group to elaborate on her drawing, Jasmine stated that she is lying on a trapdoor to hell and that a black cloud separates her from God. She added that her priest told her that people are guilty because Adam and Eve ate the apple. She explained that one must be deserving to have a relationship with God. One participant suggested that the black cloud represents the Church's rules or teachings.

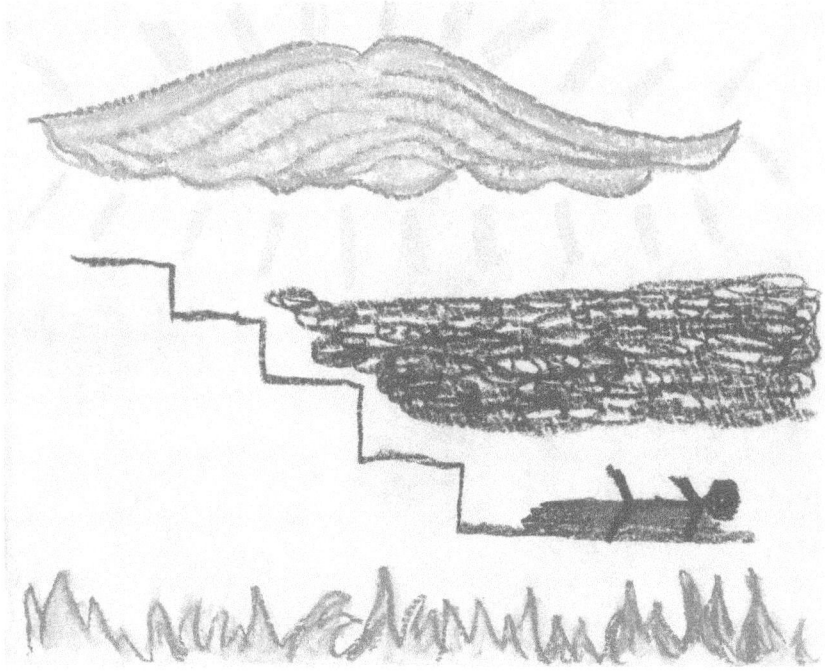

Figure 6.1 Jasmine's Drawing of Her Representation of God

By contrast, the drawing made by Hudson depicts a long, flowing, winding, and curving path constructed out of tiny words written as a stream-of-consciousness poem (see Figure 6.2):

> ... Maybe this is moving falling flows breaking flows still and in the wide wash the ever into is were am feeling in an ever in a moving winter spring blue woven fabric space the longing filling longing breathing ever and am able when I breathe the mist the evening layers over when a color fuses into trees the leaving water falling hands and hair out flying swinging center and a whisper and a child every smile open eyes and dark and whispers to the edge and black and falling into nothing into water into flowing ...

When asked to elaborate on her drawing, Hudson stated that God is flowing in and out, rhythmic, moving, not good or bad, not pleasurable or unpleasurable. God encompasses everything, but not nothing, and definitely does not include judgment.

Over the first three sessions, Jasmine explained that she would like to stop believing in the Catholic religion but would first need permission from her priest. She then launched into a massive attack on priests and their "silly" beliefs about

Figure 6.2 Hudson's Drawing of Her Representation of God

God such as the burning bush, the distinction between venial and mortal sins, and the categorization of cursing as a sin. One of the group leaders suggested that Jasmine was placing the priest in a double bind: if the priest were to refuse her permission, then she would perceive him as rigid and authoritarian; if he were to grant her permission, then she would perceive him as collusive. One of the other participants added that Jasmine might also be placing God in a double bind. Jasmine listened thoughtfully without responding.

Associating to this material, one of the group leaders asked to what extent participants felt as though their illness was a form of punishment or a hell that God has assigned them to for not following the teachings. Both Jasmine and Jessica (another group participant) strongly endorsed this view. Jasmine added that she felt as though she had no choice about what to believe. One of the group leaders drew the analogy of Jasmine as a prisoner, with God as the jailor holding the key. Jasmine replied that perhaps the Catholic Church is the jailor, not God.

It was pointed out that, earlier in the session, she said it was God who would be sending her to hell. Jasmine laughed nervously and said she was not sure. One of the group leaders mentioned that, although four of the nine participants were raised as Catholics, all four had vastly different feelings toward church and God. One of the participants suggested that these different feelings might originate in cultural and family differences.

In another session, Jasmine read a passage about a boy whose first teacher taught him the "right" way to draw a flower but whose second teacher allowed him to draw his own flower. Jasmine explained that she identified with the boy because her parents and the Catholic Church told her how to think, act, and feel and what she should believe about God. She thought she would be going to hell for all the mortal sins she had committed. One of the group leaders asked Jasmine whether God could be forgiving. Jasmine replied that the priests had also said that, but she questioned this view. What kind of God would have all these rules and regulations? She said that she had done wrong in her life and deserved hell. She explained that she had never experienced forgiveness before. This group leader asked whether she could accept God's or anyone's forgiveness, or forgive herself. She was not sure. She had done horrible things to people. Why would God like her or want to forgive her?

Another group participant suggested that Jasmine was too concerned about other people's approval. One of the group leaders asked whether Jasmine had created God in her parents' image. She answered that maybe she had because it was hard to trust God and others when all the people in her life had been untrustworthy. Jasmine asked how she could begin to trust again—she wanted answers. One of the group leaders suggested that Jasmine wanted this group leader to draw the flower for her. She and the other participants laughed. This group leader then asked Jasmine what her ideal image of God would be like. She responded that God would be like the second teacher—letting the boy draw the flower as he sees it. It would be hard to imagine such a God, however, because she had the feeling that God was going to judge her someday. This group leader responded that it would be hard to imagine that God could be any more judgmental of her than she was of herself. She thought for a moment, understanding that her image of God was similar to her experience of her parents.

Reacting to this material, Hudson offered that she liked her own image of God as water because water is pliable, not rigid like dogma. Water always flows to the lowest point; it is balanced. Her image of God is neither masculine nor feminine, a life force, "being"—a verb rather than a noun. Meagan read a passage that attributed such qualities as kindness, generosity, compassion, and love to God. Samantha, who had drawn God as formless watercolors, responded that she had tried to live a perfect life but developed obsessional eating habits that led to her hospitalization. Hudson agreed with this characterization, adding that she wanted to see these attributes in herself as well but could never achieve them. She said she was dying for forgiveness and no longer wanted to strive for perfection. In a later group session, she read a passage by a Buddhist monk depicting the life force as a river, with each individual as a whirlpool or identity in the river. Hudson explained that each person could flow within and without the river; individuals can be either in resonance or out of resonance with the life force. Another patient commented that the passage sounded beautiful but lonely. In that world, she would need to take a detour—to return to her old (and self-destructive) behaviors for excitement. One of the group leaders asked whether cutting oneself (a pre-admission symptom experienced by many group participants, including Hudson) was living in or out of resonance with the life force. Hudson responded that it was being "out of sync" because it was a destructive act, not a creative act. This group leader posed the question, "How does one shift from being in sync to being out of sync and vice versa?" Hudson replied that she made choices. She emphasized that cutting was not necessarily wrong. This choice was conditioned by the judgments and criticisms of others. Raising her voice, she declared that her image of God had nothing to do with judgment or evil. One of the group leaders later read a passage about the loss of a loved one that questioned God's presence. One of the other patients remarked that it was cruel to read something so sad. Hudson, on the other hand, stated that there was beauty in loss—that somehow the longing and pain associated with the loss make the loss more poignant.

Some Thoughts About the Group Process

Drawings from five of the patients depicted a punitive, judgmental, and demanding God Who shows love only to those who follow His rules and refuse to question His authority. These patients struggled with parental representations that sounded strikingly similar to their descriptions of their images of God. For example, Jessica reported that she struggled with a schizophrenic mother who kicked her out of the house at age 14 and strictly prohibited anger from being expressed in the household. A similar relationship was repeated with her abusive husband. On several occasions, she declared that God does not tolerate anger. In another example, Jasmine reported that her mother and father had been physically abusive toward her, and her two brothers had sexually abused her, while God idly stood by or perhaps even directed this activity. Perhaps in the interest of preserving some morsel of goodness in her parental representations (see Fairbairn, 1952), Jasmine began to perceive herself as inherently flawed, unworthy of her parents' love and deserving of her abuse. She could rail against the God/parents who threatened her existence through abuse and neglect, yet later, in the course of the group sessions, she disclosed underlying feelings of inherent badness by quietly admitting that she really did deserve hell.

The drawings of the other four patients depicted an abstract, formless life force that serves as a positive energy source in the universe. These God representations seemed to serve primarily defensive functions, reflecting a disavowal of characteristics signifying personhood. For example, Samantha struggled with anorexia and the sense that her mother failed her, yet she drew God as formless watercolors and characterized God as a mystical power that will fulfill all her needs once she gives in to it. It is easy to imagine that her image of God signified a massive idealization of a perfectionistic, demanding mother representation who finds Samantha lacking.

Struggling with feelings of longing, Hudson mentioned the death of her father and wondered whether he was still present in some way, just as she wondered whether her dear friend who had committed suicide was still present in some way. Without prompting, she denied that she was feeling any anger toward this friend. Continuing this theme of denial, Hudson engaged in a massive reaction formation (i.e., a defensive process in which a person consciously experiences an emotion opposite to the emotion they are unconsciously experiencing) that moved her to declare that there was beauty in loss and that her image of God had nothing to do with judgment or evil. During another session, however, she revealed that she was dying for forgiveness for her lack of perfection and wanted to see perfection in God, as if God were actually a person. Yet, later, during this same session, she drew the analogy of God to water—not dogmatic but pliable and balanced. Hudson's struggle as manifested in the group centered on her need to idealize God to compensate for overwhelming sadness and loss.

In essence, then, for five participants, their drawings of God corresponded rather directly to their views of their parents as harsh, angry, and abusive. For the other four patients, their drawings of God seemed to reflect defensive denial and idealization as well as a distancing by depersonification. I discovered that all four participants who presented a depersonified representation of God were diagnosed with comorbid narcissistic features in addition to their primary diagnosis of BPD. None of the other five participants had such a diagnosis. This observation between the quality of God representation and the absence or presence of narcissistic psychopathology seems consistent with Kernberg's (1986) concepts of pathological narcissism, the pathological grandiose self, and associated defensive processes of idealization and devaluation. This pathological organization, observed in narcissistic personalities with underlying borderline personality organization, robs the superego (i.e., conscience) of good, modulating elements and permits some ego integration at the cost of a deterioration of relationships. Unacceptable self-representations are split off in combination with "widespread, devastating devaluation of external objects and their representations" (Kernberg, 1986, p. 262).

Based on this theory, I speculate that the depersonified, inanimate, nebulous representations of God offered by those BPD inpatients with pathological narcissistic features suggest a distancing from the unconscious God representations formed during early childhood. The narcissism serves to defend against the mental representation of a personified God with feelings and desires, possibly even possessing hatred and condemnation. This defensive strategy is consistent with a dismissing (i.e., anxious-avoidant) attachment pattern. Through the use of idealization and denial as defensive strategies, a punitive, demanding God can be neutralized, transforming into something harmless, bland, or even mystical as in Hudson's image of flowing water. A mystical power can never find fault; on the contrary, one's needs will be magically gratified without one's having to acknowledge another person's existence. In related fashion, the four BPD inpatients with comorbid narcissistic features offered less information regarding their parental representations than the others, perhaps reflecting a denial of their parents' influence or very existence. Thus, I am suggesting that narcissistic psychopathology might be associated with the formation of defensive, "compensatory" God representations. Of course, the God representations of the other group also contain defensive aspects, but the "correspondence" of these mental representations to the parental representations quickly became obvious, often to the participants themselves.

In addition to these clinical observations from the group, I wondered whether the group could begin a process of transforming representations of God into more benevolent and personified forms. For example, in the beginning, Jasmine could not conceptualize God as anything more than the sum total of all the rules, regulations, and punishments imposed on her by her parents and priests. Jasmine was not permitted to question God, just as she was never permitted to question her parents. God does not accept skeptics, and mothers do not accept children who question their authority. By the end of the group, however, Jasmine risked articulating her ideal image of God—someone who would benevolently allow her to define her own identity. She was helped to this point in her exploration by the group leaders' and other participants' suggestions that her parents helped to create her God image for her and that she herself had created God in her parents' image. In Winnicott's (1971) spirit of the transitional object, we observed the paradox that Jasmine was re-creating an image of God who could give her permission to re-create her images of both God and herself.

I also observed that a group therapy setting seemed to facilitate this transforming work because exposure to the different religious experiences shared by the participants enabled them to question their own religious assumptions and adopt a sometimes-playful approach to their exploration and critical examination of their God representations. Without this group exposure, the openness to question the historical and emotional basis of these representations might not have developed so readily. That the two group leaders represented two different disciplines also permitted participants to observe the group leaders' openness to their own different spiritual experiences, which validated the participants' own spiritual exploration.

Finally, the group's observations of the sometimes-striking similarities between a participant's God representation and her parental and self-representations increased participants' awareness that the God representation could both differ from and even transcend parental and self-representations. This awareness, however, did not seem to help participants also to modify their parental representations. Perhaps parental representations seemed too real and, therefore, more resistant to modification, while the obviously projective nature of the God representation (and perhaps also the self-representation) was openly acknowledged and accepted.

I believe, however, that the group leaders' willingness to discuss openly the relations between representations of God and personal experiences profoundly influenced participants' motivation to examine their understanding of all their mental representations—including, but not limited to, God, parents, and self. That changes in parental representations were not observed in the group process does not necessarily mean that the group process did not produce changes in these mental representations, or at least in reflective functioning pertaining to these mental representations (Fonagy et al., 2002; see also Goodman, 2010, Chapter 6). I believe that the secure base that my co-leader and I provided for the participants also facilitated the openness to the group experience observed in the patients without narcissistic features (see Goodman, 2025b, Chapter 4). I am suggesting that the group setting afforded some of these patients the opportunity to "earn" their secure attachment (Hesse, 2018, p. 570; Main & Goldwyn, 1989) to the Higher Power of their understanding, thus paving the way to rely on their Higher Power as a safe haven and a secure base after hospital discharge, when attachment figures such as therapists and the group leaders would no longer be so readily available for comfort or protection (see Goodman, 2025b, Chapter 3).

Remarkably, we did not observe any openness to re-creating the representations of God or parents among the four participants who presented depersonified representations of God. In fact, their mental representations did not appear open to change at all during the course of the group sessions. Kernberg (1980, pp. 135–153) suggested that the pathological grandiose self, observed in narcissistic personalities with underlying borderline personality organization, does not permit the intrapersonal vulnerability necessary to benefit from psychotherapy. Only in middle age, when youth and beauty begin to fade and the narcissistic supplies begin to dwindle through the loss of their associates, do narcissistic persons seek out and benefit from psychotherapy. Perhaps these BPD inpatients were unable to make themselves sufficiently vulnerable or to decrease interpersonal distancing and devaluing to benefit from the group process, at least in this time-limited context. Returning to the correspondence and compensation hypotheses mentioned earlier (Kirkpatrick, 1999), it appears that this group model of spiritual intervention was able to initiate the process of modifying representations of God, but only among participants whose representations of God corresponded to their parental representations. Those participants who used their representations of God to compensate for their parental representations seemed content with these mental representations, using them to ward off any negative emotions associated with their parental representations. This preliminary evidence suggests that images of God that correspond to parental images might be more malleable than images of God that compensate for parental images. Systematic research is needed to support this evidence.

I want to note that the validity of the conclusions drawn from this study are limited by (1) the small group of participants ($N = 9$) and (2) the lack of an empirical method used for studying these representational phenomena. A larger number of BPD patients could be assessed for their levels of narcissism and placed into narcissistic or non-narcissistic categories. Their drawings of the representation of God, along with their descriptions of them, could be blindly assigned by raters to the punitive and depersonified categories suggested here. A statistical association could thus be calculated. The assessment of change in one's representation of God resulting from participation in a spirituality group would require a systematic method for measuring the quality and complexity of this mental representation (e.g., see Blatt et al., 1992) or the quality of this attachment relationship (e.g., see Goodman, 2025a, Chapter 6).

Despite these limitations, we believe that these clinical impressions can serve as preliminary evidence in support of the idea that a psychodynamically oriented, exploratory spirituality group can help patients identify and potentially reconstruct images of God, which, in turn, can facilitate change in self-representations. While this clinical work did not appear to re-create parental representations or to re-create any mental representations of BPD inpatients with comorbid narcissistic features, some participants were able to embark on a process of re-creating their mental representations of God and of themselves. These persons were able to encounter a God whom they could re-create—and, in doing so, a self whom they could re-create—in the potential space provided by a spirituality group.

When Is This Model of Spiritual Intervention a Good Match?

Participants in this 14-session exploratory spirituality group were originally conceived as psychiatric inpatients diagnosed with BPD who expressed interest in exploring their assumptions regarding their spirituality. The unit chief made an announcement about the group, and a flyer for the group was posted on the community bulletin board. Despite the narrow definition of group membership described in this chapter, an exploratory spirituality group that includes discussion of drawings of participants' God images could work with any clinical population, inpatient or outpatient. I could also envision this group model of spiritual intervention working with nonclinical populations in places of worship such as churches or temples. Participants interested in the parallels between their mental representations of their caregivers during childhood and their current mental representations of a Higher Power are well suited to benefit from this group experience because the group is designed both to elicit and to modify these connections through mutual exploration among participants. The necessary conditions of this nontraditional group setting would include voluntary participation and adequately trained group leaders—ideally a chaplain and a mental health professional.

Training Requirements to Become a Spiritual Group Leader

I recommend that two co-leaders lead these groups—one trained as an ordained chaplain and the other trained as a licensed mental health professional (i.e., psychiatrist, psychologist, social worker, mental health counselor or professional counselor, or psychiatric nurse practitioner) because, as seen in the case illustration, complex and challenging spiritual and mental health issues emerge in this intense group setting. It is important that two persons highly trained in spirituality and in mental health facilitate the exploration of God images. Above all, co-leaders must adopt a nonjudgmental stance toward participants' drawings and their interpretation, as well as work to protect the group from judgmental comments by participants. The co-leaders must also work well together and get along well together outside group sessions.

My friendship with the hospital chaplain in the case illustration served to ground the group process and facilitate meaningful self-disclosure among participants. She and I also completed drawings of our God images but did not share our personal histories, as that would have distracted from participants' exploration of their own God images and interpreting their meaning in the context of their own personal histories. Finally, the hospital chaplain and I always held a debriefing session at the conclusion of each group session to process what had happened in the group and to review the nature of our interventions and how they either enhanced or hindered the group process. I also took careful notes of the group process immediately following each group session for two reasons: (1) to meet state requirements for maintaining progress notes on patients receiving treatment and (2) to develop process material for writing about the group experience in this chapter.

Conclusions

Co-led by a hospital chaplain and a clinical psychologist, this 14-session exploratory spirituality group, which took place on a psychodynamically oriented psychiatric inpatient unit, can serve as a template for exploring the meaning of participants' God images in a safe space carved out in hospitals, churches, temples, nursing homes, correctional facilities, and outpatient community mental health clinics. The purposes of this spirituality group are: (1) to increase awareness of spirituality—particularly conscious and unconscious images of God—held by each participant; (2) to place these images and associated feelings and beliefs in the context of their current and past life situations and psychiatric symptoms; and (3) to provide an opportunity for participants to explore and discuss each other's image or images of God, thus potentially facilitating a re-creation and modification to a more integrated and benevolent image.

We discovered that we could classify participants' drawings and subsequent descriptions of their God images into two categories—punitive and depersonified—and that these two categories coincided with a difference in personality organization (i.e., having or not having narcissistic features). Because of the small sample size ($N = 9$), this finding requires further validation in a large, controlled research study that can build on these anecdotal observations. We concluded that this spirituality group benefited some of the participants in helping them to reflect on their God images and the connections between these images and their parental images during childhood. I believe that qualified persons can implement this model of spiritual intervention in a variety of settings to facilitate the development of more integrated and benevolent God images as those participants understand their Higher Power.

References

American Psychiatric Association. (2022). *Diagnostic and statistical manual of mental disorders* (5th ed., text rev.). Author.

Blatt, S. J., Chevron, E. S., Quinlan, D. M., Schaffer, C. E., & Wein, S. (1992). *The assessment of qualitative and structural dimensions of object representations* (rev. ed.). Unpublished manuscript, Yale University, New Haven, CT.

Bowlby, J. (1982). *Attachment and loss: Vol. 1. Attachment* (2nd ed.). Basic Books.

Cassibba, R., Granqvist, P., Costantini, A., & Gatto, S. (2008). Attachment and God representations among lay Catholics, priests, and religious: A matched comparison study based on the Adult Attachment Interview. *Developmental Psychology, 44*, 1753–1763.

Fairbairn, W. R. D. (1952). *An object-relations theory of the personality*. Basic Books.

Fonagy, P., Gergely, G., Jurist, E. L., & Target, M. (2002). *Affect regulation, mentalization, and the development of the self*. New York: Other Press.

Gallagher, R. E., Manierre, A., & Castelli, C. (1994). From the valley of the shadow of death: A group model for borderline patients. *The Journal of Pastoral Care, 48*, 45–53.

Goodman, G. (2010). *Transforming the internal world and attachment: Theoretical and empirical perspectives* (Vol. 1). Jason Aronson.

Goodman, G. (2025a). *Practical applications of transforming the attachment relationship to God: Using attachment-informed psychotherapy*. Routledge.

Goodman, G. (2025b). *Using psychoanalytic techniques to transform the attachment relationship to God: Our refuge and strength*. Routledge.

Granqvist, P. (2020). *Attachment in religion and spirituality: A wider view*. Guilford Press.

Granqvist, P., Broberg, A. G., & Hagekull, B. (2014). Attachment, religiousness, and distress among the religious and spiritual: Links between religious syncretism and compensation. *Mental Health, Religion and Culture, 17*, 726–740.

Granqvist, P., Ivarsson, T., Broberg, A. G., & Hagekull, B. (2007). Examining relations between attachment, religiosity, and New Age spirituality using the Adult Attachment Interview. *Developmental Psychology, 43*, 590–601.

Hesse, E. (2018). The Adult Attachment Interview: Protocol, method of analysis, and selected empirical studies: 1985–2015. In J. Cassidy & P. R. Shaver (Eds.), *Handbook of attachment: Theory, research, and clinical applications* (pp. 553–597). Guilford Press.

Kernberg, O. F. (1980). *Internal world and external reality: Object relations theory applied.* New York: Jason Aronson.
Kernberg, O. F. (1986). Further contributions to the treatment of narcissistic personalities. In A. Morrison (Ed.), *Essential papers on narcissism* (pp. 245–292). New York: New York University Press.
Kirkpatrick, L. A. (1999). Attachment and religious representations and behavior. In J. Cassidy & P. R. Shaver (Eds.), *Handbook of attachment: Theory, research, and clinical applications* (pp. 803–822). New York: Guilford Press.
Main, M., & Goldwyn, R. (1989). *Adult attachment rating and classification system.* Unpublished manuscript, University of California, Berkeley.
Nkara, F., Main, M., Hesse, E., & Granqvist, P. (2018). *Attachment to deities in light of attachment to parents: The Religious Attachment Interview.* Unpublished manuscript.
Rieger, K. L., Reimer-Kirkham, S., Burton, B., Howell, B., Liuta, N., Sharma, S., Smoker, S., Tuppurainen, A., Lounsbury, K., Kreiter, E., Dixon, D., Anthony, R., Bradbury, S., Hiemstra, D., Wilkinson, K., Hilton, M., & Slavutskiy, O. (2023). Arts-based spiritual care in healthcare: A participatory, scoping review. *The Arts in Psychotherapy, 84,* 102027.
Rizzuto, A.-M. (1979). *The birth of the living God: A psychoanalytic study.* Chicago: University of Chicago Press.
Winnicott, D. W. (1971). *Playing and reality.* New York: Basic Books.

Chapter 7

Spiritually Integrated Psychotherapy

Introducing Spirituality and Working Through Spiritual Struggles

To get a clearer understanding of Spiritually Integrated Psychotherapy (SIP) and how it works, these two case illustrations from my private practice include session dialogue recreated from session notes that I took immediately following several sessions. As a certified SIP therapist, I can testify to the challenging nature of both cases—challenging because neither patient is explicitly spiritual. Thus, I must rely only on implicit spiritual interventions to address their underlying spiritual needs. In the first case illustration, Blair is an atheist/Buddhist who feels abandoned by God and eventually comes to believe that science is sufficient to explain the world. I address Blair's implicit spirituality—his longing for joy—rather than any explicit spirituality. In the second case illustration, Florence is a recently divorced nominal Catholic who sees no meaning in her life other than her relationship to her dog. Again, I focus on Florence's implicit spirituality—what her life's purpose is. Both patients respond favorably to the search for deeper meaning in their lives. Exactly how does the SIP therapist address the implicit spiritual content in sessions with these types of patients?

Blair

Case Conceptualization Introduction

Treatment began in June 2019, when 44-year-old Blair (a pseudonym) sought help for internet pornography addiction. A first-generation Cuban American, Blair is a state-funded attorney whose clients are mentally ill patients committed to a psychiatry facility in Westchester County, New York, adjacent to the county where he and his family now live. He is married, with a daughter (age 12) and a son (age 10). His wife is also a state-funded attorney who works at the same psychiatric facility. Blair and his family live in a middle-income community that is a suburb of New York City. I have treated Blair in once-weekly individual psychotherapy for the past 5 years. He saw my *Psychology Today* profile and called me to schedule his first session because I practiced in his county and because I have a sex addiction therapy certification from the International Institute of Trauma and Addiction Professionals (IITAP).

Presenting Issues and Diagnosis

Blair's chief complaint at the time of the referral was that he compulsively watched internet pornography on his phone. His wife eventually caught him, and he promised to seek help for this problem. Masturbation often accompanied his porn viewing, which would take place in the bathroom or in the finished basement after everyone went to bed. I diagnosed him with compulsive sexual behavior disorder, classified by the International Classification of Diseases (ICD-11; Kraus et al., 2018; World Health Organization [WHO], 2020), with moderate depressive symptoms. Blair also consumed excessive quantities of alcohol during his 20s, but this behavior diminished considerably after he got married. As of this writing, Blair's internet pornography use is now only very sporadic. We have now shifted to discussing issues related to Blair's identity as a person, father, husband, and son.

Spiritual Assessment

Blair grew up in a practicing Catholic family in Westchester County, New York. As a child, Blair and his family attended church every Sunday, and he and his two brothers attended Catholic schools throughout childhood and adolescence. During his 20s, Blair remembers that his attitude toward God was that God did not care about him or the world and had in fact abandoned him and the world; this gradually evolved into an attitude of not believing in God. Blair came to believe that science is sufficient to explain the world and his place in it.

This denial of a personal God Who abandoned him created a different problem—the deprivation of a potential spiritual resource to help him overcome his addiction. Blair currently identifies as an atheist, but he and his family occasionally attend a Universalist/Unitarian church that espouses his secular humanist values. He also considers himself a Buddhist, trying to live his life in accordance with the Buddha's teachings. According to Blair, Buddhism is how he currently makes sense of his life. Since entering treatment, Blair has attended Buddhist workshops and retreats and has tried meditation to calm his mind. He reports that he enjoys these activities and partially credits them for the success that he has experienced in remaining sober from watching pornography. Meditation helps him to let go of the craving for pornography.

Shortly after entering treatment, I recommended 12-step meetings of Sex Addicts Anonymous (SAA) or Sexaholics Anonymous (SA), which I thought would provide him with both spiritual and peer support in his recovery from sex addiction. He attended several SAA meetings but stopped going, initially stating that he could not get past this fellowship's belief in a Higher Power but later acknowledging that he does not want to rely on others for help because part of him does not want to be "seen." Blair has often discussed implicitly spiritual topics such as his life's purpose and his mortality.

Interventions

I typically use mentalizing clarifications (i.e., labeling emotions, connecting behaviors to underlying mental states) and interpretations (i.e., proposing causal connections between his symptoms [e.g., cravings for pornography] and his underlying wishes, expectations, and fears about his wife's and others' reliability in meeting his emotional needs). Because he is an atheist, I do not make any explicit spiritual interventions. In a recent session, I asked him if he ever experiences joy. He reflected on that question for a long time and, in the following two sessions, referenced this same question, which suggests that he pondered it between sessions (see below). During one of these sessions, Blair expressed a wish that joy would find him. I replied that he might be making it hard for joy to find him. That statement seemed to stop him in his tracks. He eventually agreed that he does make himself invisible to joy.

We also discussed his earlier relationship to God. In his late adolescent years, Blair considered joining the priesthood but grew disillusioned with God because God does not care about him. God only abandons. I interpreted this negative perception of God as a projection of his experiences with his earthly father onto God. Blair agreed but then pointed to all the suffering in the world and concluded that a loving God would not stand for it.

Session Excerpts (May 10, 17, 23, 2024)

May 10

Blair: Everything going on in the world is tragic.
Me: It sounds as though you're feeling depressed. There seems to be no joy in your life.
Blair: (pause) Well, I find joy in my children's lives. I don't think I'm depressed, but you're right that I feel little joy in my life. It reminds me of the C. S. Lewis book, *Surprised by Joy*. I read that book in college. I do need to pay more attention to experiences of joy in my life.

May 17

Blair: My daughter is now insisting that we call her [masculine variant of her given name]. It makes me wonder what I've done as a parent to cause her to act this way. I might have been able to stop it if I had only been less open-minded.
Me: Your daughter seems to be acting out your own unconscious, repressed wishes to be visible and recognized, not hiding herself as you did as a child.
Blair: You're probably right. I just wish I didn't have to be a trans parent. (long pause) I wish joy would find me.

Me:	You might be hiding from joy. In fact, you might be making yourself hard to find from joy.
Blair:	(long pause) I never thought of that before.

May 23

Blair:	I want to find joy in my life. This new job I'm applying for could stretch me in new ways—that feels exciting to me. Even my daughter has been more tolerant of me lately.
Me:	Seek and ye shall find!

My Spirituality and Therapeutic Process With This Patient

My awareness of my patients' and my own spirituality sets the foundation for any explicit or implicit spiritual intervention. Other than privately praying for Blair, I have not used my explicit spiritual resources in my work with him. I have suggested a community resource—SAA or SA 12-step programs—but he has rejected this idea. Blair can freely address spiritual matters, however, and, when he does, I communicate that I can speak his language because of my own religious and spiritual searching. Both of us have struggled with addiction, which 12-step programs explicitly label as a spiritual problem that requires a spiritual solution. I abandoned agnosticism to embrace this worldview, whereas Blair has embraced atheism and Buddhism and has rejected the 12-step worldview. Despite this divergence in our spiritual paths, I hope to learn how to help Blair find and maintain his own spiritual path. In these session excerpts, I personify joy as a symbol of a Higher Power, which seems to stimulate his implicit spirituality and open the door for more conversation about it. I also use the familiar biblical phrase spoken by Jesus, "Seek and ye shall find" (which I know that he would be familiar with) to allude to the spiritual dimension of his search for joy. The SIP therapist often uses subtle interventions to create opportunities for spirituality to manifest itself in sessions.

Florence: Case Conceptualization Introduction

At the beginning of treatment in November 2018, Florence (a pseudonym) was a 25-year-old Irish American registered nurse living on Long Island with her future ex-husband, whom she had married just 3 months earlier. She lived in a two-bedroom top-floor apartment in a house with her future ex-husband and described herself as having a middle-income socioeconomic status. I have been treating Florence in once-weekly individual psychotherapy for the past 5½ years. The Soldiers Project, a nonprofit organization that provides free psychotherapy for military veterans and their spouses, referred her to me. Florence's future ex-husband, David (a pseudonym), had returned from deployment to South Korea and Afghanistan in June 2016.

Presenting Issues and Diagnosis

Florence's chief complaint at the time of referral was that she was experiencing difficulty adjusting to her husband's return from deployment. She was experiencing anxiety generalized to many different situations, including her marriage, the longevity of her friendships from college, and interactions with her in-laws, particularly her mother-in-law. Florence also suffered from compulsive worries about having turned off the stove. She often takes a photo of the on/off switch to reassure herself when she goes to work that she has indeed turned off the stove. I have assigned her psychiatric diagnoses of generalized anxiety disorder and obsessive-compulsive disorder (American Psychiatric Association, 2022).

Spiritual Assessment

Florence grew up in a nominally Catholic family on Long Island. She and her family seldom attended church when she was a child, and she does not attend church as an adult. She does not explicitly talk about religious or spiritual issues during sessions, and religion and spirituality do not seem to play an active role in her life. Florence's one "spiritual" resource is her close relationship to her dog, Magnolia (a pseudonym), whom Florence describes as her best friend and daughter. Magnolia often makes an appearance during our online therapy sessions, and it is obvious that Florence adores this dog. Florence has close relationships to her parents, who live fewer than 5 miles away, and a small cadre of friends from college. Recently, Florence has discovered that she has not consciously defined any purpose for her life, which puzzles her. Many of her friends are getting married or having babies, while she is divorced with a dog, and I believe that she might be feeling envy toward these friends. She seems to feel that her life is stagnating, while her friends are moving forward in their lives. Florence has not mentioned wanting to explore her spirituality during sessions.

Interventions

I typically use mentalizing clarifications (i.e., labeling emotions, connecting behaviors to underlying mental states) and interpretations (i.e., proposing causal connections between her symptoms [e.g., anxiety] and her underlying wishes, expectations, and fears about her future). I do not make any explicit spiritual interventions. Implicitly, I have emphasized the deep meaning of relationships in Florence's life and her tendency to misunderstand these relationships as non-reciprocal. She places others above herself and then feels exploited when others sense her weakness in asserting herself and thus take emotional advantage of her. Florence has not used these words, but it is as if others' betrayal of her kind-heartedness robs her soul of vitality and optimism. While agreeing with me that others betray her, Florence usually resists my attempts to identify her role of passivity and lack of self-assertion in this relationship pattern. Despite the resistance I have encountered, Florence does evidence a greater ability to set boundaries and tell others how she is really feeling. Her divorce after 5 miserable years of marriage demonstrates that she is listening and absorbing my interpretations and making behavioral changes, despite her denials in sessions. In the session excerpt below, I draw attention to the lack of conscious purpose in her life, which gets her to contemplate what her life is all about.

Session Excerpt (May 18, 2024)

Florence: I don't have anything to talk about today.
Me: Okay, maybe it's a good time to talk about your remaining goals for our work together.
Florence: I still have too much anxiety, and I like to have a place where I can talk about it.
Me: Let me ask you a bigger question: what do you think your life's purpose is?
Florence: I don't know. (long pause) I don't like thinking about it because it makes me feel anxious. I just feel apathetic about most things in my life. I think it goes back to sometime after I got married. I was wondering what would come next in my life. I got married to David because a lot of my friends were getting married at around the same time. It was just something I was supposed to do. But after I got married, I didn't know what that next thing was. Maybe my purpose in life is to be Magnolia's mommy.
Me: Magnolia gives your life meaning.
Florence: Exactly. I'm a nurse—I guess that also gives me a purpose. But most times, it's a boring job. I like my job because my hours are great, but I wouldn't say I'm excited to go to work every day.
Me: If you limit yourself just for today, what do you think your desire for today is?
Florence: Going back to bed. (laughs)
Me: I hear you telling me that you're feeling depressed.
Florence: Yeah, you're probably right; that could be what's going on.
Me: Do you feel as though you want to hurt yourself?
Florence: I have no plans to kill myself, but at the same time, I don't know why I'm living. I just live my life day by day; I don't have a larger purpose. The problem is that I have nothing to look forward to.

My Spirituality and Therapeutic Process With This Patient

My awareness of my patients' and my own spirituality sets the foundation for any explicit or implicit spiritual intervention. Other than privately praying for Florence, I have not used my explicit spiritual resources in my work with

Florence. I privately hope that I exude a Christlike presence in my encounters with Florence. I am always punctual and attentive. I radiate warmth, understanding, and patience with Florence. Finally, I believe that she knows that I care for her deeply and accept her unconditionally, even with all her resistances. Florence is challenging me to find creative ways to envelop her in an atmosphere of spiritual curiosity. In this session excerpt, I do not intervene in a heavy-handed way but rather ask her what her life's purpose is. I reflect her insight about her relationship to her dog. I then bring her back to the here and now and point out her moderate depressive symptoms. A SIP therapist must strive for poignancy rather than cleverness.

Description of Spiritually Integrated Psychotherapy

SIP is a therapeutic attitude cultivated in the therapist in which the therapist looks for opportunities to discuss spirituality with the patient in a psychotherapy session. According to one of the SIP architects (Pargament, 2011), therapists practicing from various theoretical orientations can implement clinical techniques that facilitate the search for the spiritual in the therapy session and in the patient. In the SIP literature (e.g., Griffith, 2010; Jones, 2019; Pargament, 2011; Pargament & Exline, 2022), the words "spirituality," "sacred," "spiritual strivings," and "spiritual struggles" are frequently used; thus, it is necessary to spend time defining them before proceeding with a deeper description of SIP.

SIP authors tend to give "spirituality" the broadest possible definition. According to Pargament and Exline (2022), the essence of spirituality is "the capacity to see domains of life ... through a sacred lens, imbuing them with deeper divine-like character and significance" (p. 6). Earlier in his career, Pargament defined "spirituality" as "a search for the sacred" (Pargament, 1999, p. 12). Pargament (2011) defines "sacred" as "invested with divine qualities (e.g., transcendence, boundlessness, ultimacy) or ... perceived to be manifestations of the divine" (p. 51). One could then ask Pargament to define "divine." Giving "spirituality" the broadest possible definition risks circularity. If everything is spiritual, then nothing is not spiritual. As I was going through my SIP training program, I asked one of my supervisors what is not spiritual. He replied, "Anything that the patient is not engaged by" (Wayne Gustafson, personal communication, October 3, 2024). He affirmed that "spirituality" is "the quality of a person's relatedness." Given this definition, it is easy to see why Pargament and Exline (2022) argue that therapists from every theoretical orientation can practice SIP: all therapists try to keep the patient engaged and improve their quality of relatedness. A therapist does not have to be SIP-trained to do this work.

Griffith (2010) expresses his exasperation at this broadest possible definition of "spirituality": "Nearly anything providing meaning and connection can count as 'my spirituality'" (p. 21). The problem with this definition, as Griffith (2010) sees it, is that it has difficulty "distinguishing between saints and demons when both are drawing energy from sources greater than themselves" (p. 21). Thus, Griffith (2010) mercifully narrows the definition of "spirituality" to distinguish between Mother Teresa and the Nazi Heinrich Himmler: "A commitment to person-to-person relatedness independent of any social categorization and an ethic of compassion that extends to all persons, even those outside one's own religious or social group" (p. 21). Of course, this definition of "spirituality" represents an ideal to strive for rather than a reality for most therapists. SIP therapists can use this definition as a therapeutic goal: therapists want their patients to reach across the aisle of social categorization to show compassion to "the other," whether "the other" differs by gender, race, class, age, educational level, sexual orientation, gender identity, or religious affiliation. In my experience as a certified SIP therapist, my clinical techniques are not what makes me "spiritually integrated"; rather, it is *my awareness* of my patients' moving closer to or further away from spirituality during a session.

"Spiritual strivings" and "spiritual struggles" are phrases used by Pargament and his colleagues (Pargament, 2011; Pargament & Exline, 2022) to denote the spiritual motivations and conflicts that patients bring to psychotherapy sessions. They make a strong argument for the thesis that all persons "are born with spiritual potential, the potential to seek out the sacred. In this sense, everyone is a spiritual being. ... Spirituality is, in short, a critical and distinctive dimension of human motivation" (Pargament, 2011, p. 60). In support of this thesis, Barrett (2012) summarizes many research studies to support the conjecture that young children naturally believe in a Higher Power, and only much later do some children stop believing. In other words, believing in a Higher Power is the default position in the human mind (for a detailed discussion, see Goodman, 2025b, Chapter 3). If all persons are born with spiritual motivation, then all patients come to sessions with spiritual strivings—whether or not they are aware of them. The SIP therapist, through a heightened awareness cultivated by their extensive training, looks for and seizes opportunities to discuss these strivings, even if unconscious to the patient. In my case illustrations, Blair is seeking joy as an antidote to this tragic world, while Florence is seeking a larger purpose. According to these authors, these patients are expressing spiritual strivings.

In the session excerpts, Blair declares that "the world is tragic." He holds this view only because he can envision a more just world with no poverty, sickness, or death. Why is God not restoring the world to conform to his vision of what should be? He is striving to understand why God has abandoned this world (and, more specifically, him). Florence carefully avoids the elephant in the room—her therapeutic goals—which I gently ask her to reflect on. Perhaps her anxiety is related to her not knowing what her life's purpose is, which I suspect is her spiritual striving. Spiritual struggles come in many forms. What are these different forms?

Spiritual struggles are "experiences of tension, conflict, or strain that center on whatever people view as sacred (Exline, 2013; Pargament et al., 2005)"

(Pargament & Exline, 2022, p. 6). These authors identify six categories of spiritual struggles: (1) divine, (2) ultimate meaning, (3) doubt, (4) moral, (5) demonic, and (6) interpersonal. Briefly, divine struggles are related to anger or disappointment with a Higher Power and typically include feelings of divine punishment, abandonment, and lack of divine love. "Why does God allow suffering in my life? Does God love me? Why do bad things happen to good people?" In my case illustration, Blair concluded that God abandoned him and afterward decided not to believe in God anymore. Ultimate meaning struggles have to do with finding a larger purpose in life. Florence alluded to this spiritual struggle in our therapy session. She seems to be asking, "Does life really matter?" Doubt struggles are related to confusion or doubts about a person's spiritual or religious beliefs. "Is the Bible infallible if it supports misogyny in places?" Existential anxiety often accompanies both ultimate meaning struggles and doubt struggles. Moral struggles include conflicts over following a person's moral principles and falling short of cherished ideals. "Why do I keep drinking alcohol during work hours? How can I leave this dead marriage when my child needs me every day?" These conflicts are often associated with tension and guilt. Demonic struggles are related to anxiety that demons are malevolent supernatural forces that are tormenting the person. "Satan seems to take over my control when I enter a casino." Interpersonal struggles include conflicts with others regarding sacred issues or religious institutions. "How can the pastor of my church support an immoral person like Donald Trump?" "Why does the chair of the music committee refuse to add a contemporary worship service on Sunday morning?" "How could the priest have sexually abused me?" These are the categories of spiritual struggles with which all of us struggle from time to time.

Lest the reader conclude that spiritual struggles afflict only spiritual persons, research suggests that even atheists experience spiritual struggles. Atheists might encounter derision from their spiritually minded friends and acquaintances because they do not believe in spirituality. This set of conflicts would fall under the interpersonal category. Atheists can also experience divine struggles. In his autobiography, *Surprised by Joy*, C. S. Lewis (1955) reflects on his young adulthood as an atheist:

> I was at this time living, like so many Atheists or Antitheists, in a whirl of contradictions. I maintained that God did not exist. I was also very angry with God for not existing. I was equally angry with Him for creating a world. (p. 115)

Lewis's divine struggle is excruciatingly palpable.

Research also suggests that some atheists experience interpersonal, moral, and ultimate meaning struggles (Sedlar et al., 2018) as well as negative emotion around the idea of God (Bradley et al., 2015, 2017), including anger toward God (Exline et al., 2011). If we accept the presupposition that spirituality is an inborn human motivation (Pargament, 2011) on a par with sexuality, aggression, and attachment (e.g., Lichtenberg, 1989), then it stands to reason that atheists—who consciously deny this part of their motivational system—would also experience spiritual struggles. Atheists are denying a fundamental part of their human nature; thus, the spiritual conflict is not only interpersonal but also intrapersonal.

One of the many challenges of addressing spiritual struggles in SIP is knowing when a spiritual struggle is genuinely spiritual in nature and when a spiritual struggle is a manifestation of a psychological issue. For example, a person diagnosed with schizophrenia might be experiencing auditory hallucinations (i.e., hearing voices) that seem to be coming from the devil, telling them that they are an evil person. This struggle is more psychological than spiritual. In many circumstances, however, spiritual struggles overlap with psychological struggles so significantly that it is difficult to tease them apart. Half of older adults diagnosed with depression report spiritual struggles (Murphy et al., 2016). Almost half of outpatients getting treatment for a mood disorder also report spiritual struggles (Rosmarin et al., 2014), as do one-third of college students getting treatment at college counseling centers (Johnson & Hayes, 2003). For example, Blair feels depressed about all the suffering in the world—and in himself—without a Higher Power to lend a helping hand. If spiritual struggles often co-exist, then why would therapists ignore spiritual struggles in their sessions?

Pargament and Exline (2022) identify three categories of spiritual struggles: primary, secondary, and complex. Primary spiritual struggles cause psychological problems such as higher levels of emotion dysregulation and distress. Secondary spiritual struggles are caused by psychological problems such as higher levels of emotion dysregulation and distress. Finally, complex spiritual struggles both cause and are caused by psychological problems such as higher levels of emotion dysregulation and distress. In their literature review, Pargament and Exline (2022) conclude that most spiritual struggles are complex because they are so intimately intertwined with psychological problems. This close connection makes it difficult for researchers to study the phenomenon of spiritual struggles in isolation. SIP therapists are, therefore, ideally situated to address spiritual struggles because they are already trained to identify and treat psychological problems. Although highly trained to address spiritual struggles, pastoral counselors are often not adequately trained to treat psychological problems (see below).

What can research tell us about the causality between spiritual struggles and psychiatric symptoms? Can researchers determine when a spiritual struggle is primary, secondary, or complex? Are certain categories of spiritual struggles more likely to be primary than others? Prediction might imply causation, but it is impossible to conclude with confidence that spiritual struggles cause psychiatric symptoms. To demonstrate causation, researchers would need to randomly assign a large sample of persons to two conditions, one of which includes exposure to and development of spiritual struggles. Later, persons in both conditions would complete measures of depression and anxiety. If spiritual struggles cause psychiatric symptoms, then we would expect the group exposed to spiritual struggles to experience higher levels of depression and anxiety than the non-exposed group. Of course, such a study would be not only unethical but also impossible to conduct. How would a researcher induce spiritual struggles in participants? Thus, researchers must show how spiritual struggles predict rather than cause psychiatric symptoms.

One compelling research design that points in the direction of causation is known as a longitudinal design, where researchers assess a sample at an initial time point and then follow up with this sample years later to find out what happened to them. For example, researchers assessed first-year college students for levels of self-esteem, depression, and anxiety and then reassessed them in their third year for levels of spiritual struggles as well as these same symptoms. Even after adjusting for levels of self-esteem, depression, and anxiety from their first year, the third-year students with higher levels of spiritual struggles experienced higher levels of psychiatric symptoms (Bryant & Astin, 2008). In a sample of African Americans, researchers assessed levels of spiritual struggles and psychiatric symptoms at baseline and once again 2½ years later. After adjusting for levels of psychiatric symptoms measured at the first assessment, the participants with higher levels of spiritual struggles were experiencing higher levels of psychiatric symptoms than the participants with lower levels of spiritual struggles 2½ years later (Park et al., 2018). After conducting their exhaustive literature review, Pargament and Exline (2022) conclude: "Spiritual struggles may lead to greater distress and disorientation" (p. 63). If spiritual struggles can lead to patient distress, then why would therapists *not* address spirituality in therapy?

Psychiatric symptoms assessed at baseline can also predict spiritual struggles at follow-up. For example, in a sample of adolescents diagnosed with either cystic fibrosis or diabetes, depression predicted spiritual struggles in both groups 2 years later (Reynolds et al., 2014). Similarly, in a sample of African Americans who had experienced the death of a loved one by homicide, more severe grief reactions predicted spiritual struggles 6 months later (Neimeyer & Burke, 2011). All these studies suggest that spiritual struggles both influence and are influenced by psychiatric symptoms. The evidence is clear that the therapist's awareness of patients' spirituality and therapeutic interventions that address this spirituality falls within the purview of the practice of psychotherapy. If SIP is so sorely needed in our spiritually starving society, then why are you, the reader, probably just now hearing about it?

History of Spiritually Integrated Psychotherapy

With the publication of Pargament's (2011) seminal book, *Spiritually Integrated Psychotherapy*, in 2007, SIP entered the pastoral counseling conversation as a viable treatment option for spiritually curious persons who want help with their spiritual struggles. The history of SIP, however, reaches further back in time. According to Snodgrass (2019), SIP rose from the ashes of the pastoral counseling movement. After decades of informal "counseling" conducted by clergy who recognized the intertwined spiritual and emotional needs of their congregations, the American Association of Pastoral Counselors (AAPC) was founded in 1963. Pastoral counselors filled the vacuum created by mainstream psychotherapy dominated by a rigid sectarianism. The three theoretical titans of 20th-century psychotherapy—Sigmund Freud (1927), John B. Watson (1936), and B. F. Skinner (1976)—founded psychoanalysis and behaviorism, the two most recognizable brand names of psychotherapy. All three of these men openly espoused atheism. These three men and many other prominent atheist psychologists cast a long, dark shadow over psychotherapy training, forbidding the exploration of spiritual issues in psychotherapy and thus creating fertile ground for pastoral counseling to sprout.

Unfortunately, AAPC did not recognize or collaborate with like-minded organizations (Snodgrass, 2019). Dissatisfied with the atheistic zeitgeist surrounding psychotherapy, some members of the American Psychological Association founded Division 36—the Society for the Psychology of Religion and Spirituality—in 1946. Some members of the American Counseling Association founded the Association for Spiritual, Ethical, and Religious Values in Counseling (ASERVIC) in 1951. Some psychologists and counselors were expressing a professional interest in exploring the relation between psychology and spirituality.

Perhaps the most decisive event for AAPC took place in 1974, when its leadership voted not to pursue state licensure (Snodgrass, 2019; Townsend, 2015). State licensure for mental health professionals was becoming mandatory; mental health professionals must have the proper academic credentials, supervision hours, and continuing education credits to attain and maintain state licensure. Because AAPC removed itself from this licensure process, pastoral counseling was not included in states' scope of practice, and pastoral counselors, therefore, could not call themselves "psychotherapists." In the 1990s, managed care companies took over the healthcare industry, reimbursing customers' psychotherapy claims only if they were conducted by state-licensed mental health professionals who held malpractice insurance policies. Only state-licensed mental health professionals could obtain malpractice insurance in the first place. With no recognition from the healthcare industry and no malpractice insurance coverage, pastoral counseling became a relic of the unregulated history of mental healthcare.

To survive, AAPC looked for opportunities to merge with another organization (Snodgrass, 2019). In 2019, AAPC members voted to consolidate with the Association for Clinical Pastoral Education (ACPE), effectively dissolving AAPC as a separate legal entity. This merger opened the door for SIP. The consolidated ACPE voted to shift the focus away from pastoral counseling, which the organization viewed as recognition not only of market-driven forces but also of a new emphasis on inclusiveness of religious affiliation rather than on the exclusive Christian emphasis that "pastoral counseling" suggests. Historically, pastoral counseling has been "guided by the truths and authority of a particular religious tradition" (Pargament, 2011, p. 131). In contrast, patients in SIP have the right "to define truths as they see them [which is] perhaps the most basic of all truths that therapists live by" (p. 131). Regarding patients' current spiritual needs, Snodgrass (2019) writes, "In hospitals and other institutional settings ... spiritual care professionals occupy diverse religious locations and serve patients and clients of any or no faith" (p. 154). Thus, SIP serves a more diverse array of patients than pastoral counseling, and its practitioners represent a more diverse array of spiritual and religious affiliations. The SIP therapist allows their patients to discover spiritual truths for themselves rather than influence them to accept the therapist's own spiritual truths.

Perhaps the most important difference between SIP and pastoral counseling is that only state-licensed or license-eligible mental health professionals can practice SIP. While pastoral counselors typically have a theological education such as a Master of Divinity (MDiv) degree, SIP mental health professionals have at a minimum a mental health master's degree, a state license to practice psychotherapy, malpractice insurance, and a certification in SIP (see later section). Health insurance companies do not reimburse patients treated by pastoral counselors because they lack state licensure and malpractice insurance.

Seminary faculty and students are beginning to recognize this reality of licensure. In the US alone, there are 17 dual-degree programs that offer both a MDiv degree and a Master of Social Work (MSW) degree. These students learn how to integrate spirituality into their work with their patients once they assume a therapeutic role, whether those patients are congregants, hospital patients, military veterans, or unhoused persons. In the training program for certification, SIP offers mental health professionals an exposure to working with spirituality in treatment without having to receive a theological education in a seminary or school of theology. The SIP certification compensates for the lack of spirituality training in graduate schools that provide mental health education (e.g., clinical psychology doctoral programs) and the obsolescence of pastoral counseling programs.

In summary, SIP satisfies a spiritual hunger in both therapists and patients and helps patients make meaning of their experience. SIP authorities such as Pargament (2011; Pargament & Exline, 2022), Griffith (2010), and Jones (2019) are leading the way in defining this new field and shaping its curriculum for generations of mental health professionals who want to address explicit and implicit spirituality in their psychotherapy sessions. In the current marketplace, pastoral counseling might no longer be a viable treatment option, but SIP has gained traction in its wake. Both seminaries and graduate schools of mental health could incorporate the SIP curriculum into their own training so that future mental healthcare providers will become more aware of spiritual issues in their work with patients.

Practical Application of Spiritually Integrated Psychotherapy

If we accept the first presupposition that spirituality is an inherent motivational system that all humanity shares, and if we accept the second presupposition that psychotherapy facilitates the patient's exploration of human motivation, then it follows that spirituality naturally emerges in most or all psychotherapy treatments. In psychotherapy, spirituality takes the form of spiritual strivings and struggles (see earlier section). If SIP is effective in helping patients address their spiritual struggles, then how would we know it? Pargament (2011) suggests that spirituality must be "well-integrated" (p. 134). In other words, the component parts of spirituality "work together in synchrony with each other" (p. 134). This definition becomes clearer when Pargament (2011) remarks that "a person can hold very different images of the sacred simultaneously. The same individual can view God as loving at one level, punitive at another, and detached at still another" (p. 143).

The reader will recall from Chapter 1 that insecure attachment patterns reflect a lack of narrative coherence. This lack is manifested when an interviewer questions insecurely attached persons about relationships to their caregivers during childhood. For example, a person might describe their relationship to their mother during childhood as "loving" but, when the interviewer asks for a specific memory to support this adjective, the person might have nothing to offer: "I don't really have many memories from my childhood, but I just know she was loving." Such persons are known to have an anxious-avoidant attachment pattern. Consciously, the person holds an emotionally positive image of this relationship in mind, yet, on an unconscious level, the person often holds an emotionally negative image of this same relationship in their mind. In the second case illustration, Florence describes her father as "loving," yet, in one session, she casually mentions that he refused to take her to the hospital after she injured her arm because he did not think it was serious. Only after her mother took her to the hospital did the family learn that Florence's arm was broken. One incident does not make a parent loving or unloving, but Florence's emotional reaction of nonchalance while recounting this story suggests incoherence between her "semantic memory" of her father's emotional responsiveness—"loving"—and her "episodic memory" of her father's dismissal of her physical pain. When asked about her feelings about her father's dismissal, Florence in turn dismisses her father's behavior and her own unconscious feelings of rejection by giving him a pass.

Quite plausibly, images of our attachment relationship to a Higher Power can also suggest incoherence (Goodman, 2025a, 2025b; Pargament, 2011; Rizzuto, 1979). How does the SIP therapist go about integrating these disparate images of a Higher Power to facilitate this "well-integrated spirituality"? The first step is to conduct a spiritual assessment.

Conducting a Spiritual Assessment

The SIP literature is united in recommending that all therapists conduct a spiritual assessment. This assessment includes questions designed to situate the patient in their spiritual journey (or lack of journey) and to understand the nature of the patient's spiritual struggles, if any. The ACPE SIP training manual (ACPE, 2024, p. 286) suggests asking nine questions as part of a comprehensive spiritual assessment:

- Does the client consider themselves spiritual or religious, or not?
- What groups does the client belong to?
- What is their image of God or Ultimate Reality?
- What are the client's implicit and explicit spiritual resources?
- What are features of the client's spiritual personality?
- What are the client's spiritual struggles?
- What are the "heart of the matter" issues?
- Is spirituality/religion helping, harming, or both? (Include here how the client's spirituality interacts, positively or negatively, with any mental health diagnoses.)
- Does the client want to address spirituality in therapy?

The goal of this spiritual assessment is "to develop a concrete plan of action for addressing spirituality in psychotherapy" (Pargament, 2011, p. 201). Of course, not every patient wants to address spiritual issues in their treatment, and the therapist needs to be prepared for that possibility. Instead, the SIP therapist needs to conduct an implicit spiritual assessment, using the broadest possible definition of spirituality. In both case illustrations, I use an implicit spiritual assessment. I ask Blair if he ever experiences joy. Joy is an emotion commonly associated with the spiritual self. In fact, in later sessions, my question opened up an explicit spiritual conversation about the joy that he experiences during Buddhist retreats and meditation sessions. I ask Florence what she thinks her life purpose is. This question prompts her to reflect on the lack of purpose that she has been experiencing.

I would call these interventions "reorientations to the spiritual realm." I am using the broadest possible definition of spirituality espoused in this chapter by helping these patients imbue their lives with "deeper divine-like character and significance [which is] the essence of spirituality" (Pargament & Exline, 2022, p. 6). Thus, spiritual assessment continues long after the intake sessions. As these case illustrations demonstrate, spiritual assessment goes hand in hand with spiritual intervention.

Therapist Qualities Facilitating and Hindering SIP

We can all imagine ourselves as patients in psychotherapy, wanting our therapists to have a certain temperament or personality that will help us to get the most out of the therapeutic experience. As a long-time patient in psychotherapy,

I especially value my therapist's ability to understand me, helping me to feel understood. We can also imagine other therapist qualities that would facilitate contact with our spiritual nature. SIP trainers emphasize several temperamental and personality qualities that therapists need to cultivate to conduct a meaningful SIP session. Before discussing these qualities, however, I want to explore a question that seems not to have a definitive answer in the literature. Can a nonspiritual therapist conduct SIP? And, if so, can their patients experience relief from, or at least become more aware of, their spiritual struggles?

On the one hand, therapists who acknowledge their own spirituality will be more likely to understand their patients' spirituality. These "spiritual" therapists will be naturally more capable of empathizing with their patients' spirituality than nonspiritual therapists. On the surface, this statement makes sense. For example, a Christian therapist is going to understand a patient's spiritual experience of taking communion because this therapist has also probably taken communion. On the other hand, this Christian therapist might make invalid assumptions about the patient's Christian experience that a non-Christian therapist might not make. For example, in my case illustration of Blair, I observe that there seems to be no joy in his life. He responds by mentioning C. S. Lewis's *Surprised by Joy*, a book that I read years ago as a Christian and understood as a Christian; Blair also read this book when he was a Christian, before he became an atheist. I assume that he shares my understanding of this book, even though he no longer views himself and the world from a Christian perspective. If I were not a Christian and had not read this book, I might have asked him to share with me what the book means to him. This inquiry might have opened up new avenues of understanding that I, as a Christian, do not explore because I assume that we share the same experience as Christians having read this book.

This problem of shared and nonshared therapist and patient spiritual identity is not unique to SIP. Researchers have investigated the advantages and disadvantages of shared assumptions among therapists and patients with shared and nonshared racial identities (Sue, 1998), therapist case conceptualizations of patients with shared and nonshared racial identities (Neufeldt et al., 2006), and psychologist school consultation of students with shared and nonshared racial identities (Ingraham, 2003). Overall, the findings suggest that racial matching of therapist and patient (or consultant and student) has benefits for the therapeutic alliance but also limitations, such as the perception of shared assumptions that are not truly shared. For example, an African American therapist working with a Ugandan patient might unconsciously assume shared experiences based on race, when their experiences might be quite different. Similarly, a white American therapist working with an Irish patient might make the same false unconscious assumptions. A therapist can make the same false unconscious assumptions about a patient's religious background if they generally share a religious identity. A mainline Protestant therapist working with an evangelical Protestant patient might unconsciously assume shared experiences based on the Protestant label; however, their views on Christianity might be radically different.

We can then ask the question whether a nonspiritual therapist can work with a spiritual patient. The foregoing discussion about racial identity in therapy suggests that a nonspiritual therapist might be protected from unconsciously making false assumptions about a spiritual patient but have more difficulty establishing a therapeutic alliance. Pargament (2011) seems to equivocate in his answer to this question. On the one hand, he writes that "the spiritually integrated therapist can draw on his or her understanding of and approach to spirituality as a powerful resource of change," while the spiritually dis-integrated therapist "may overlook valuable opportunities for change or unwittingly exacerbate the client's problems" (p. 187). On the other hand, "empirical studies have shown that even presumably secular psychotherapies result in changes in clients' images of God (e.g., Tisdale et al., 1997)" (p. 195). Pargament (2011) also cites a research study that demonstrated that nonreligious therapists outperformed religious therapists in a religious CBT treatment condition (Propst et al., 1992), concluding that "nonreligious therapists can be effective in delivering spiritually integrated psychotherapy" (p. 331).

Perhaps we can resolve this tension if spiritually integrated therapists can also be nonreligious. Regardless of their religious commitments, therapists must be "spiritually integrated." Extrapolating from Pargament's definition of "spiritually integrated" discussed earlier, a spiritually integrated therapist must have an internally coherent image of the sacred, even if this therapist is not committed to a religious identity. Clearly, additional research is sorely needed to determine whether a spiritually integrated therapist, regardless of religious affiliation, is more therapeutically successful than a spiritually dis-integrated therapist, regardless of religious affiliation. We could categorize therapists into four treatment conditions—spiritually integrated/religious, spiritually integrated/nonreligious, spiritually dis-integrated/religious, and spiritually dis-integrated/nonreligious—to determine which therapist category outperforms the others. Of course, the patient's spirituality and religious background might also contribute to the results, making for an exceedingly complex research design consisting of 16 conditions. It is no wonder that so few researchers study this question!

Beyond this therapist quality of spiritual integration, what other therapist qualities facilitate SIP? Pargament (2011, p. 190) lists spiritual knowledge, openness and tolerance, self-awareness, and authenticity as four essential qualities of the SIP therapist. Seeking knowledge about a patient's spirituality is critical to facilitating an empathic connection to the patient. I am currently treating Séamus (a pseudonym), a patient who practices Hinduism and regularly discusses his "kundalini energy" (Goodman, 2025c). I assiduously studied the concept of kundalini energy so that I could understand what he was telling me about this deeply personal experience. I believe that this effort helped him to feel more deeply understood. Openness and tolerance of a patient's spirituality help the patient to feel accepted and not judged for their spiritual experiences. My open and tolerant stance in therapy sessions reassured Séamus that I would treat anything that he told me about his energic spiritual experiences with respect and curiosity without pathologizing these experiences.

Self-awareness is critical to the SIP process because knowing my spiritual values can keep me from imposing these values onto my patients. Because Hinduism is not consistent with my own spiritual values, I need to be especially aware of any biases against Séamus's spiritual values. Self-awareness can help to protect the therapist from negative countertransference, or negative emotional reactions aroused by the patient's emotions or beliefs expressed during sessions. Finally, authenticity, when practiced in the context of these other three therapist qualities, facilitates a deep sense of trust that the therapist has foregrounded the patient's interests and is not pretending to help only because the patient pays for therapy. For example, I believe that Séamus knows that I am genuinely interested in his spiritual struggles and want to help him to overcome them. That I sought his permission to write about him (Goodman, 2025c) indicates my genuine interest in his welfare and desire to understand him better.

Of course, regardless of whether a therapist is practicing SIP, every therapist should possess these qualities. In the middle of the last century, Carl Rogers (1957) identified three necessary and sufficient conditions of therapeutic personality change: empathy, genuineness, and unconditional positive regard. These conditions easily map onto Pargament's (2011) therapist qualities necessary to practice SIP. What are the therapist qualities that hinder SIP and the patient's spiritual integration?

Therapist qualities that hinder SIP and the patient's spiritual integration are more specific to the practice of SIP. Pargament (2011, p. 333) lists spiritual bias, spiritual myopia, spiritual timidity, spiritual overenthusiasm, spiritual cockiness, and intolerance of ambiguity as the six hindrances of the SIP therapist. Spiritual bias, which is closely related to negative countertransference (see above), is holding stereotyped views of the patient's spirituality or religion, what Griffith (2010) refers to as "meeting a patient ... as a category" (p. 79), not as a person. Spiritual myopia suggests a difficulty with detecting explicit or implicit spiritual needs buried within the clinical material presented by the patient. Spiritual timidity indicates an unwillingness to discuss spirituality, perhaps related to fears of patient rejection or the therapist's own perceived lack of spiritual knowledge or experience. Spiritual overenthusiasm refers to the reflexive tendency to interpret all clinical material as spiritual and to treat spirituality as the solution to all clinical problems (e.g., telling the compulsive handwasher to turn the problem over to Jesus). Spiritual cockiness is related to therapists steeped in their own religious backgrounds who overestimate their competence to work with patients from different religious backgrounds. Intolerance of ambiguity refers to a tendency to offer simple, often formulaic solutions to spiritual struggles without truly understanding the underlying complexity of the patient's conflict.

All SIP therapists succumb to these hindrances at one time or another; thus, I recommend specific SIP training and ongoing supervision to increase therapist awareness of these hindrances to the patient's spiritual integration (see below).

Sacred Qualities of the Therapeutic Relationship

Not only must SIP therapists possess specific qualities to facilitate the search for the sacred in SIP, but also, paradoxically, the sacred must permeate the therapeutic relationship for the duration of this search. In some treatment models, especially those originating in the psychodynamic tradition, the therapeutic relationship is the fulcrum of change in psychotherapy. Elsewhere (Goodman, 2025a, 2025b), I discuss how to use Attachment-Informed Psychotherapy (AIP) to establish a therapeutic relationship conducive to exploring spiritual struggles, especially divine struggles related to the quality of a person's attachment relationship to a Higher Power. Thus, particularly in the psychodynamic tradition, the effectiveness of SIP critically depends on the sacred qualities that imbue the therapeutic relationship.

If an explicit or implicit discussion of spirituality belongs in the therapeutic conversations between therapist and patient, then how can the therapist facilitate spiritual healing in their therapeutic relationships with patients who have experienced spiritual struggles? Pargament (2011) suggests three sacred qualities of the therapeutic relationship—grace, deep acceptance, and reassuring presence—that can help to heal these spiritual struggles, which, as I have suggested, are also associated with psychiatric symptoms. Grace and deep acceptance suggest closely related interventions in the sense that the therapist demonstrates to the patient, through careful listening, a nonjudgmental attitude, and nonreactivity, an unconditional acceptance of the patient's entire being. Reassuring presence suggests that the therapist will not avert their gaze or withdraw their acceptance but instead bear witness to the patient's pain, even when being with the patient might be painful.

Pargament (2011) points out that these three sacred qualities of the therapeutic relationship do not exclude the importance of gently confronting patients when needed. In fact, using these sacred qualities to intervene in a patient's life could be disorienting to a patient unfamiliar with them. For example, a patient diagnosed with histrionic personality disorder might interpret reflective listening, empathy, genuineness, and unconditional positive regard (Rogers, 1957) as invitations of seduction, while the patient diagnosed with narcissistic personality disorder might interpret these sacred qualities as condescending. A patient diagnosed with paranoid personality disorder might interpret them as a preparation for exploitation. Thus, the therapist must consider the patient's personality organization and adjust their interventions accordingly—even the sacred ones.

In summary, the SIP therapist channels the sacred qualities of the therapeutic relationship as a human representative of the divine. Patients often attribute sacred qualities to therapists (Pattison, 1982), whether deserved or undeserved. Using language from attachment theory, the patient might be trying to establish an attachment relationship to the therapist that resembles their attachment relationship to a Higher Power. For example, the patient might idealize their relationships both to the therapist and to God, which conceal underlying worries of abandonment in both relationships. This type of attachment relationship would be considered anxious-avoidant (see Chapter 1), reflecting a deep-seated insecurity about God's—and the therapist's—steadfast presence.

To these three sacred qualities, I would therefore add a fourth—a mutual sacred awareness of the influence of attachment relationships to the caregivers during childhood and to a Higher Power—even if belief in a Higher Power is denied. Attachment theory is ideally suited to addressing existential problems of survival and death. Even as infants, all humans (in fact, all mammals) seek proximity to a "stronger and/or wiser" (Bowlby, 1988, p. 120) caregiver perceived as having the capacity to protect them from existential harm such as a predator or severe weather. Thus, attachment theory is at its core an existential theory. Mikulincer (2019) presents compelling research evidence that suggests that study participants who are subliminally primed for mortality salience (i.e., an unconscious awareness of one's own mortality) show an activation of the attachment system characterized by seeking proximity to stronger, wiser others or mental representations of relationships to these others to reduce existential anxiety caused by mortality salience. Pargament and Exline (2022) argue that "life's most fundamental existential questions often do become fraught with sacred power and significance. And when they do, struggles become spiritual struggles" (p. 7). If existential struggles are at their core spiritual struggles, then attachment theory can certainly make a critical contribution to an understanding of spiritual struggles. A mutual sacred awareness of the influence of attachment relationships to those caregivers (both human and sacred) who are sought out for protection from existential dangers is, therefore, a key component of the process of spiritual healing in SIP.

These therapist qualities serve the primary goal of integrating the patient's spirituality—"one whose component parts work together in synchrony with each other" (Pargament, 2011, p. 134). From an attachment perspective (Hesse, 2018), that would mean developing the ability to tell a coherent spiritual narrative that reflects an underlying organization consistent with Grice's (1989) four conversational maxims. The first conversational maxim is quality: be truthful and have evidence for what you say. Florence's describing her father as loving during childhood but not providing any specific memories to support this description would violate the maxim of quality. The second conversational maxim is quantity: be succinct and yet complete. Describing my mother as loving using many meandering sentences or just one or two words would violate the maxim of quantity. The third conversational maxim is relevance: be relevant to the topic as presented. Describing my mother as loving and then abruptly changing the subject would violate the maxim of relevance. The fourth conversational maxim is manner: be clear and orderly. Describing my mother in vague terms (e.g., "great") or using psychological jargon (e.g., "having a positive affective valence") would violate the maxim of manner. Thus, from an attachment perspective, I would consider a patient who discusses their attachment relationship to a Higher Power while maintaining these four conversational maxims as exhibiting a high degree of narrative coherence, which captures the essence of a well-integrated spirituality.

Empirical Evidence Supporting the Effectiveness of SIP

The empirical evidence supporting the effectiveness of SIP is gradually accumulating. One of the challenges of conducting research to assess SIP's effectiveness is the wide variety of treatment models that claim the brand name "SIP." Therapists practicing popular treatment models such as Psychodynamic Therapy (PDT) or Cognitive-Behavioral Therapy (CBT) can use their respective arsenals of clinical techniques in the service of spiritual integration. How do researchers assess treatment effectiveness in integrating a patient's spirituality when these two popular treatment models have so little in common (Goodman, 2013)? Some SIP researchers have developed treatment manuals articulating therapeutic interventions that any spiritually respectful, curious therapist can use to treat their patients. For example, *Solace for the Soul* (Murray-Swank & Pargament, 2005), designed to treat sexually abused women, and *Re-Creating Your Life* (Cole & Pargament, 1998), designed to treat persons diagnosed with serious mental illness, explicitly incorporate spirituality into psychotherapy sessions. Despite these advances in defining SIP for specific patient populations, the unstandardized treatment protocol of SIP makes the task of its assessment difficult across patient populations.

Nevertheless, several meta-analyses have suggested that SIP—regardless of treatment model—is effective in treating common psychiatric symptoms such as anxiety and depression. A meta-analysis is an increasingly common methodological tool in the researcher's arsenal in which the researcher leverages the statistical power of multiple treatment effectiveness studies by testing SIP's effectiveness using the combined sample sizes of all such studies. For SIP, the results are encouraging. A meta-analysis of 31 studies indicated that the average effect size was .56 (Smith et al., 2007), which the research literature considers to be a large effect size (Cohen, 1992). More recently, Gonçalves and his colleagues (Gonçalves et al., 2015) identified 23 studies that satisfied their inclusion criteria and found that SIP was associated with very significant reductions in stress, alcoholism, depression, and especially anxiety. The authors caution, however, that "the diversity of protocols and outcomes associated with a lack of standardization of interventions point to the need for further studies" (p. 2937). In a meta-analysis consisting of 16 studies, faith-adapted CBT (F-CBT) outperformed standard CBT on measures of anxiety and depression; however, the authors caution against drawing firm conclusions because of significant methodological limitations of the selected studies (Anderson et al., 2015). A 97-study meta-analysis indicated that religious or spiritual-adapted psychotherapy (R/S-adapted psychotherapy) did not outperform standard psychotherapy in reducing psychological distress but did outperform standard psychotherapy in improving spiritual well-being (Captari et al., 2018). Perhaps R/S-adapted psychotherapy is more adept at treating what Pargament and Exline (2022) call "spiritual struggles" (see earlier discussion) than standard psychotherapy. Finally, in the most recent meta-analysis published to date (Bouwhuis-Van Keulen et al., 2024), religious and spiritually-based (R/S) therapy outperformed standard psychotherapy only for "patients with a strong religious and spiritual affiliation" (p. 339).

These meta-analyses suggest that SIP is effective in treating common psychiatric symptoms such as anxiety and depression. In some meta-analyses, SIP outperforms standard psychotherapy without qualification; in others, SIP outperforms standard psychotherapy only in improving spiritual well-being, or outperforms standard psychotherapy only for spiritually grounded patients. It makes intuitive sense that spiritually grounded patients would respond better to SIP than standard psychotherapy, perhaps because they feel more deeply understood by SIP therapists. The challenge identified in all these meta-analyses is to formulate a standardized definition of SIP to facilitate its assessment. I envision a future of multiple models of SIP, each with its own coherent set of principles and protocol. Chapter 8 defines one specific model of SIP—AIP—that seeks to transform the patient's attachment relationships to a Higher Power and to their parents during childhood from insecure to secure. Other specific models of SIP are sure to proliferate.

Spiritually Integrated Psychotherapy Viewed in the Context of Attachment Theory

As I already mentioned, attachment theory has much to offer a spiritually informed therapist who wants to practice SIP. Helping a patient to experience their Higher Power as a safe haven to turn to in distress and as a secure base from which to explore their surroundings would facilitate a well-integrated spirituality. A patient must first experience their therapist as reliable and emotionally responsive before they can ever experience their Higher Power this way. Alice Walker's (1982) *The Color Purple* provides a beautiful illustration of the African American protagonist Celie's transformation of her attachment relationship to God. Initially, Celie writes letters to the God she knows—"big and old and tall and graybearded and white ... trying to chase that old man out of my head" (pp. 165, 168)—which perfectly mirrors the mental images of her earthly male oppressors. Later in her spiritual journey, Celie meets Shug Avery, an African American woman who loves Celie unconditionally—a love that she never experienced before. Through the healing power of this unconditional love, Celie's attachment relationship to God changes from constricted and insecure to expansive and secure. By the end of the novel, Celie writes, "Dear God. Dear stars, dear trees, dear sky, dear peoples. Dear Everything. Dear God" (p. 242). Above all, a SIP therapist needs to provide this same emotionally corrective experience (Alexander & French, 1946) to their patients to facilitate this spiritual transformation (see below and Chapter 8).

Chapter 8 articulates one specific treatment model for addressing spirituality in psychotherapy—AIP. AIP assumes that both patients and therapists have mental images of a Higher Power and mental images of a relationship to a Higher Power. These mental images, or mental representations, profoundly influence a person's spiritual and psychological lives, including spiritual practices (or absence of practices) and psychiatric symptoms. Theologian Ann Belford Ulanov writes: "Our God-images are as idiosyncratically personal as is our handwriting, our breathing, or our walking" (Ulanov, 2001, p. 96). While these mental representations are as unique as snowflakes, we can nevertheless detect patterns of mental representations that certain groups of persons have in common. Just as all snowflakes are geometrically configured to have six sides, all persons who belong to a particular group share a certain "mode of primary relatedness" (Slade, 1999, p. 588) directly related to the specific quality of these persons' attachment relationships to their caregivers during childhood.

Studying these commonalities among early attachment relationships to caregivers, Ainsworth and her colleagues (1978) identified three attachment patterns (i.e., secure, anxious-resistant, anxious-avoidant) that seem to follow a developmental trajectory into adulthood (Waters et al., 2000). Main and Solomon (1986, 1990) later identified a fourth attachment pattern (i.e., disorganized/disoriented). Together, these four attachment patterns represent all the types of attachment relationships thus far identified throughout the world (Mesman et al., 2018). Although persons' mental representations of their attachment relationship to a Higher Power are unique, we can identify certain commonalities across these unique mental representations. Thus, we can implement intervention strategies that address the identifying characteristics of each of these groups rather than apply a set of boilerplate interventions to all patients or, on the other hand, make continual attempts to reinvent the wheel by creating a novel set of unique interventions for each patient (see Chapter 2).

These attachment patterns, developed in relation to our caregivers during the earliest months of our lives, can increase or decrease our risk of developing psychopathology later in life. The quality of these early attachment relationships can expose us to or protect us from psychiatric symptoms. Specifically, secure attachment relationships can act as a buffer from adverse life events that might otherwise cause psychiatric symptoms (e.g., anxiety, depression), whereas insecure attachment relationships (i.e., anxious-resistant, anxious-avoidant, disorganized/disoriented) can exacerbate our vulnerability to such symptoms (for a summary of findings, see Stovall-McClough & Dozier, 2018).

Furthermore, the quality of a person's early attachment relationships is also associated with the quality of their attachment relationship to a Higher Power. Either the type of attachment security or insecurity to the caregivers during childhood corresponds to the type of attachment security or insecurity to a Higher Power, or a Higher Power serves as a surrogate attachment figure, compensating for insecure attachment relationships to the caregivers during childhood (for a summary of findings, see Granqvist, 2020; Granqvist & Kirkpatrick, 2018). If the quality of a person's attachment relationships to the caregivers during childhood is related to both their psychiatric symptoms and the quality of their attachment relationship to a Higher Power, then it stands to reason that the quality of a person's attachment relationship to a Higher Power is also associated with their psychiatric symptoms. Preliminary evidence suggests the viability of this relationship (Granqvist, 2020; Granqvist & Kirkpatrick, 2018); however, the studies supporting this hypothesis used self-report assessments of attachment quality, which are known to suffer from poor construct validity (Roisman et al., 2007). Further research is obviously needed to establish the connection between the quality of a person's attachment relationship to a Higher Power and their psychiatric symptoms. From a therapeutic perspective, it also seems reasonable to hypothesize that targeting the quality of a person's attachment relationship to a Higher Power in psychotherapy might bring symptomatic relief to spiritually curious or spiritually grounded patients. In my first case illustration, Blair's depression might lift if he can find joy in his relationship to a Higher Power.

Psychotherapy for Spiritually Curious Persons

If human beings are maturationally hard-wired to believe in a Higher Power, and if awareness of mortality, suffering, loss, and insecure attachment relationships to parents sometimes interfere with a relationship to this Higher Power, then it follows that a potential treatment goal of psychotherapy would be to help a person to restore their default setting to a secure attachment relationship to the Higher Power of their understanding. SIP as defined by its pioneers (e.g., Griffith, 2010; Jones, 2019; Pargament, 2011; Pargament & Exline, 2022) is designed to restore spiritual integration, but it does not leverage the explosion of knowledge about attachment theory and attachment relationships. Attachment researcher Arietta Slade (2018) explained it this way:

> Therapists who are able to provide a secure and safe base for their patients, to remain emotionally present and compassionate while managing complex and potentially intense affects within a therapy session, are likely to be those who best facilitate their patients' development. (p. 769)

Psychotherapy is not designed to last forever. When the work is completed, does the patient simply mourn the therapist's loss and move on without this critical attachment relationship?

A secure attachment relationship to God, however, would continue beyond a person's therapeutic relationship and potentially sustain the person through all kinds of suffering for which the therapist had previously provided comfort and security. Thus, a spiritually informed therapist, in addition to providing a "secure and safe base," would facilitate a secure attachment relationship to a Higher Power that would endure beyond the temporal limitations of psychotherapy. This work would naturally include making connections between a person's attachment relationships to parents and their attachment relationship to their Higher Power, as I did in my reflection on my autobiographical narrative (see Goodman, 2025a, Chapter 1). Thus, there is a need for a SIP that capitalizes on the latest advances in attachment theory by applying them to this spiritual therapeutic context. Chapter 8 is an attempt to present a model of SIP that incorporates the latest insights of attachment theory into its healing process.

In secular circles, AIP is designed to transform a person's attachment relationships to parents from insecure to secure, which presumably generalizes to other emotionally significant relationships in the person's life. In this treatment model, "Change in attachment status itself becomes the target of treatment" (Slade, 2018, p. 771). If we consider the relationship to God to be emotionally significant, then we would also expect this relationship to change from insecure to secure. Persons who were probably insecurely attached to parents during early childhood and become securely attached later in life owing to the life-changing experience of a loving relationship or psychotherapy are later classified as "earned secure" (Hesse, 2018). In other words, these persons worked on themselves to overcome their early attachment insecurity with parents and have developed the capacity to form secure attachment relationships and, potentially, a secure attachment relationship to God.

Can an insecurely attached person become securely attached later in life owing to the life-changing experience of a loving relationship to God? The literature usually suggests only one direction of causality, with a secure attachment relationship to God as an outcome of the self-work required for the shift to occur from insecurity to security. AIP, in a spiritual context, acknowledges the bidirectionality of causality—that earning security in one attachment relationship can affect the security in another.

Because AIP privileges the acknowledgment of a sacred personified mental image to whom a person can establish an attachment relationship, nontheistic patients might feel more deeply understood participating in a SIP that relies on a broader definition of the sacred than AIP does. In my second case illustration, I ask Florence what her life's purpose is, not what her image of God is. Thus, although I might be promoting AIP as a SIP par excellence, I welcome the proliferation of various models of SIP that might suit spiritually curious patients who do not hold theistic beliefs about a Higher Power. In the words of prominent psychotherapy researcher Sydney Blatt, "Different kinds of folks may need different kinds of strokes" (Blatt & Felsen, 1993, p. 245).

When Is This Model of Spiritual Intervention a Good Match?

SIP is a good match when a person is experiencing emotional and spiritual conflicts that rise above the level of an adjustment disorder. Persons with adjustment disorders might find that SIP represents a higher level of care than they actually need. Support programs such as Stephen Ministry (see Chapter 2) facilitate the processing of grief, loss, and moderate depression but not more chronic problems that require a deeper exploration of both conscious and unconscious processes. A trial of SIP might benefit persons struggling with severe depression, chronic anxiety, sexual dysfunction, or impulsivity, to name a few diagnoses.

SIP would also be especially well suited for spiritually grounded and spiritually curious persons who want to explore their spirituality with a therapist. Perhaps these persons even recognize the intimate connection between their spirituality and their psychological problems. SIP is especially suitable for patients experiencing one or more of the six categories of spiritual struggles discussed earlier in this chapter. Perhaps less obviously, however, SIP might also be suitable for persons who have rejected a personified God but who nevertheless value spirituality in the broadest possible sense. My patient Blair labels himself an atheist, yet spirituality spontaneously emerges often in our therapy sessions. This case illustration answers the question whether SIP can treat atheists.

The reader should not view SIP as a stand-alone treatment. Many psychological problems do not improve with SIP alone. Psychopharmacotherapy (i.e., medication), couples therapy, group therapy, and support groups such as 12-step programs (see Chapter 4) often serve as collateral treatments for SIP patients because 45 minutes of weekly psychotherapy represent only about 0.4% of a person's life. Many diagnoses such as substance and behavioral addictions require much more attention than weekly SIP alone can provide.

My father, an evangelical Christian who once considered the ministry, viewed my decision to attend graduate school in clinical psychology skeptically. He believed that, because the Bible does not explicitly mention SIP, then it obviously represents "the wisdom of this world" which is "foolishness in God's sight" (I Corinthians 3:19, NIV). Thus, SIP is probably not well suited to many persons who come from fundamentalist faith traditions. Such persons would probably feel more comfortable speaking informally to a clergy person and not calling it "psychotherapy." After all, isn't psychotherapy for "psychos"? Griffith (2010) provides several key case illustrations that suggest that even the most skeptical religious persons can participate in SIP if the therapist approaches them with empathy, genuineness, unconditional positive regard, and an authentic desire to learn more about their religious beliefs and attitudes. In summary, the patient agrees to their SIP participation by providing informed consent to any explicit discussion of these beliefs and attitudes (Hawkins & Bullock, 1995). SIP is therefore a good match for persons who have chronic, complex emotional and spiritual conflicts and who want to talk about their spirituality in psychotherapy, either explicitly or implicitly.

Training Requirements to Practice Spiritually Integrated Psychotherapy

Based on the discussion about SIP and pastoral counseling that began this chapter, it should come as no surprise that a SIP therapist must be licensed as a mental health professional in their state. Licensed mental health professionals include psychiatrists; clinical, counseling, and school psychologists; social workers; psychiatric nurse practitioners; marriage and family therapists and counselors; mental health counselors; and professional counselors (I apologize if I have omitted any licensed mental health professions from this list). Each of these mental health professions has their own graduate school training and licensure procedures. Length of graduate school training can vary widely; for example, a psychiatrist must attend 4 years of medical school and 4 years of psychiatry residency before being able to use the label "psychiatrist." A mental health counselor must attend only 2 years of graduate school and, depending on the state, receive a certain number of hours of clinical supervision with a licensed mental health professional. The reader should check their state's licensure requirements to become a licensed mental health professional in that state.

After a person becomes licensed in the mental health profession of their choice, the training to become a SIP therapist does not end there. As already mentioned, graduate schools seldom train their graduate students to competency as practitioners of this type of therapy. Thus, the licensed mental health professional must obtain this training in a SIP certificate program. The certification to become a SIP therapist requires significant additional work. The completion of such a program certifies that the licensed mental health professional is competent to practice SIP in their state.

At least two US organizations provide SIP training. The Solihten Institute (solihten.org), based in Denver, offers ad hoc 2-hour SIP webinars designed to improve the therapist's awareness of spiritual issues that emerge in psychotherapy practice. Webinar titles include "Impact of Trauma on Spirituality and Religious Beliefs" and "Integrating Religion Into Cognitive Behavioral Therapy." Each webinar costs $125, and there is a significant discount for registering for all six currently advertised webinars ($425).

On the other hand, ACPE (acpe.edu), based in Atlanta, sponsors a rigorous SIP certification program that includes several facets. Therapists must complete two 15-hour online SIP curriculum training modules (Modules 1 and 2), 20 hours of online or in-person SIP consultation (ACPE's word for "supervision") with a SIP trainer (of which 12 hours can be group consultation with a SIP trainer), and a final 2-hour presentation of a case from the therapist's own practice, wherein the therapist demonstrates engagement of the ten core SIP competencies. These ten core SIP competencies (ACPE, 2024, p. 9) include:

1. Appreciation of spiritual and religious diversity and ability to work across spiritual and religious difference;
2. Ability to work with clients holistically from a bio-psycho-social-spiritual perspective;
3. Ability to integrate spirituality into psychotherapy in an ethically appropriate manner;
4. Ability to conduct spiritual assessment;
5. Ability to help clients leverage healthy spiritual resources;
6. Ability to use a variety of spiritual interventions;
7. Ability to help clients engage with spiritual struggles;
8. Ability to address harmful spirituality and religion in the context of psychotherapy;
9. Ability to articulate how their personal spirituality is a resource in understanding clients, themselves, and the therapeutic process;
10. Ability to be aware of and make therapeutic use of spiritual countertransference.

For the final presentation, the therapist must prepare a four-page case presentation using the ACPE SIP case consultation template (ACPE, 2024, p. 286) as well as a 600-word personal statement that includes the context in which the therapist practices, the most important knowledge that they have gained from the SIP training, and an assessment of their strengths and "growing edges" in the practice of SIP (p. 11).

After completing the SIP certificate program, SIP therapists must renew their certification every 3 years by fulfilling continuing education (CE) requirements and joining and participating in a community of practice. A community of practice consists of a group of certified SIP therapists and trainees who meet online or in person to discuss their SIP cases. These groups would be known in non-ACPE contexts as peer-group supervision. In a 3-year span, the SIP therapist must attend a community of practice for 9 hours and must complete 9 hours of CE, which can include both ACPE-sponsored and ACPE-approved webinars and workshops. ACPE membership (required for certification) costs $100 per year. Each SIP module costs $400, and the 20 hours of SIP consultation cost me $1,885 (although SIP trainers' fees slightly vary). Thus, the total cost of my SIP training experience was $2,785. Considering the 50 hours of investment, significant sticker price, and relative lack of meaning that this certificate has in the psychotherapy marketplace, the therapist must really want this training to learn how to work with patients' spirituality in psychotherapy.

Conclusions

SIP is a model of spiritual intervention ideally suited for persons experiencing both psychological and spiritual struggles that require the knowledge, skill, and experience of a licensed mental health professional certified in SIP. Unlike Stephen Ministry, SIP is sufficiently versatile to work with persons from a variety of faith traditions, including persons with no faith. As Pargament and Exline (2022, p. 15) point out, even atheists can experience spiritual struggles and seek help for resolving these struggles. The case illustration of Blair presented at the beginning of this chapter demonstrates an atheist's need to explore their spirituality. The case illustration of Florence also demonstrates how SIP can highlight a nonspiritual person's lack of purpose and offer a search for purpose. SIP can become a sandbox of spiritual play, where patients feel comfortable exploring their implicit or explicit spirituality and experience the therapist's acceptance, regardless of what they discover about themselves—even if what they discover is no God at all.

Basic Therapist Stance Toward Spiritually Integrated Psychotherapy

A therapist seeking to help a spiritually curious patient to establish a secure attachment relationship to a Higher Power and simultaneously to experience emotional and spiritual well-being must practice grace, deep acceptance, and reassuring presence during their sessions. Regardless of their spirituality, the therapist must first cultivate a spiritual curiosity, not only about the patient's spiritual beliefs, practices, and relationship to a Higher Power but also about the language that the patient uses to describe their spiritual experiences. The therapist must develop a conversational familiarity with this spiritual language, just as a person who takes a Portuguese course might immerse themselves in the culture and street life of São Paulo to develop a conversational familiarity with Portuguese. The patient observes the therapist's empathic effort and gradually trusts the therapist enough to open up about their authentic spirituality.

Second, the therapist must evaluate the patient's spirituality to determine whether it is benefiting or harming the patient. A stage actress who prays to her Higher Power before the curtain goes up to calm her nerves is benefiting from her spirituality, while a woman who refuses to allow her daughter to receive a smallpox vaccination because it is against God's will is not benefiting from her spirituality but, instead, is placing her daughter's life at risk. In this chapter, I place such moral dilemmas in the context of the attachment relationship to a Higher Power. What do a patient's spiritual practices say about the quality of their attachment relationships to the caregivers during childhood and to a

Higher Power? How can the therapist help the patient to improve the quality of these attachment relationships? I am suggesting that these moral dilemmas work themselves out when a secure attachment relationship to a Higher Power is gradually restored.

Finally, therapists must turn on their "spiritual radars" (Pargament, 2011, p. 217). Whenever a patient begins to discuss any topic of ultimate importance, conveying a profound sense of transcendence, boundlessness, or the eternal, then the therapist's spiritual radar should be beeping, signaling that spirituality has entered the therapeutic relationship. The question is whether the therapist will capitalize on these opportunities to discuss the patient's spirituality. In my professional career, I have wasted many opportunities to notice spirituality with my patients. Like an old-fashioned merry-go-round, however, if I miss the brass ring, another one will always be waiting for me the next time around. In psychotherapy, chances to notice spirituality abound.

Both this chapter and Chapter 8 focus on the therapeutic techniques that help patients improve the quality of their attachment relationships to the caregivers during childhood as well as to a Higher Power. I argue that these relationships are intertwined such that working through attachment relationships to the caregivers during childhood influences the attachment relationship to the sacred and vice versa. The quality of the patient's attachment relationships has everything to do with the quality of their emotional and spiritual well-being. Therapists expand their arsenal of therapeutic techniques to use with their spiritually curious and spiritually grounded patients in AIP. The therapeutic goal is to help patients to "develop images of God that accentuate the loving generosity of a personal God who not only gifts us with life but is intimately present as a support for the development of that life" (Au & Au, 2006, p. 127). For healing to occur, the patient must become aware of their spiritual and attachment needs and then develop the vulnerability to risk meeting these needs. The therapeutic relationship becomes the fulcrum of this change.

How do I define my own basic therapist stance toward SIP? In my psychotherapy sessions, I offer empathy, patience, self-awareness, understanding, insight, acceptance, compassion, relationship, and a secure base and safe haven to persons suffering from burdens too heavy to carry alone (Galatians 6:2, NIV). I compare myself to a container into which my patients pour their unbearable feelings. My task is to detoxify these feelings and make them easier to understand and tolerate. I help my patients to use healthy relationships to others, including their Higher Power, to meet their emotional and spiritual needs and the emotional and spiritual needs of others. This work includes identifying the ways in which my patients have created God in their parents' image (see Chapter 8). I aspire to treat my patients as if they were Jesus in disguise (Matthew 25:35–40, NIV). I want to be the face of Jesus to my patients.

What Have I Learned in My Spiritually Integrated Psychotherapy Certificate Program?

Having just completed my SIP certificate program at ACPE, I can share what I learned through this experience. First, I learned that God's Spirit resides in everyone, and, therefore, everyone brings the Spirit into their psychotherapy sessions—even the atheist. I would define the Spirit as the manifestation of God in all persons as beings created in God's image (Genesis 1:27, NIV). An innate spirituality is present in all human beings and is not just a curiously quirky evolutionary by-product (Goodman, 2025b). According to contemplative writer Beverly Lanzetta (2019), "'The spirit' is intrinsic to all people and all human endeavors. ... Creation is not alone, separate from its source, but deeply and mysteriously imbued with spirit in every aspect of mind, soul, and matter" (pp. 2, 7).

Second, I learned that this Spirit is always flowing through both the SIP therapist and the patient, regardless of any religious or spiritual beliefs or nonbelief consciously held by either one. The SIP therapist can access this spiritual energy through a heightened self- and other-awareness and love that transcend words, venturing into the realm of intuition and spirituality. The SIP therapist is like a jazz musician, improvising their solos to express their moment-to-moment feelings in the context of the other band members. The jazz musician goes wherever the Spirit leads them. In a recent interview, jazz singer Dianne Reeves explained:

> Jazz, specifically for me, is a very spiritual music because it's beyond the page. It's this intimate exchange of ideas that is a language without words, that you can feel, that you can speak through an instrument, that you can share. And it becomes a spirit-to-spirit, soul-to-soul experience with your audience. It's because of these things that I know there's something greater than I am. (Thomas, 2024, April 29)

The SIP therapist channels this spiritual energy into plumbing the depths of the patient's—and their own—soul to discover modes of relatedness unknown to both participants. This is what it means to be a SIP therapist.

Third, I learned that the SIP therapist has broad latitude to intervene in the moment-to-moment interactions with the patient. The SIP therapist must follow their spiritual intuition in both listening and responding to the patient's verbal and nonverbal communications, especially their emotional expressions. Just as a jazz musician follows wherever the Spirit leads them, so too does the SIP therapist rely on their spiritual intuition to intervene based on the moment-to-moment feelings experienced by the patient. The prophet Elijah waited to hear God's "gentle whisper" (I Kings 19:12, NIV). Did the whisper come from without or within? No one knows. Regardless of the location, the SIP therapist follows this gentle whisper—their spiritual intuition—in response to the patient's emotional expressions.

Finally, I want to share a significant difference in clinical technique between how I practice SIP and how I was taught to practice SIP. It involves the role of questioning the patient. In my SIP certification program, there was tremendous emphasis on not assuming that the SIP therapist knows what the patient means when they discuss spiritual concepts. Words and phrases such as God, slain in the Spirit, sin, covenant, heaven, hell, the devil, washed in the blood of the lamb, and redeemed can have different meanings to different patients, and so it is important to elicit the patient's idiosyncratic meanings of these words and phrases as they emerge in the treatment. The thinking goes that the patient will experience a deep feeling of having been understood when the SIP therapist makes the effort to understand the patient's meaning of these words. As discussed in this chapter, empathy is a healing agent in SIP. I once treated a rabbi, and, in one of our sessions, he used the word "mikvah." I had no idea what "mikvah" meant, so I asked. Understanding the meaning of the word eventually helped me to understand the nature of his marital conflict.

Questioning, however, is a double-edged sword. Who assumes control of both the content and the flow of the session when the SIP therapist peppers the patient with questions? Would a patient leave such a session feeling understood if they never received the opportunity to set the session agenda? Might the SIP therapist be forfeiting the opportunity to hear what the patient really wants to talk about in the session by adopting a basic therapist stance of questioning? Renowned child-centered play therapist Garry Landreth (2012) also urges against a questioning stance when working with children. He writes, "Questions keep the therapist in the lead. The child-centered play therapist allows the child to lead the experience and the relationship to where the child needs to be and therefore avoids questions" (p. 181). Questioning keeps the SIP therapist in charge.

There is another approach that I often use in SIP sessions. I limit questioning and instead use interpretations—statements that provide meaning to the patient's experience. Am I always right? Of course not! But the patient can then correct me when I am wrong, and I can then rephrase my interpretation. In my psychoanalytic training, one of my supervisors, Bill Greenstadt, compared this process to an archer using a quiver of arrows to hit the bullseye. The archer aims at the bullseye, and, instead of hitting the mark, the arrow hits one of the outer circles on the target. The patient then takes this arrow and moves it closer to the bullseye. The archer then shoots another arrow, but this one hits closer—just outside the bullseye, and so on. Through this iterative process, the SIP therapist and patient are collaborating on a mutual understanding of the patient's psychological and spiritual struggles. This approach strengthens the therapeutic alliance and, I believe, the overall empathic connection with the patient. I prefer this approach to the questioning approach taught in my SIP certification program. In this interpretive or hermeneutic approach, championed by pastoral counseling theologian Charles Gerkin (1984), the patient always remains in control of the content and the flow of the session. When a session using this approach is moving along smoothly, these interpretive statements facilitate spontaneous material from the patient that the SIP therapist and patient can explore together. The reader should try out both approaches and determine which one works better for which patients.

SIP is a therapeutic attitude that consists of attending to the patient's psychological and spiritual strivings and struggles. The SIP therapist must then form hypotheses about how these struggles interact with each other. Blair could not find joy in his life, which made him susceptible to sex addiction and depressive symptoms. Florence could not find purpose in her life, which made her susceptible to anxiety. The SIP therapist maintains awareness of both sets of problems and addresses them when the time is right for the patient. A genuine connection to the sacred is the treatment goal of SIP. This connection might not include an attachment relationship to God. In the next chapter, I discuss AIP, a specific SIP treatment model designed for patients who experience psychological and spiritual struggles in their attachment relationship to a Higher Power.

References

ACPE. (2024). *ACPE Spiritually Integrated Psychotherapy (SIP) program participant manual*. Unpublished manuscript. ACPE: The Standard for Spiritual Care.

Ainsworth, M. D. S., Blehar, M. C., Waters, E., & Wall, S. (1978). *Patterns of attachment: A psychological study of the strange situation*. Erlbaum.

Alexander, F., & French, T. M. (1946). *Psychoanalytic therapy: Principles and application*. Ronald.

American Psychiatric Association. (2022). *Diagnostic and statistical manual of mental disorders* (5th ed., text rev.). Author.

Anderson, N., Heywood-Everett, S., Siddiqi, N., Wright, J., Meredith, J., & McMillan, D. (2015). Faith-adapted psychological therapies for depression and anxiety: Systematic review and meta-analysis. *Journal of Affective Disorders, 176*, 183–196.

Au, W., & Au, N. C. (2006). *The discerning heart: Exploring the Christian path*. Paulist Press.

Barrett, J. L. (2012). *Born believers: The science of children's religious belief*. Free Press.

Blatt, S. J., & Felsen, I. (1993). Different kinds of folks may need different kinds of strokes: The effect of patients' characteristics on therapeutic process and outcome. *Psychotherapy Research, 3*, 245–259.

Bouwhuis-Van Keulen, A. J., Koelen, J., Eurelings-Bontekoe, L., Hoekstra-Oomen, C., & Glas, G. (2024). The evaluation of religious and spirituality-based therapy compared to standard treatment in mental health care: A multi-level meta-analysis of randomized controlled trials. *Psychotherapy Research, 34*, 339–352.

Bowlby, J. (1988). *A secure base: Parent–child attachment and healthy human development*. Basic Books.

Bradley, D. F., Exline, J. J., & Uzdavines, A. (2015). The god of nonbelievers: Characteristics of a hypothetical god. *Science, Religion and Culture, 2*(3), 120–130.

Bradley, D. F., Exline, J. J., & Uzdavines, A. (2017). Relational reasons for nonbelief in the existence of gods: An important adjunct to intellectual nonbelief. *Psychology of Religion and Spirituality, 9*(4), 319–327.

Bryant, A. N., & Astin, H. S. (2008). The correlates of spiritual struggle during the college years. *Journal of Higher Education, 79*, 1–27.

Captari, L. E., Hook, J. N., Hoyt, W., Davis, D. E., McElroy-Heltzel, S. E., & Worthington, E. L., Jr. (2018). Integrating clients' religion and spirituality within psychotherapy: A comprehensive meta-analysis. *Journal of Clinical Psychology, 74*, 1938–1951.

Cohen, J. (1992). A power primer. *Psychological Bulletin, 112*, 155–159.
Cole, B. S., & Pargament, K. I. (1998). Re-creating your life: A spiritual/psychotherapeutic intervention for people diagnosed with cancer. *Psycho-Oncology, 8*, 395–407.
Exline, J. J. (2013). Religious and spiritual struggles. In K. I. Pargament, J. J. Exline, & J. W. Jones (Eds.), *APA handbook of psychology, religion, and spirituality (Vol. 1): Context, theory, and research* (pp. 459–476). American Psychological Association.
Exline, J. J., Park, C. L., Smyth, J. M., & Carey, M. P. (2011). Anger toward God: Social-cognitive predictors, prevalence, and links with adjustment to bereavement and cancer. *Journal of Personality and Social Psychology, 100*(1), 129–148.
Freud, S. (1927). The future of an illusion. In J. Strachey (Ed. and Trans.), *The standard edition of the complete psychological works of Sigmund Freud* (Vol. 21, pp. 1–56). Hogarth Press.
Gerkin, C. V. (1984). *The living human document: Re-visioning pastoral counseling in a hermeneutical mode.* Abingdon Press.
Gonçalves, J. P. B., Lucchetti, G., Menezes, P. R., & Vallada, H. (2015). Religious and spiritual interventions in mental health care: A systematic review and meta-analysis of randomized controlled clinical trials. *Psychological Medicine, 45*, 2937–2949.
Goodman, G. (2013). Is mentalization a common process factor in transference-focused psychotherapy and dialectical behavior therapy sessions? *Journal of Psychotherapy Integration, 23*, 179–192.
Goodman, G. (2025a). *Practical applications of transforming the attachment relationship to God: Using attachment-informed psychotherapy.* Routledge.
Goodman, G. (2025b). *Using psychoanalytic techniques to transform the attachment relationship to God: Our refuge and strength.* Routledge.
Goodman, G. (2025c). A yogi in attachment-informed psychotherapy: A spiritually informed case conceptualization. *Pastoral Psychology, 74*, 263–278.
Granqvist, P. (2020). *Attachment in religion and spirituality: A wider view.* Guilford Press.
Granqvist, P., & Kirkpatrick, L. A. (2018). Attachment and religious representations and behavior. In J. Cassidy & P. R. Shaver (Eds.), *Handbook of attachment: Theory, research, and clinical applications* (pp. 917–940). Guilford Press.
Grice, H. P. (1989). *Studies in the way of words.* Harvard University Press.
Griffith, J. L. (2010). *Religion that heals, religion that harms: A guide for clinical practice.* Guilford Press.
Hawkins, I. L., & Bullock, S. L. (1995). Informed consent and religious values: A neglected area of diversity. *Psychotherapy, 32*, 293–300.
Hesse, E. (2018). The Adult Attachment Interview: Protocol, method of analysis, and selected empirical studies: 1985–2015. In J. Cassidy & P. R. Shaver (Eds.), *Handbook of attachment: Theory, research, and clinical applications* (pp. 553–597). Guilford Press.
Ingraham, C. L. (2003). Multicultural consultee-centered consultation: When novice consultants explore cultural hypotheses with experienced teacher consultees. *Journal of Educational and Psychological Consultation, 14*, 329–362.
Johnson, C. V., & Hayes, J. A. (2003). Troubled spirits: Prevalence and predictors of religious and spiritual concerns among university students and counseling center clients. *Journal of Counseling Psychology, 50*(4), 409–419.
Jones, R. S. (2019). *Spirit in session: Working with your client's spirituality (and your own) in psychotherapy.* Templeton Press.
Kraus, S. W., Krueger, R. B., Briken, P., First, M. B., Stein, D. J., Kaplan, M. S., Voon, V., Abdo, C. H. N., Grant, J. E., Atalla, E., & Reed, G. M. (2018). Compulsive sexual behaviour disorder in the ICD-11. *World Psychiatry, 17*(1), 109–110.
Landreth, G. L. (2012). *Play therapy: The art of the relationship* (3rd ed.). Routledge.
Lanzetta, B. (2019). *Foundations in spiritual direction: Sharing the sacred across traditions.* Blue Sapphire Books.

Lewis, C. S. (1955). *Surprised by joy: The shape of my early life.* Harcourt Brace Jovanovich.

Lichtenberg, J. D. (1989). *Psychoanalysis and motivation.* Analytic Press.

Main, M., & Solomon, J. (1986). Discovery of an insecure-disorganized/disoriented attachment pattern. In T. B. Brazelton & M. W. Yogman (Eds.), *Affective development in infancy* (pp. 95–124). Ablex.

Main, M., & Solomon, J. (1990). Procedures for identifying infants as disorganized/disoriented during the Ainsworth Strange Situation. In M. T. Greenberg, D. Cicchetti, & E. M. Cummings (Eds.), *Attachment in the preschool years: Theory, research, and intervention* (pp. 121–160). University of Chicago Press.

Mesman, J., van IJzendoorn, M. H., & Sagi-Schwartz, A. (2018). Cross-cultural patterns of attachment: Universal and contextual dimensions. In J. Cassidy & P. R. Shaver (Eds.), *Handbook of attachment: Theory, research, and clinical applications* (pp. 852–877). Guilford Press.

Mikulincer, M. (2019). An attachment perspective on managing death concerns. In C. Routledge & M. Vess (Eds.), *Handbook of terror management theory* (pp. 243–257). Elsevier Academic Press.

Murphy, P. E., Fitchett, G., & Emery-Tiburcio, E. E. (2016). Religious and spiritual struggle: Prevalence and correlates among older adults with depression in the BRIGHTEN program. *Mental Health, Religion and Culture, 19*(7), 713–721.

Murray-Swank, N. A., & Pargament, K. I. (2005). God, where are you? Evaluating a spiritually-integrated intervention for sexual abuse. *Mental Health, Religion, and Culture, 8*, 191–204.

Neimeyer, R. A., & Burke, L. A. (2011). Complicated grief in the aftermath of homicide: Spiritual crisis and distress in an African American sample. *Religions, 2*, 145–164.

Neufeldt, S. A., Pinterits, E. J., Moleiro, C. M., Lee, T. E., Yang, P. H., Brodie, R. E., & Orliss, M. J. (2006). How do graduate student therapists incorporate diversity factors in case conceptualization? *Psychotherapy: Theory, Research, Practice, Training, 43*, 464–479.

New International Version. (1978). *The Holy Bible, new international version.* Zondervan.

Pargament, K. I. (1999). The psychology of religion and spirituality? Yes and no. *International Journal for the Psychology of Religion, 9*, 3–16.

Pargament, K. I. (2011). *Spiritually integrated psychotherapy: Understanding and addressing the sacred* (paperback ed.). Guilford Press.

Pargament, K. I., & Exline, J. J. (2022). *Working with spiritual struggles in psychotherapy: From research to practice.* Guilford Press.

Pargament, K. I., Murray-Swank, N. A., Magyar, G. M., & Ano, G. G. (2005). Spiritual struggle: A phenomenon of interest to psychology and religion. In W. R. Miller & H. D. Delaney (Eds.), *Judeo-Christian perspectives on psychology: Human nature, motivation, and change* (pp. 245–268). American Psychological Association Press.

Park, C. L., Holt, C. L., Le, D., Christie, J., & Williams, B. R. (2018). Positive and negative religious coping styles as prospective predictors of well-being in African Americans. *Psychology of Religion and Spirituality, 10*, 318–326.

Pattison, E. M. (1982). Management of religious issues in family therapy. *International Journal of Family Therapy, 4*, 140–163.

Propst, L. R., Ostrom, R., Watkins, P., Dean, T., & Mashburn, D. (1992). Comparative efficacy of religious and nonreligious-behavioral therapy for the treatment of clinical depression in religious individuals. *Journal of Consulting and Clinical Psychology, 60*, 94–103.

Reynolds, N., Mrug, S., Hensler, M., Guion, K., & Madan-Swain, A. (2014). Spiritual coping and adjustment in adolescents with chronic illness: A two-year prospective study. *Journal of Pediatric Psychology, 39*, 542–551.

Rizzuto, A.-M. (1979). *The birth of the living God: A psychoanalytic study*. Chicago: University of Chicago Press.
Rogers, C. R. (1957). The necessary and sufficient conditions of therapeutic personality change. *Journal of Consulting Psychology, 21*, 95–103.
Roisman, G. I., Holland, A., Fortuna, K., Fraley, R. C., Clausell, E., & Clarke, A. (2007). The Adult Attachment Interview and self-reports of attachment style: An empirical rapprochement. *Journal of Personality and Social Psychology, 92*, 678–697.
Rosmarin, D. H., Malloy, M. C., & Forester, B. P. (2014). Spiritual struggle and affective symptoms among geriatric mood disordered patients. *International Journal of Geriatric Psychiatry, 29*(6), 653–660.
Sedlar, A. E., Stauner, N., Pargament, K. I., Exline, J. J., Grubbs, J. B., & Bradley, D. F. (2018). Spiritual struggles among atheists: Links to psychological distress and well-being. *Religions, 9*(8), 242.
Skinner, B. F. (1976). *Particulars of my life*. Knopf.
Slade, A. (1999). Attachment theory and research: Implications for the theory and practice of individual psychotherapy with adults. In J. Cassidy & P. R. Shaver (Eds.), *Handbook of attachment: Theory, research, and clinical applications* (pp. 575–594). Guilford Press.
Slade, A. (2018). Attachment and adult psychotherapy: Theory, research, and practice. In J. Cassidy & P. R. Shaver (Eds.), *Handbook of attachment: Theory, research, and clinical applications* (pp. 759–779). Guilford Press.
Smith, T. B., Bartz, J., & Richards, P. S. (2007). Outcomes of religious and spiritual adaptations to psychotherapy: A meta-analytic review. *Psychotherapy Research, 17*, 643–655.
Snodgrass, J. L. (2019). The future of spiritually integrated psychotherapy in the AAPC tradition. *Journal of Pastoral Care & Counseling, 73*, 153–156.
Stovall-McClough, K. C., & Dozier, M. (2018). Attachment states of mind and psychopathology in adulthood. In J. Cassidy & P. R. Shaver (Eds.), *Handbook of attachment: Theory, research, and clinical applications* (pp. 715–738). Guilford Press.
Sue, S. (1998). In search of cultural competence in psychotherapy and counseling. *American Psychologist, 53*, 440–448.
Thomas, M. (2024, April 29). *Dianne Reeves lauds the spiritual power of jazz that goes "beyond the page."* Chicago Symphony Orchestra Experience webpage. Retrieved on May 17, 2024. https://cso.org/experience/article/9432/dianne-reeves-lauds-the-spiritual-power-of-ja
Tisdale, T. C., Keys, T. L., Edwards, K. J., Brokaw, B. F., Kemperman, S. R., Cloud, H., Townsend, J., & Okamoto, T. (1997). Impact of treatment on God image and personal adjustment, and correlations of God image to personal adjustment and object relations adjustment. *Journal of Psychology and Theology, 25*, 227–239.
Townsend, L. (2015). Pastoral counseling's history. In E. A. Maynard & J. L. Snodgrass (Eds.), *Understanding pastoral counseling* (pp. 17–37). Springer.
Ulanov, A. B. (2001). *Finding space: Winnicott, God, and psychic reality*. Westminster John Knox Press.
Walker, A. (1982). *The color purple*. Harcourt Brace Jovanovich.
Waters, E., Merrick, S., Treboux, D., Crowell, J., & Albersheim, L. (2000). Attachment security in infancy and early adulthood: A twenty-year longitudinal study. *Child Development, 71*, 684–689.
Watson, J. B. (1936). John Broadus Watson [autobiography]. In C. Murchison (Ed.), *A history of psychology in autobiography* (Vol. 3, pp. 271–281). Clark University Press.
World Health Organization. (2020). *International classification of diseases for mortality and morbidity statistics* (11th rev.). Retrieved from https://icd.who.int/browse11/l-m/en

Chapter 8

Attachment-Informed Psychotherapy

Transforming Attachment Relationships to a Higher Power and to Parents

The following treatment presents me with an ideal opportunity to demonstrate how to use Attachment-Informed Psychotherapy (AIP) to work with a patient who manifests a distressing somatic symptom with a clearly discernible spiritual component. I trace the layers of this man's spirituality from early childhood through adolescence to middle adulthood and demonstrate how each layer might play a role in this symptom. Because this treatment is ongoing, not all the perplexities posed by this symptom, nor the other symptoms experienced by this patient, have been resolved. Perhaps they never will be resolved. This case illustration raises the question: how does a spiritually informed therapist practicing AIP leverage this dimension of experience to facilitate the spiritual journey of a man whose complex spirituality is literally screaming to be understood? I attempt to answer this question in this brief case conceptualization.

Séamus

Presenting Issues and Diagnosis

Séamus (a pseudonym) is a 38-year-old college graduate of Irish American descent. Séamus was raised in an intact, two-parent household in a middle-income suburb of New York City. He has a brother born 2 years earlier. Séamus identifies as cisgender and heterosexual. Currently, he works as a finance executive at an upscale clothing company in Manhattan and, in his spare time, as a bartender in his Brooklyn neighborhood. He used to have his own yoga studio but gave that up at the beginning of the pandemic. He still practices yoga, however.

Séamus's chief complaint was that there was an energy located in his pelvis that shouts, "I'm gay!" He first experienced this sensation in early 2020 as a yoga instructor during a session. Séamus had asked the students, "What is your deepest desire?" and, at that moment, he experienced a sensation in his "Sacral Chakra" (pelvic region) accompanied by the words, "To be gay." Séamus reported that he experiences this sensation nearly every day, which causes him both anxiety and depression. Previous therapy was not effective in treating this symptom. On one of his psychedelic trips prior to beginning treatment with me, he developed the belief that a male authority figure from his childhood had sexually abused him. Séamus expressed anger toward his father for not protecting him from this alleged abuse. Based on his reading of psychological literature and previous therapy experience, he formulated a tentative hypothesis that his symptom—"I'm gay!"—has something to do with this alleged childhood sexual abuse. Séamus has always maintained that this somatic experience, coupled with the thought "I'm gay!" is intensely uncomfortable. I quickly determined that Séamus had not had a psychotic break. He was oriented to time, person, and place, seemed to have good judgment, and was a reliable reporter of his experience. He denied suicidal and homicidal ideas or intentions as well as delusions and hallucinations. He seemed highly motivated for treatment because he wanted to "release this energy inside me" (session notes, December 1, 2023).

Based on the persistence of his somatic symptom that causes him significant pain, I believe that he warrants a diagnosis of somatic symptom disorder, moderate (SSD; code 300.82; American Psychiatric Association, 2022). Interestingly, risk factors associated with SSD include "a reported history of sexual abuse or other childhood adversity" (American Psychiatric Association, 2022, p. 313).

Session Excerpt (February 29, 2024)

I have italicized the sentences that reflect Séamus's possible references to his transference (i.e., feelings about childhood attachment figures transferred onto the therapist).

Séamus: I planned to travel to Florida for a shuffleboard tournament, but I changed my mind when I learned that some of my friends had backed out of the tournament. I feel like I'm losing interest in this activity and maybe also in this group of friends.
Me: Mm hm.
Séamus: I talked to my dad recently. I feel like I'm beginning to understand him better. *I really think he's doing his best.* I didn't tell you—I went on a psilocybin trip last month, and all this anger and sadness came up. It's blocking my kundalini energy from bursting forth. My dad restricted my expression of kundalini energy—I couldn't be joyful, flamboyant, and free.
Me: It would be really challenging for you to forgive your father because that would make you feel vulnerable to more rejection and shame from him.
Séamus: That's right. I'm remembering an incident a couple of years ago with him. I had a great conversation with him about all the pain I was going through and specifically how his lack of emotional connectivity as a parent, and the way he yelled at me sometimes as a kid, is part of the healing process I'm going through now. We had a pretty good conversation, and it felt like he was actually starting to accept the fact

and show some remorse. Then as I left to drive home, he made a joke about me being a couple of pounds overweight. Like, "So are you gonna hit the gym when you get back and shed a few pounds?" And then I think he even said, "Just kidding." I think it was his unconscious way of trying to dig at me a little bit after I had yelled at him and called him out for a couple of hours in our conversation that day. And also weirdly his way of trying to connect in some way to show he cares about me and my health, but he doesn't know how to do that in an emotionally mature way. What enraged me when he made his comment was like, "You're part of the reason I'm going through this pain, and you don't even get it, and then you have the nerve to say something like that to me after I've come up here and bared my soul to you." So that's what pissed me off.

Me: And forgiving him might make you vulnerable to another attack.
Séamus: Right.
Me: On the one hand, you want to understand your dad, but on the other hand, you still feel enraged and needing to protect yourself from being hurt by your dad again.
Séamus: I do feel like I understand my dad better, but the pain of his controlling behavior is still with me. *It isn't going away.*
Me: You needed to hide your feminine, flamboyant self from your father to earn his love.
Séamus: I look at it a bit differently. I wasn't trying to earn my father's love so much as trying to avoid his shaming and yelling.
Me: You had to hide that part of yourself—your true self—and now, it's leaking out in this thought-energy that "I'm gay!"
Séamus: Yes, and not only the feminine energy. The masculine energy is also coming to the surface—I've noticed that I'm being more assertive at work now.
Me: Your father restricted both masculine and feminine energy—two important parts of yourself—that you're now trying to release and assimilate into a broader sense of yourself.
Séamus: Right.
Me: I wonder how all this ties in to your connection to God.
Séamus: I grew up learning about a male God that I never believed in. Growing up, my understanding was that God was this omnipotent white male figure that had a bunch of rules, and we were kinda in trouble if we didn't follow them. Since starting yoga in 2014, though, I've come to believe in a God that can be feminine and even gender-neutral.
Me: I can imagine it might feel difficult to have a relationship with a masculine God, given that all you know about male authority figures is through your relationship to your father.

Séamus:	Yeah, it's hard to conceptualize an all-loving God when my own father has been so controlling and shaming. *I want to continue working toward releasing this energy, which feels stuck in my chest, neck, and jaw area.*
Me:	You're in pain. Let's keep working on it.
Séamus:	Okay.

Session Excerpt Commentary on Psychotherapy Process

Near the beginning of this session excerpt, Séamus tells me about a recent conversation with his father, after which he provides an assessment of his father: "I really think he's doing his best." At that moment, I had not considered this comment as transference material but, while writing my session notes, I recognized this possible reference. Does he think that I am a well-meaning, fatherly psychologist who is doing his best but who nevertheless is not helping him? Later in this excerpt, there is tentative evidence for the conjecture that he does not feel helped by me. First, he lets me know that the pain of his father's controlling behavior "isn't going away." He could be saying, "Aren't you supposed to be relieving me of this suffering at the hands of my father, or are you just another ineffectual old man?" Later, Séamus returns to his chief complaint—his somatic symptom: "I want to continue working toward releasing this energy, which feels stuck in my chest, neck, and jaw area." He reminds me of his somatic suffering in nearly every session. Again, he could be saying, "Aren't you supposed to be relieving me of this suffering in my own body?" Unconsciously, Séamus might be viewing father = therapist = God: an unholy symbolic equation of ineffectual old men who cannot or will not help him to stop suffering. I have not yet made these potential connections with him in our work together.

I do not sense a strong influence of my countertransference (i.e., therapist's peculiar emotional reactions to the patient) in this session, but I want to comment on what might be faint traces of them in a couple of my interventions. First, early in this excerpt, I point out that "it would be really challenging for you to forgive your father." The idea of forgiveness is coming from me, not him. He might not be considering forgiveness; moreover, he might never want to forgive his father. My motives for bringing it up are twofold: (1) I know that forgiveness will most likely lead him to let go of his anger toward his father and thus bring him relief and (2) I feel helpless and want to accelerate the process to alleviate this feeling in myself as quickly as possible. The latter motive directly relates to my countertransference feeling, which might have stimulated this intervention. Second, near the end of this session excerpt, I interpret his difficulty in having a relationship with a masculine God as having to do with his difficult relationship with his father. One possible implication of this interpretation is that a resolution of Séamus's difficult relationship with his father might occasion a restoration of Séamus's nonexistent relationship with a masculine God. I need to be aware of my own belief in a personified God and not allow this belief to influence my interventions with Séamus.

Despite a possible transference–countertransference matrix of helpless boy–ineffectual father figure observed in the psychotherapy process, I believe that I have successfully contained his anxiety and rage and have, at times, deactivated his attachment system when it was hyperactivated. I also believe that he is aware of my role in this deactivating process. In a future session, I could ask him how he feels about the effectiveness of our work together and his perceptions of me as his therapist. I could interpret the potential parallels among his relationships to his father, to God, and to me and see where that interpretation might lead us. The therapeutic goal would be to make Séamus aware of the possibility that remaining in a helpless (angrily preoccupied) state of mind protects him from becoming an intentional agent whose actions on his own behalf—including the action of forgiveness—might make him "vulnerable to another attack" or at least expose him to "more rejection and shame." Reviewing this chapter, Séamus highlighted his fear of rejection and shame, "and because of that I've been wearing all these masks to fit it. And the 'true self'… is screaming to be heard and seen" (Séamus, personal communication, April 10, 2024).

I am gradually helping Séamus to develop a new, secure attachment relationship by remaining committed to this process and by allowing him to share any anger that he might feel toward me for not helping him yet—in the ways that he wants to be helped. This permission that I am giving him to express himself without restrictions sharply contrasts with his father's attitude of toxic masculinity, which has often led him to deflect and deny Séamus's feelings, especially his negative feelings, when confronted. Having also had a father who sometimes yelled at me and a mother who mostly observed and seldom intervened, I believe that I understand Séamus's resentment and tendency not to trust the effectuality of others. I have faith that he will work through his feelings and develop a deeper connection to God, however he understands God. Wallin (2007) writes that enactments—transference–countertransference matrices—are inevitable. How can I use my awareness of our enactment to bring spiritual and emotional healing to this man?

Caregiver–Infant Attachment Relationship as Metaphor for Therapist–Patient Relationship

British psychoanalyst John Bowlby (1977b, 1988) argues that the primary purpose of the therapist is to provide the patient with a secure base from which they can explore themselves and their relationships to others. In attachment theory, the secure base in the person of the caregiver provides protection for the infant as they explore the environment. The caregiver's safe haven, a complementary concept, offers comfort when internal or external threats to homeostasis cause the infant to become distressed. Concepts similar to the secure base as identified by other writers include conditions of safety (Weiss & Sampson, 1986), atmosphere of safety (Schafer, 1983), and background of safety (Sandler, 1960). The therapeutic relationship proceeds when the patient uses the therapist to explore themselves and their relationships and for comfort when confronted by distressing internal and external threats.

Attachment theory and research have spawned the application of still other facets of the caregiver–infant attachment relationship to the therapist–patient relationship (Amini et al., 1996; Diamond et al., 1999; Diamond, Clarkin, et al., 2003; Diamond, Stovall-McClough, et al., 2003; Farber et al., 1995; Holmes, 1996, 1998; Lyons & Sperling, 1996; Mackie, 1981; Mallinckrodt, 2000; Mallinckrodt et al., 1995; Mallinckrodt et al., 1998; Mallinckrodt et al., 2005; Mitchell, 1999). Parish and Eagle (2003) identified seven facets in addition to secure base and safe haven: proximity-seeking, separation protest, stronger/wiser, availability, strong feelings, particularity, and mental representation.

Proximity-seeking refers to the infant's need to seek proximity to the caregiver for protection when faced with an internal or external danger (Bowlby, 1982). Parish and Eagle (2003) do not define what proximity-seeking looks like for the therapist–patient relationship; however, we might regard a patient's request for additional sessions after a therapist or patient vacation as an adult form of proximity-seeking.

Separation protest refers to the distress experienced by the infant when separated from the caregiver and the infant's protest about it (Bowlby, 1982). In the therapist–patient relationship, the patient might protest a therapist's upcoming vacation.

One of the ingredients of an attachment relationship, according to Bowlby (1977a), is that the infant perceives the caregiver as stronger and wiser than they are. Similarly, in the therapist–patient relationship, the patient perceives the therapist as having knowledge of the patient's problems and ways to resolve them that exceed the patient's own knowledge.

Availability refers to the caregiver's emotional and physical availability to meet the infant's attachment needs (Bowlby, 1982). The therapist also meets the patient's emotional needs through attentive listening, regularly scheduled appointments, interpretations that foster a sense of being understood, and many other manifestations of the therapist's availability unique to each therapist–patient dyad.

An infant also expresses strong feelings toward a caregiver (Bowlby, 1982). The infant is looking for the caregiver to facilitate the regulation of these strong feelings so that they can begin to tolerate them. The patient also looks to the therapist for assistance with strong feelings stimulated by the therapist–patient relationship. Freud (1915) describes the patient's strong feelings of romantic love for the therapist, although he does not view them as products of an attachment relationship.

Particularity refers to the child's preference for the primary caregiver over other persons, which begins practically at birth. Infants at 10 days have shown a preference to be fed by the primary caregiver rather than by a substitute (Burns et al., 1972). Patients demonstrate the same preference for their therapists. A therapist covering for a vacationing therapist meets with the vacationing therapist's patient only in an emergency. In other words, therapists are not interchangeable. For instance, after taking a hiatus from therapy for over a year, Séamus returned to therapy with me because he had developed a preference for me over a stranger/therapist.

Mental representation refers to the child's reliance on an internalized image of the caregiver for comfort or guidance in the caregiver's absence (Bowlby, 1973; Mahler et al., 1975). The patient also relies on this internalized image of the therapist in certain situations outside therapy. When one of my patients diagnosed with borderline personality disorder (BPD) gets an urge to drink alcohol, an image of me asking her what she is feeling at that moment comes into her mind. Mental representation resembles safe haven as an internalized image of comfort when internal or external threats arise.

Another clinical concept from the psychoanalytic literature thought to reflect facets of an attachment relationship between the therapist and patient is the "working alliance" (e.g., Greenson, 1965; Mackie, 1981). Freud (1912a) foreshadowed this concept in his discussion of the dynamics of transference. He defined three components of transference: a negative component, a positive component, and an "unobjectionable" component (p. 105). The first two components are unconscious and serve as resistances to the treatment, while the third component consists of friendly or affectionate feelings admissible to consciousness and serves the treatment as its "vehicle of success" (p. 105). The unobjectionable positive transference represents "a belief in the value of treatment, based on widely held views of analysis as a discipline and of the analyst as a professional practitioner [which] facilitates the work" (Greenberg, 2001, p. 367). Greenberg (2001) has questioned whether Freud's concept has stood the test of time and has argued that the contemporary patient enters treatment seeking a relationship rather than seeking someone who simply relieves symptoms.

Regardless of whether the patient is seeking a practitioner or a relationship, the concept seems to encompass a sense of trust in the benevolence of the therapist who "exhibits a serious interest" in and "sympathetic understanding" for the patient over time and establishes a "proper rapport" with them (Freud, 1913, pp. 139–140). Using Parish and Eagle's (2003) list of attachment concepts applicable to the therapist–patient relationship, strong feelings, stronger/wiser, secure base, and availability are either implicitly or explicitly present in Freud's original idea. Freud (1913) suggested that the patient's attachment to the therapist is a prerequisite for the emergence of the unconscious components of transference: "[The patient] will of himself form such an attachment and link the doctor up with one of the imagos of the people by whom he was accustomed to be treated with affection" (pp. 139–140). The link between the unobjectionable positive transference and the caregiver–infant attachment relationship is implied.

Freud's (1912a) original concept reemerged in the literature as "the therapeutic alliance" (Zetzel, 1956) and "the working alliance" (Greenson, 1965). These terms were defined as capturing elements of the real relationship to the therapist not distorted by transference. Horvath and Greenberg (1989) later sought to measure this working alliance by constructing the Working Alliance Inventory (WAI), which consists of three subscales—task, goal, and bond. "Task" refers to the level of agreement between the therapist and patient about what to do in sessions. "Goal" refers to the level of agreement about the desired outcome of treatment. "Bond" refers to the level of positive personal feelings between patient and therapist. The "bond" subscale most closely resembles Freud's (1912a) original definition of the unobjectionable positive transference.

Research has repeatedly identified the working alliance as highly predictive of successful treatment outcome (Bordin, 1994; Horvath & Symonds, 1991; Luborsky, 1994; Martin et al., 2000; Safran & Muran, 2000), and even teletherapy outcomes (although more modestly; see Aafjes-van Doorn et al., 2024). The concept of the working alliance has been associated with the concepts of secure attachment and transference because all three concepts seem to reflect similar mental representations, emotions, and strategies for emotion regulation activated by the relationship to the therapist and its correspondence with relationships to past caregivers (Bradley et al., 2005; Westen & Gabbard, 2002). Whether these concepts overlap conceptually or operate at different levels of abstraction is a matter of debate.

For example, in Séamus's treatment (which is ongoing), we have a good working alliance: we agree on his goals for treatment and the mutual task of his free association and my interpretation of his material. Séamus is also securely attached to me: he uses me as a safe haven when he feels confused about the identity of his alleged abuser and as a secure base from which to start his own wellness community center. Séamus's transference toward me, however, contains both positive and negative emotions. He views me as reliable and caring but perhaps somewhat ineffectual in my ability to help him. These emotional valences can vary across—or even within—sessions, whereas the working alliance and secure attachment to me are much more stable phenomena.

Limitations of the Caregiver–Infant Attachment Relationship Metaphor

Of course, every metaphor has a breaking point—a point at which the parameters no longer fit. Such is the case with the metaphor of the caregiver–infant attachment relationship. The therapist is not a caregiver per se, nor is the patient an infant. The therapist provides a service paid for by the patient, which takes place in a limited time. Ironically, these treatment arrangements both allow the metaphor to exist and immediately invalidate it. One of my patients diagnosed with BPD revealed a fantasy—concretely experienced by her as an expectation—that therapists should not charge for their services. In fact, she reminded me that therapists take a vow of poverty, like Mother Teresa, to conduct this work. I must have missed that ceremony in graduate school! By informing her that I would be raising my fee next year, I was invalidating this fantasy. She immediately reminded me that she had abruptly ended her previous treatment when she discovered that her previous therapist, who wanted to raise the patient's fee to $80 per session, drove a Mercedes-Benz. The fantasy of the all-nurturing, selfless caregiver conflicts with the reality of the professional aspects of the relationship. We continued working on this issue of my projected fee increase and its meanings for her for many sessions.

The therapeutic relationship is unique because of financial, temporal, spatial, logistic, and ethical boundaries—boundaries that do not exist in the caregiver–infant relationship (Farber et al., 1995; Goodman, 2006). We can imagine an Orwellian world in which the mother says to the infant, "Time's up! You've had your fill of milk for the day." Or, "Stop being a baby and get off my lap!" Or, "You can't sleep in my bed; you'll get too used to that!" Anyone familiar with ferberization techniques (Ferber, 1990, 2006) will recognize the sound of these statements from behaviorally oriented psychologists already applying the model of the therapeutic relationship to child rearing practices well suited to the regimented corporate world for which these children are being trained. The establishment of boundaries such as time, money, and, perhaps most important, therapist availability between sessions structures the therapeutic relationship in interesting ways. The expectations of contact-maintenance, caressing, fondling, holding, and primary caregiver preoccupation—all provided to the infant gratis—do not apply in the therapeutic context.

These arrangements—unique to the therapeutic relationship—might differentially affect patients according to their attachment quality. An anxious-resistant (preoccupied) patient (entangled in parental relationships from childhood) might respond to these boundaries with indignation and resentment and create an interaction structure (i.e., pattern of reciprocal interaction) in which he or she perceives the caregiver/therapist as withholding emotional support. An anxious-avoidant (dismissing) patient (dismissing the importance of parental relationships from childhood), on the other hand, might feel a sense of relief that strict therapeutic boundaries are in place—at least until the defensive processes against closeness to the therapist are analyzed. The therapeutic boundaries established by the therapist—fee, schedule, unavailability outside of session, lack of physical contact—are unilateral decisions that structure the responses that patients of various attachment patterns will have toward the therapy. These parameters do not exist in the caregiver–infant relationship. As therapists, we must be aware of the differential effects of these parameters on our patients; these can provide us with diagnostic and attachment-related information and strategies for intervention. The manner in which we establish and maintain these boundaries reflects our own use of secondary attachment strategies (i.e., hyperactivating/preoccupied vs. deactivating/dismissing; see Goodman, 2025b, Chapter 3) that interact with our patients' strategies to create unique interaction structures that can facilitate or hinder the treatment.

In addition to the parameters inherent to every therapeutic relationship, factors such as gender and race also make important contributions to the construction of the therapeutic relationship that might interact with the patient's attachment quality in interesting ways. Following the work of Jessica Benjamin (1987), the resolution of the Oedipus complex for little boys in Western society often results in a rigid identification with the father and a wholesale repudiation of the mother and, by extension, women, femininity, and dependence. Whereas the mother, in infancy, is typically perceived as the all-powerful primary caregiver—the secure base and safe haven—this mental representation of the mother changes as the infant enters the preschool years. Boys no longer perceive her as all-powerful and all-protecting—the hallmarks of felt security—but rather as a diminished presence in the household in comparison with the father. This transformation of the maternal representation could have an impact on the patient's perception of the female therapist. One might be less likely to feel secure in a therapeutic relationship with a woman whom society has deemed "less than." Farber and Geller (1994) have observed, "Our culture seemingly 'allows' women to serve as protectors of infants and young children but not to inhabit roles that require the provision of wisdom, strength, or protection of adults" (p. 206).

Reflections on the Caregiver–Infant Attachment Relationship as Metaphor for the God–Patient Relationship

I have discussed the limitations of the caregiver–infant attachment relationship in relation to the therapist–patient relationship. Specifically, I noted that the metaphor appears to break down when the financial, temporal, spatial, logistic, ethical, and linguistic boundaries of treatment are considered. Unlike a therapist, however, God does not charge for caring, has no temporal or spatial limitations, always interacts with humans ethically (that is God's "brand"), and, owing to God's omniscience, understands humans at both the presymbolic and symbolic levels of communication. Thus, on these dimensions, the God–patient relationship seems to conform more closely to the caregiver–infant attachment relationship than the therapist–patient relationship does.

Furthermore, the God–patient relationship transcends the metaphor of the caregiver–infant attachment relationship for one obvious reason: God's love for humans far exceeds a caregiver's love for their infant. God's love is perfectly responsive to humans' emotional needs. The psalmist writes: "How priceless is your unfailing love, O God! People take refuge in the shadow of your wings"

(Psalm 36:7, NIV). Similarly, "For as high as the heavens are above the earth, so great is his love" (Psalm 103:11, NIV). From the New Testament, the author of the apostle John's first letter expresses this sentiment succinctly as "God is love" (I John 4:16, NIV). In his letter to the Romans, the apostle Paul underscores the steadfastness of God's love: "Neither death nor life, neither angels nor demons, neither the present nor the future, nor any powers, neither height nor depth, nor anything else in all creation, will be able to separate us from the love of God" (Romans 8:38–39, NIV).

The Hebrew Bible also contains many examples of God's perfect caregiving. Through the prophet Hosea, God speaks as a caregiver: "I led them with cords of human kindness, with ties of love. To them I was like one who lifts a little child to the cheek, and I bent down to feed them" (Hosea 11:4, NIV). Similarly, "As a mother comforts her child, so will I comfort you" (Isaiah 66:13, NIV). Through the prophet Isaiah, God declares that God's caregiving skills supersede those of a mother: "Can a mother forget the baby at her breast and have no compassion on the child she has borne? Though she may forget, I will not forget you" (Isaiah 49:15, NIV). Thus, according to these sacred texts, the God–patient relationship transcends the caregiver–infant attachment relationship and does not present the limitations imposed on the therapist–patient relationship. Long after the therapist–patient relationship is over, long after parents die, the God–patient relationship endures. With Séamus, he also turned to a Higher Power when he first experienced his somatic symptom coupled with the words "I'm gay!" Connecting to the kundalini energy of the Divine became his purpose for being. One of the attractions of this connection for Séamus was the unlimited access to the perfect love of the Divine—a perfect love that he never felt with his childhood caregivers.

Thus, it would be expedient for the therapist to help the patient to connect to a Higher Power to fulfill the patient's ongoing attachment needs outside the therapy office and beyond treatment termination. As Bowlby (1977a) suggests, attachment behavior "is held to characterize human beings from the cradle to the grave" (p. 203). The patient's reliance on a Higher Power to meet these needs might help the patient to consolidate and sustain the psychological gains made while participating in the therapist–patient relationship. According to the psalmist, God seems to be the ultimate Container: "The Lord is compassionate and gracious, slow to anger, abounding in love. ... He does not treat us as our sins deserve or repay us according to our iniquities" (Psalm 103:8, 10, NIV). God is the exemplar of love, compassion, and forgiveness—emotions ideally suited to help contain a patient's emotional distress. The therapist can facilitate the transfer of this containment function from onself to a Higher Power during the termination phase.

AIP, and psychodynamic therapy more generally, increases a patient's awareness of how and why their mind works as it does. The patient engages in and shares with the therapist ongoing interactions with significant others (including a

Higher Power). The patient also engages in ongoing interactions with the therapist. The therapist might ask the patient to interpret the underlying intentions of these significant others (including a Higher Power) and of the therapist, which would enhance the patient's mentalizing capacity. Mentalization is the ability to interpret others' (and one's own) behaviors as products of others' (and one's own) mental states (i.e., wishes, desires, intentions, beliefs, fantasies; Fonagy et al., 2002). A closely related concept, theory of mind, is the ability to determine that the beliefs in one's own mind can differ from the beliefs in another person's mind (see Goodman, 2025b, Chapter 3; see also Baron-Cohen, 1995). A patient's belief that they can interpret with absolute certainty the meaning of others' interactions and behaviors might make that patient feel momentarily in control. Unfortunately, however, this belief also diminishes the ability of a Higher Power to place others' interactions and behaviors into a broader context that serves a greater good. In his letter to the Romans, the apostle Paul also reveals his understanding of this truth: "And we know that in all things God works for the good of those who love him" (Romans 8:28, NIV), but, in a different letter, he encourages the Thessalonians to "give thanks in all circumstances" (1 Thessalonians 5:18, NIV).

Working therapeutically with a patient on their understanding of God's omnibenevolence could generalize to oneself and significant others—not to trust oneself and others blindly but to learn how to give oneself and others the benefit of the doubt. Conversely, working therapeutically with a patient on their understanding of the imperfect benevolence of significant others could generalize to trusting in God's omnibenevolence. These insights might open the patient to new experiences unfiltered by the potential distortions emanating from the patient's (and therapist's) mental representations of old, familiar attachment relationships. A goal of AIP is to develop the ability to tolerate the ambiguity of the meaning of people's interactions and behaviors without automatically resorting to typecasting these interactions and behaviors to confirm the biases pre-established by these old, familiar attachment relationships (see Goodman, 2025b, Chapters 5 and 6).

The Therapist's Secure Base Provision and the Patient's Underlying Attachment Needs

One of the therapist's most important functions in producing therapeutic change is to provide a secure base for the patient (Bowlby, 1988; Parish & Eagle, 2003). Providing a secure base, however, is not identical to emotional sensitivity and responsiveness. In examining the mediating role of caregiver sensitivity in the well-established relation between the caregiver's attachment organization and the infant's attachment organization, De Wolff and van IJzendoorn (1997) conducted a meta-analytic study in which they concluded, "[Caregiver] sensitivity has lost its privileged position as the only important causal factor" (p. 583) in determining attachment security in infancy. Referred to as a "transmission gap," the other causal factors, besides parenting behavior, that account for the quality of infant attachment have puzzled attachment researchers for decades. Classical attachment theory has always asserted that caregiver sensitivity to the infant's emotional needs helps the infant develop expectations of caregiver reliability and security, which in turn coalesces into a secure attachment by 12 months.

One solution to this transmission gap is to consider caregiving behavior only in attachment-activating situations as influencing the quality of infant attachment (Cassidy et al., 2005). For example, an otherwise insensitive caregiver mobilizes their latent emotional responsiveness and understanding when the infant falls off the bed and hurts their knee, offering comfort, consolation, and holding contact. It is secure base provision—the extent to which the caregiver provides a secure base in moments of fear, injury, or loss—that determines the quality of infant attachment, not emotional sensitivity and responsiveness when the attachment system is not activated (e.g., when the infant is eating with family).

In the same manner, the therapist's provision of a secure base must meet the specific needs of the patient in moments of crisis. The therapist must discern these specific needs even though the patient might miscue the therapist and obscure these needs (Cooper et al., 2005; Eagle, 2006; Hoffman et al., 2006). A therapist could respond to a patient in line with that patient's expectations developed from childhood experiences when the attachment system is activated, or respond in defiance of these expectations. The quality of the secure base, which the therapist provides, is likely to determine whether a sufficient context for therapeutic change is established.

When Séamus took a hiatus from treatment, for instance, I soon learned that I had failed to interpret this decision as a test of my concern for him. Instead, I offered little resistance to his rationalizations for leaving—(1) having accomplished his therapeutic goal by unmasking his alleged abuser during an LSD trip and (2) needing to save money. I behaved like his inconsistent father during childhood, who either yelled or behaved indifferently toward Séamus. He took over a year to return to treatment, eventually realizing that he had left prematurely. I would not make that mistake again.

The therapist must discern a patient's attachment needs, which are gently whispering beneath the din of defensive processes and clamoring to distract the patient (and therapist) from hearing them. The therapist's discernment depends on various factors, some of which have nothing to do with the patient, others of which interact with the patient's characteristics to produce interaction structures (Jones, 2000) unique to the therapeutic dyad. These interaction structures can facilitate or disrupt the therapist's secure base provision. Sometimes, a therapist's own personality organization can interact with their theoretical orientation to limit the treatment's effectiveness (Crastnopol, 2001; Kantrowitz, 1995). For example, a therapist alienated from their feelings might be inclined to practice Cognitive-Behavioral Therapy (CBT), a treatment model that de-emphasizes the processing of feelings. Whether the therapist's and patient's characteristics are complementary or noncomplementary and how this matching influences treatment process and outcome have recently garnered considerable attention in the psychotherapy research literature. Freud's one-size-fits-all technical recommendations fail to account for therapist–patient matching, which undoubtedly affects treatment outcomes.

Since Luborsky and his colleagues (1975) first claimed that all psychotherapy models produce generally equivalent outcomes (see also Rosenzweig, 1936), psychotherapy researchers have attempted to identify therapist and patient characteristics that might improve treatment effectiveness. Out of over 200 therapist and patient characteristics studied, therapist–patient matching accounts for a higher proportion of variance in treatment outcomes than any therapist or patient characteristic (Beutler, 1991). Matching on demographic variables such as gender, ethnicity, and first language is associated with successful treatment outcomes (Berzins, 1977; Beutler et al., 1991; Flaskerud, 1990; Nelson & Neufeldt, 1996). Similarly, matching on personal values, beliefs, attitudes, coping styles, expectations, and self-concept is also associated with successful treatment outcomes (Beutler et al., 1986; Nelson & Neufeldt, 1996; Reis & Brown, 1999; Talley et al., 1990).

On interpersonal variables, however, it is therapist–patient *mismatching* that produces successful treatment outcomes (Arizmendi et al., 1985; Beutler et al., 1991; Charone, 1981). For example, dissimilarity on values related to interpersonal security and sexual relationships produces successful treatment outcomes (Beutler et al., 1978). Similarly, treatments are more effective when therapists who value autonomy are matched with dependent patients or when therapists who value connection are matched with patients who value autonomy than when both parties have similar interpersonal traits (Berzins, 1977). Evidently, these contrasting interpersonal traits between the therapist and patient provide the patient with the corrective emotional experience (Alexander & French, 1946) required for a successful treatment outcome (Bernier & Dozier, 2002).

In those situations in which the caregiver does not provide a secure base or safe haven, the child goes to "Plan B"—an alternative to the straightforward proximity-seeking and contact-maintaining behaviors that represent the hallmarks of secure attachment relationships. Plan B comes in two varieties: deactivating and hyperactivating (Kobak et al., 1993). When proximity-seeking and contact-maintaining behaviors fail to deactivate the attachment system, the child can deactivate the attachment system by dismissing their attachment needs and avoiding the caregiver. Adults who routinely use this secondary attachment strategy minimize, devalue, or dismiss the emotional importance of attachment relationships (Main & Goldwyn, 1994). The child can also hyperactivate the attachment system by exaggerating their attachment needs and expressing anger toward the caregiver. Adults who routinely use this secondary attachment strategy are angrily preoccupied with attachment relationships (Main & Goldwyn, 1994).

Although we would expect most therapists to have secure states of mind with respect to attachment (Diamond, Stovall-McClough, et al., 2003; Tyrrell et al., 1999) by virtue of having had either emotionally responsive caregivers during childhood or a long-term, intensive psychotherapy where a corrective emotional experience could occur, most therapists also use a secondary attachment strategy sometimes. For secure adults, these secondary attachment strategies are partially captured in the Adult Attachment Interview (AAI) secure subclassifications (Main & Goldwyn, 1994), which range from F1 (somewhat restricting or setting aside of attachment) to F5 (somewhat resentful or preoccupied with attachment). Wherever therapists lie on this deactivating-hyperactivating continuum partially determines how they regulate their emotional lives and relate to others (Kobak et al., 1993; Slade, 1999). Patients also use these secondary attachment strategies. Anxious-avoidant (dismissing) patients use the deactivating strategy, while anxious-resistant (preoccupied) patients use the hyperactivating strategy. Therapeutic dyads are defined as "noncomplementary" when the therapist's secondary attachment strategy does not match the patient's secondary attachment strategy.

This therapeutic principle of noncomplementarity has emerged in the attachment literature (Bernier & Dozier, 2002; Bernier et al., 2005; Dozier, 2003; Dozier & Bates, 2004; Dozier et al., 1994; Dozier & Tyrrell, 1998; Tyrrell et al., 1999). Dozier and her colleagues have demonstrated that noncomplementary secondary (defensive) attachment strategies (see Goodman, 2025b, Chapter 3) between case managers and patients produced more successful treatment outcomes than complementary secondary attachment strategies. In their first study, Dozier and her colleagues (1994) administered the AAI to 27 patients diagnosed with thought or mood disorders and 18 case managers of these patients to determine their attachment patterns using the Attachment Q-Set (AQS; Kobak et al., 1993). The AQS codes AAI narratives on two orthogonal dimensions: security–insecurity (primary attachment strategy) and deactivating–hyperactivating (secondary attachment strategy). Dozier and her colleagues (1994) interviewed the case managers regarding their most recent interventions with their patients. These interviews were coded for depth of intervention and attention to dependency needs.

The results indicated that case managers rated as insecurely attached intervened in greater depth with the hyperactivating (anxious-resistant) patients than case managers rated as securely attached, who tended to intervene in less depth with this same type of patient. Similarly, case managers rated as insecurely attached attended more to the greater dependency needs of their hyperactivating (anxious-resistant) patients than case managers rated as securely attached, who attended to fewer dependency needs in this same type of patient. In their discussion, the authors concluded that securely attached case managers "seem able to attend and respond to clients' underlying needs, whereas case managers who are more insecure respond to the most obvious presentation of needs" (Dozier et al., 1994, p. 798). These insecurely attached case managers have difficulty resisting "the strong pull from the client to respond in ways that confirm existing [internal working] models" (p. 793). In other words, offering a noncomplementary relational experience to the patient is more likely to occur with a securely attached therapist because of "their willingness to intervene in ways that may be uncomfortable for themselves" (p. 798). The authors also pointed out that securely attached case managers responded more to the dependency needs of deactivating (anxious-avoidant) patients than to those of hyperactivating (anxious-resistant) patients. In my treatment with Séamus, I provide a calming, noncomplementary experience whenever he becomes emotionally dysregulated in speaking about his father. This calming intervention enables him to regulate his emotions.

This idea is consistent with the work of Diamond, Clarkin, and her colleagues (2003), who, in their work with patients with BPD, "remain attuned to the often fleeting emergence of ... secure states [of mind] that may emerge" (p. 167). Like a "gentle whisper" (I Kings 19:12, NIV), the need to rely on the therapist or a Higher Power as a secure base is often hard to hear above the din of noise—the denials of dependency—that distracts the therapist from making a noncomplementary intervention. One of my analytic patients, diagnosed with BPD, denied that she missed me after vacations (for a full discussion of this case, see Goodman, 2010, Chapter 3). According to her, she enjoyed sleeping in and not having to analyze everything. Despite this patient's dismissing attitude, she came four times per week, seldom missed a session, and was seldom late. She called me once to tell me that she was feeling ill and was canceling the following day's session. At our next session, she chastised me for not calling her back to check on her. It took several days for us to work through what she perceived as my unavailability to her. It is not my practice to call patients back under such circumstances but, in retrospect, I agree that I should have called back this patient because, unbeknownst to me, she was using me as a safe haven during her illness. In subsequent sessions, she ignored such interpretations and focused instead on my "obligation" to patients to return their telephone calls. All therapists have had similar experiences in their practices. The question is whether therapists can allow themselves to respond differentially to patients based on their patients' secondary attachment behavior—to nurture the gentle whisper of primary secure attachment behavior and its associated state of mind rather than silence it.

The therapeutic principle of noncomplementarity makes intuitive clinical sense. The therapist responds to the patient's underlying needs, not to their miscues (Cooper et al., 2005; Eagle, 2006; Hoffman et al., 2006) governed by defensive processes. Securely attached therapists are more likely to tolerate discomfort in the interaction and gently challenge the patient's characteristic mode of relatedness to others than insecurely attached therapists would. Do we know, however, whether noncomplementary interventions actually produce more successful treatment outcomes than complementary interventions?

In their second study, Dozier and her colleagues (Tyrrell et al., 1999) administered the AAI to 54 patients diagnosed with thought or mood disorders and 21 case managers of these patients to determine their attachment patterns with the AQS (Kobak et al., 1993). The study design differed from the first study, however, because the case managers assessed treatment outcomes, defined as the quality of working alliance, global life satisfaction, and global assessment of functioning (GAF). Deactivating (anxious-avoidant) case managers and their hyperactivating (anxious-resistant) patients tended to have a higher quality of working alliance than deactivating (anxious-avoidant) case managers and their deactivating (anxious-avoidant) patients. Conversely, hyperactivating (anxious-resistant) case managers and their deactivating (anxious-avoidant) patients tended to have a higher quality of working alliance than hyperactivating (anxious-resistant) case managers and their hyperactivating (anxious-resistant) patients. Patients who belonged to noncomplementary dyads also experienced greater global life satisfaction and higher GAF than patients who belonged to complementary dyads. The authors (Tyrrell et al., 1999) argue that this study provides empirical evidence for Bowlby's (1988) therapeutic goal to disconfirm the patient's usual interpersonal and emotional strategies and expectations. In noncomplementary dyads, this goal is accomplished because case managers "have different ways of approaching relationships and regulating emotions than their clients. ... The development of these more effective strategies can then lead to enhanced quality of life and better psychological, social, and occupational functioning for clients" (Tyrrell et al., 1999, pp. 731–732).

One of the fascinating facets of this study is that therapist–patient correspondence on attachment patterns predicted treatment outcomes without any knowledge of the nature of the interventions made by the therapists. The authors (Tyrrell et al., 1999) conclude, "The therapeutic process that mediates the relationship between client–case manager attachment dissimilarity and positive treatment outcomes needs to be investigated more thoroughly" (p. 732). I suspect that emotion regulation, produced by a noncomplementary correspondence on attachment patterns, occurs through behavioral as well as verbal channels of communication. A therapist's facial expressions, body language, and tone of voice, and the office's seating arrangement all communicate a level of tolerance or intolerance of a patient's pattern of emotion regulation. The timing of the therapist's verbal interventions also communicates this tolerance or intolerance, irrespective of verbal content. The findings of this study suggest that a corrective emotional experience (Alexander & French, 1946), mediated by a noncomplementary correspondence of attachment patterns, produces enhanced treatment outcomes. In other words, new implicit procedural knowledge (see Goodman, 2025b, Chapter 4), acquired by the patient through the nonverbal emotion-regulatory interactions with the therapist, can produce therapeutic change independent of the acquisition of new symbolic (verbal) knowledge that can increase insight. In this case, my effort to enable Séamus to forgive his father might be less essential to his treatment outcome than my nonverbal interventions that help him to deactivate his dysregulated emotions.

These important studies conducted by Dozier and her colleagues need to be replicated with skilled therapists in traditional psychotherapy settings with less disturbed patients to improve the generalizability of the results (Diamond, Clarkin, et al., 2003; Dozier et al., 1994). Toward this end, Bernier and her colleagues (2005) conducted a similar study with 90 first-year college students and ten professors who volunteered as academic counselors. The counselor-professors worked together with the students in regularly scheduled one-to-one sessions throughout the fall semester to provide mentoring and to discuss social and emotional adjustment problems. Students were administered the AAI, while counselor-professors completed a self-report attachment questionnaire. The authors assessed outcomes as students' adaptive behaviors and perceptions in mentoring and grade-point average at the end of the semester.

The results paralleled those of the previous studies: hyperactivating (anxious-resistant) students paired with deactivating (anxious-avoidant) counselor-professors tended to have more adaptive behaviors and perceptions in mentoring and higher grades than deactivating (anxious-avoidant) students paired with deactivating (anxious-avoidant) counselor-professors. Conversely, deactivating (anxious-avoidant) students paired with hyperactivating (anxious-resistant) counselor-professors tended to have more adaptive behaviors and perceptions in mentoring and higher grades than hyperactivating (anxious-resistant) students paired with hyperactivating (anxious-resistant) counselor-professors. Thus, Bernier and her colleagues (2005) essentially replicated the findings of Dozier and her colleagues (Dozier et al., 1994; Tyrrell et al., 1999) with a sample of college students receiving academic mentoring. Unfortunately, a self-report attachment questionnaire was administered to the counselor-professors, which renders the study's findings suspect because of the low correlation ($r = .09$) between the AAI and self-report measures of attachment (Roisman et al., 2007).

These empirical findings suggest that the therapist must respond differently to patients, depending on their mode of emotion regulation. Because a therapist typically uses only one secondary (defensive) attachment strategy (hyperactivating or deactivating), while their patients use either strategy, both complementary and noncomplementary dyadic therapeutic relationships will be established in any given patient caseload. With noncomplementary patients, therefore, a therapist "must have the ego strength and flexibility necessary to respond to the client ... even if it is uncomfortable for the clinician at the time" (Dozier & Tyrrell, 1998, p. 240). If we acknowledge that "the clinician's state of mind ... affects the client's expectation of availability" (Dozier & Bates, 2004, p. 173), then therapists need to have their own personal psychotherapy experience and self-analysis to acquaint themselves with their preferred attachment strategies and modes of emotion regulation—something that psychoanalytic institutes have incorporated into their training programs for almost 100 years (Freud, 1912b; Szajnberg & Crittenden, 1997).

Applying these insights to AIP for spiritually curious or spiritually grounded patients, the therapist must assess not only the patient's and their own secondary (defensive) attachment strategies used in their attachment relationships to the caregivers during childhood but also the patient's and their own secondary (defensive) attachment strategies used in their attachment relationship to God. The attachment relationship to God can correspond with or compensate for the attachment relationships to the caregivers during childhood (see Chapter 6). The therapist's awareness of the quality of their own attachment relationship to a Higher Power can aid in the selection of appropriate interventions that can provide a "gentle challenge" (Dozier & Bates, 2004, p. 174; see also Dozier, 2003, p. 254) to the patient's secondary (defensive) attachment strategy in their attachment relationship to God.

Let me provide a brief illustration. A therapist (perhaps belonging to a church that emphasizes doctrinal purity or ritual) is aware of having developed an anxious-avoidant (dismissing) attachment relationship to God, while the patient (perhaps belonging to a church that emphasizes cathartic emotional expression) has developed an anxious-resistant (preoccupied) attachment relationship to God. The therapist must assemble an array of intervention strategies consistent with their own anxious-avoidant (dismissing) mode of relatedness that might help the patient to shift into a more reflective mode of mental functioning and, ultimately, a more secure attachment relationship to God. On the other hand, the compensation pathway predicts that the quality of a person's attachment relationships to their caregivers during childhood might differ qualitatively from the quality of the person's attachment relationship to God. Thus, the therapist must select intervention strategies that gently challenge the insecure attachment relationship under discussion—either to the caregivers during childhood or to a Higher Power.

In the illustration above, the therapist must rely on their awareness of their preferred secondary (defensive) attachment strategy of anxious-avoidance to select intervention strategies that will aid in transforming both the patient's anxious-resistant attachment relationships to their caregivers during childhood and their attachment relationship to God into secure attachment relationships. If the patient's attachment relationships to the caregivers during childhood and to God are noncomplementary (i.e, insecure and secure, or secure and insecure), then the therapist needs to use intervention strategies to gently challenge the insecure attachment relationships, whether to the caregivers during childhood or to God. Ideally, the patient will use the secure attachment relationships to the caregivers or to God as well as to the therapist to generalize to the insecure attachment relationship so that all these attachment relationships are consistently secure. The added layer of complexity comes with the therapist's awareness of the quality of their own attachment relationship to God and their use of this awareness to formulate intervention strategies that gently challenge the patient's insecure (anxious-avoidant or anxious-resistant) attachment relationship to God.

The goal is to create a noncomplementary therapeutic experience that produces a transformation in all attachment relationships from insecure to secure (for a full discussion, see Goodman, 2025b, Chapter 6).

While Freud focused on the therapist's technical behaviors in characterizing the nature of clinical practice, the (albeit sparse) literature on the role of attachment relationships in therapist–patient relationships suggests that the attachment histories of both therapist and patient influence not only the process but also the outcome of treatment (Bernier & Dozier, 2002; Bernier et al., 2005; Dozier, 2003; Dozier & Bates, 2004; Dozier et al., 1994; Dozier & Tyrrell, 1998; Tyrrell et al., 1999). Dozier and her colleagues articulate the principle of noncomplementarity to characterize the optimal therapist–patient match vis-à-vis attachment relationships. Their research suggests that therapists are optimally effective with patients whose secondary (defensive) attachment strategy differs from their own. Conversely, therapists are less effective with patients whose secondary attachment strategy resembles their own. These secondary attachment strategies are patterns of emotion regulation and modes of relatedness to others based on countless attachment-activating experiences with the caregivers during childhood.

The essence of AIP is the therapist's awareness of these interaction structures and the application of this awareness in formulating therapeutic interventions. I am proposing a 2 × 2 typology of interaction structures formed by these therapist and patient secondary attachment strategies (see Table 8.1). Four possible cells exist: deactivating therapists paired with deactivating patients (Cell

Table 8.1 Typology Presenting Four Interaction Structures Based on the Secondary Attachment Strategies of Therapist and Patient

Patient	Therapist	
	Deactivating Dismissing (Ds)	Hyperactivating Preoccupied (E)
Deactivating Dismissing (Ds)	(1) Sterile (complementary): low depth, high smoothness, low arousal, rigid boundaries, overdifferentiation, overregulated affect	(2) Expressive (noncomplementary): high depth, high smoothness, moderate arousal, flexible boundaries, optimal differentiation, expressed affect
Hyperactivating Preoccupied (E)	(3) Containing (noncomplementary): high depth, high smoothness, moderate arousal, firm boundaries, optimal differentiation, contained affect	(4) Chaotic (complementary): high depth, low smoothness, high arousal, loose boundaries, undifferentiation, underregulated affect

1; "sterile"), hyperactivating therapists paired with deactivating patients (Cell 2; "expressive"), deactivating therapists paired with hyperactivating patients (Cell 3; "containing"), and hyperactivating therapists paired with hyperactivating patients (Cell 4; "chaotic"). Psychoanalysts from the relational school (e.g., Greenberg, 2001; Hoffman, 1994; Kantrowitz, 2001) argue in favor of the uniqueness of the therapist–patient relationship, which has been compared to "a snowflake" in which "no two are alike" (Kantrowitz, 2001, p. 403). If the therapist–patient relationship is unique, then it follows that the processes that facilitate therapeutic change would also vary from relationship to relationship. Nevertheless, just as every snowflake has six sides, so too does every therapist–patient relationship have a particular shape.

In fact, I am proposing that every therapist–patient relationship can have four possible shapes. Specifying a range of shapes can also help to specify a range of clinical interventions that accompany each of these shapes. I have conceptualized these four broadly defined shapes not to minimize the uniqueness of the therapist–patient relationship but rather to delineate patterns within the uniqueness that could facilitate the development of broadly defined technical principles that therapists could use beyond a single case.

Of course, this 2 × 2 typology of interaction structures also applies to the therapist's and patient's attachment relationships to a Higher Power. In most cases, the quality of attachment relationships to the caregivers during childhood and to a Higher Power correspond to each other; thus, the four possible cells created by this typology (see Table 8.1) also apply to the therapist's and patient's attachment relationship to God (for discussion about the correspondence pathway, see Chapter 6). In some cases, however, the quality of attachment relationship to a Higher Power compensates for the quality of attachment relationships to the caregivers during childhood; thus, the four possible cells created by this typology (see Table 8.1) might not apply to the therapist's and patient's attachment relationship to God (for discussion about the compensation pathway, see Chapter 6). When the compensation pathway accounts for the therapist's or patient's attachment relationship to God, the quality of attachment relationship to God is typically secure, while the quality of attachment relationships to the caregivers during childhood is typically insecure (i.e., anxious-avoidant, anxious-resistant, or disorganized/disoriented).

Conversely, secure attachment relationships to the caregivers during childhood and an insecure attachment relationship to a Higher Power (typically anxious-avoidant) would occur only when the caregivers are not religious or spiritual (see Granqvist's [2020] socialized correspondence theory discussed in Goodman, 2025b, Chapter 3). Only when suffering from an adjustment disorder (caused by overwhelming psychosocial stressors that produce psychiatric symptoms) would a securely attached patient seek psychotherapy because most securely attached patients, having experienced emotionally responsive caregiving, do not experience a pattern of emotional dysregulation implicated in most psychiatric illnesses. Thus, when a patient's attachment relationship to a Higher Power is insecure, it is likely that this person's attachment relationship to the caregivers during childhood is also insecure (unless the caregivers during childhood were not religious or spiritual). This 2 × 2 typology would, therefore, also apply to the therapist's and patient's attachment relationship to a Higher Power.

I divide the four cells into two groups: complementary interaction structures and noncomplementary interaction structures. Complementary interaction structures are patterns of reciprocal therapist–patient interaction in which the therapist and patient match on their secondary attachment strategy ("sterile" and "chaotic"; see Table 8.1). Conversely, noncomplementary interaction structures are patterns of reciprocal therapist–patient interaction in which the therapist and patient do not match on their secondary attachment strategy ("expressive" and "containing"; see Table 8.1). Dozier and her colleagues (Bernier & Dozier, 2002; Bernier et al., 2005; Dozier, 2003; Dozier & Bates, 2004; Dozier et al., 1994; Dozier & Tyrrell, 1998; Tyrrell et al., 1999) suggest that noncomplementary matches are more therapeutically effective than complementary matches. Identifying these interaction structures in the early treatment phase can aid therapists in selecting the most effective intervention strategies for transforming a patient's attachment relationships—both to the caregivers during childhood and to a Higher Power—from insecure to secure.

When Is This Model of Spiritual Intervention a Good Match?

AIP is a good match for spiritually curious and spiritually grounded patients ready to explore their attachment relationships to significant others, the caregivers during childhood, the therapist, and their Higher Power. This treatment model is contraindicated, however, for patients who experience psychotic episodes (i.e., featuring poor reality testing, or the inability to distinguish fantasy from reality). Stabilizing these patients is key to their initial treatment, which might include supportive psychotherapy and an appropriate medication regimen (Griffith, 2010).

AIP is also contraindicated for patients who experience complex posttraumatic stress disorder (PTSD) or dissociative identity disorder (DID). These persons often struggle to distinguish past from present experiences, especially when they become distressed. For these persons, I would recommend a treatment model that serves to ground the person in present experience (e.g., Brand et al., 2022; Chefetz, 2015). Patients who begin to feel grounded in present experience with one of these treatment models can later benefit from AIP and the exploration of attachment relationships, including their attachment relationship to a Higher Power. My own patient Séamus manifested anxious-resistant (preoccupied) attachment relationships to his parents and to God and was thus suitable for AIP (for more information on the assessment of Séamus's quality of attachment relationships to his caregivers during childhood and to God, see Goodman, 2025a, Chapter 6).

Training Requirements to Become an AIP Therapist

An AIP therapist must be a licensed mental health professional (i.e., psychiatrist, psychologist, social worker, mental health counselor or professional counselor, psychiatric nurse practitioner), preferably with extensive training in attachment theory and Spiritually Integrated Psychotherapy (SIP; see Chapter 7). Most importantly, an AIP therapist must receive clinical supervision from an experienced therapist who uses attachment theory and SIP to inform their therapeutic work. Individual instruction in the application of this treatment model to actual psychotherapy cases is indispensable in becoming a skilled AIP practitioner.

Conclusions

The four interaction structures I have outlined—sterile, chaotic, expressive, and containing—are, of course, caricatures of therapy sessions conducted by prototypical therapists and patients, each of whom falls on one of two ends of a continuum of secondary attachment strategies that range from deactivating to hyperactivating (Kobak et al., 1993, p. 235). Ideally, a therapist is sufficiently secure and flexible in their attachment pattern that they can challenge whatever strategy a patient presents by adopting a noncomplementary strategy to provide a corrective emotional experience for the patient (Alexander & French, 1946). A therapist who tends to use a hyperactivating attachment strategy must behave in a slightly deactivating manner with a hyperactivating patient to produce effective personality change, not only in their verbal interventions but also in their nonverbal interventions. In my own work with Séamus, I provide a calming, noncomplementary experience whenever he becomes emotionally dysregulated in speaking about his father. This calming intervention enables him to regulate his emotions. Using my provision of safety and calm, Séamus continues to work through his alleged sexual abuse, his contentious relationship to his father (both the external father and the internalized father), and his somatic symptom.

Conversely, a therapist who tends to use a deactivating attachment strategy must behave in a slightly hyperactivating manner with a deactivating patient to produce effective personality change. Researchers could assign therapists and patients randomly to these four cells to verify the principle of noncomplementarity (Bernier & Dozier, 2002; Bernier et al., 2005; Dozier, 2003; Dozier & Bates, 2004; Dozier et al., 1994; Dozier & Tyrrell, 1998; Tyrrell et al., 1999). Clinical training programs could assess the attachment pattern of trainees (and their supervisors) and patients and use this information to help trainees learn how to provide noncomplementary psychotherapy experiences for their patients. However instructive these four broadly outlined interaction structures might be for the conduct of and training in psychotherapy, they can never substitute for the unique shape of each individual therapist–patient attachment relationship.

As I have illustrated, the spiritually informed therapist can also use this typology in planning intervention strategies for working with patients who have insecure attachment relationships to their Higher Power. Secondary attachment strategies (i.e., deactivating and hyperactivating) can gently challenge the patient's noncomplementary secondary attachment strategies to assist the patient in relying on the primary attachment strategy of proximity-seeking and finding protection and comfort in their attachment relationship to their Higher Power. The therapist uses these same strategies that they use when the patient is discussing their attachment relationships to the caregivers during childhood. I have found that these noncomplementary intervention strategies can produce effective change in the patient's attachment relationship to their Higher Power, not only in their verbal descriptions but also in their deep emotional knowing of this Higher Power.

Despite my promotion of one particular treatment model—AIP—I want to suggest therapeutic flexibility. Freud (1913) was right that psychotherapy is like a game of chess in which there are an "infinite variety of moves" (p. 123) that can lead to therapeutic success. Despite diagnostic similarities, patients' needs and responses to therapeutic interventions vary widely, regardless of whether the patient is working on their relationships to significant others, the therapist (often a symbolic representative of caregivers during childhood), or a Higher Power. To meet these diverse needs, therapists need to implement intervention strategies tailored to the unique characteristics of each patient rather than boilerplate strategies designed for every patient. Therapeutically effective therapists adjust their technical approaches "on the fly" when they feel that their patients can benefit from a change in their intervention strategies. These technical modifications do not come from a treatment manual but from clinical intuition—the reflection on one's own countertransference reactions or possibly a more broadly conceptualized empathic connection with the patient.

Specifically, treatments of patients with various levels of disturbance or different constellations of symptoms, treatments in various settings (e.g., inpatient, day treatment, outpatient), and treatments that systematically take advantage of pairings of therapist and patient attachment relationships (reflecting patterns of emotion regulation) are beginning to yield findings in which adherence to particular treatment modalities varies according to "conditions on the ground" (i.e., movements of "Spirit-undercurrents"). Slavish adherence to a boilerplate training manual can spell disaster, as Castonguay and his colleagues (Castonguay et al., 1996) learned. While taking this inexorable journey, we have discovered an important clinical reality: treatment purity (whether psychoanalysis or CBT) might not be most effective for certain types of patients. Trainees need to be empathically and spiritually attuned to their patients' unique emotional and spiritual needs so that they can become aware when their treatment approach becomes counterproductive. Training in global clinical skills such as empathy, countertransference awareness (including spiritual countertransference awareness; see also Goodman, 2025b, Chapter 6), and awareness of potential interaction structures would more suitably position trainees to become effective therapists than training them how to apply a treatment manual. Instead of training trainees to be slaves to a treatment manual, clinical supervisors need to be training them to be its master. The field needs fewer technicians and more artists.

Teaching therapist adherence to two or three broad treatment approaches (e.g., psychodynamic therapy and CBT) should become a vital aspect of clinical training; however, teaching therapist adherence to narrowly focused treatment models such as bedtime noncompliance (Ferber, 2006) ensnares the field in the "narcissism of minor differences" (Freud, 1918, p. 199) and immerses trainees in memorizing procedures rather than experiencing relationships and paying attention to the movements of "Spirit-undercurrents." The endless proliferation of manualized psychotherapies that emphasize their uniqueness obscures the broadly conceptualized therapeutic processes common to all effective psychotherapies. Psychotherapy process researchers need to focus on the common therapeutic ingredients of all effective psychotherapies and organize under a unified banner rather than splinter the field by each promoting their own treatment approach. Examining therapeutic processes that actually work moves the field "beyond brand names" and inevitable sectarian strife and instead unites the field in a common objective—to help relieve patients of their suffering, both emotional and spiritual.

AIP—the treatment model I espouse in this book—is sufficiently broad to leverage global clinical skills such as empathy, countertransference awareness, and awareness of potential interaction structures to facilitate the emotional and spiritual journey of healing in patients. Perhaps most importantly, AIP easily accommodates the therapist's awareness of their own and their patients' quality of attachment relationships to a Higher Power in promoting the spiritual journey of healing that can activate the healing of the whole person—body, mind, and soul. Healing of the attachment relationships to the caregivers during childhood and healing of the attachment relationship to a Higher Power synergize each other in spiritually grounded and spiritually curious patients. Why would we even consider working with only one type of attachment relationship at the expense of the other?

References

Aafjes-van Doorn, K., Spina, D. S., Horne, S. J., & Békés, V. (2024). The association between quality of therapeutic alliance and treatment outcomes in teletherapy: A systematic review and meta-analysis. *Clinical Psychology Review, 110,* 102430.

Alexander, F., & French, T. M. (1946). *Psychoanalytic therapy: Principles and application.* Ronald.

American Psychiatric Association. (2022). *Diagnostic and statistical manual of mental disorders* (5th ed., text rev.). Author.

Amini, F., Lewis, T., Lannon, R., Louie, A., Baumbacher, G., McGuinness, T., & Schiff, E. Z. (1996). Affect, attachment and memory: Contributions toward psychobiologic integration. *Psychiatry, 59*, 213–239.

Arizmendi, T., Beutler, L., Shanfield, S., Crago, M., & Hagaman, R. (1985). Client–therapist value similarity and psychotherapy outcome: A microscopic analysis. *Psychotherapy, 22*, 16–21.

Baron-Cohen, S. (1995). *Mindblindness: An essay on autism and theory of mind.* MIT Press/Bradford Books.

Benjamin, J. (1987). The decline of the Oedipus complex. In J. M. Broughton (Ed.), *Critical theories of psychological development* (pp. 211–244). New York: Plenum Press.

Bernier, A., & Dozier, M. (2002). The client–counselor match and the corrective emotional experience: Evidence from interpersonal and attachment research. *Psychotherapy: Theory/Research/Practice/Training, 39*, 32–43.

Bernier, A., Larose, S., & Soucy, N. (2005). Academic mentoring in college: The interactive role of student's and mentor's interpersonal dispositions. *Research in Higher Education, 46*, 29–51.

Berzins, J. I. (1977). Therapist–patient matching. In A. S. Gurman & A. M. Razin (Eds.), *Effective psychotherapy: A handbook of research* (pp. 222–251). Pergamon.

Beutler, L. E. (1991). Have all won and must all have prizes? Revisiting Luborsky et al.'s verdict. *Journal of Consulting and Clinical Psychology, 59*, 226–232.

Beutler, L. E., Clarkin, J. F., Crago, M., & Bergan, J. (1991). Client–therapist matching. In C. R. Snyder & D. R. Forsyth (Eds.), *Handbook of social and clinical psychology: The health perspective* (pp. 699–716). Pergamon.

Beutler, L. E., Crago, M., & Arizmendi, T. G. (1986). Therapist variables in psychotherapy process and outcome. In S. L. Garfield & A. E. Bergin (Eds.), *Handbook of psychotherapy and behavior change* (3rd ed., pp. 257–310). New York: Wiley.

Beutler, L. E., Pollack, S., & Jobe, A. M. (1978). "Acceptance," values, and therapeutic change. *Journal of Consulting and Clinical Psychology, 46*, 198–199.

Bordin, E. S. (1994). Theory and research on the therapeutic working alliance: New directions. In A. O. Horvath & L. S. Greenberg (Eds.), *The working alliance: Theory, research, and practice* (pp. 13–37). New York: Wiley.

Bowlby, J. (1973). *Attachment and loss: Vol. 2. Separation: Anxiety and anger.* New York: Basic Books.

Bowlby, J. (1977a). The making and breaking of affectional bonds. I. Aetiology and psychopathology in the light of attachment theory. *British Journal of Psychiatry, 130*, 201–210.

Bowlby, J. (1977b). The making and breaking of affectional bonds: II. Some principles of psychotherapy. *British Journal of Psychiatry, 130*, 421–431.

Bowlby, J. (1982). *Attachment and loss: Vol. 1. Attachment* (2nd ed.). New York: Basic Books.

Bowlby, J. (1988). *A secure base: Parent–child attachment and healthy human development.* New York: Basic Books.

Bradley, R., Heim, A. K., & Westen, D. (2005). Transference patterns in the psychotherapy of personality disorders: Empirical investigation. *British Journal of Psychiatry, 186*, 342–349.

Brand, B. L., Schielke, H. I., Schiavone, F., & Lanius, R. A. (2022). *Finding solid ground: Overcoming obstacles in trauma treatment.* Oxford University Press.

Burns, P., Sander, L. W., Stechler, G., & Julia, H. (1972). Distress in feeding: Short-term effects of caretaker environment of the first 10 days. *Journal of the American Academy of Child Psychiatry, 11*, 427–439.

Cassidy, J., Woodhouse, S. S., Cooper, G., Hoffman, K., Powell, B., & Rodenberg, M. (2005). Examination of the precursors of infant attachment security: Implications for early intervention and intervention research. In L. J. Berlin, Y. Ziv, L. Amaya-Jackson, & M. T. Greenberg (Eds.), *Enhancing early attachments: Theory, research, intervention, and policy* (pp. 34–60). Guilford Press.

Castonguay, L. G., Goldfried, M. R., Wiser, S., Raue, P. J., & Hayes, A. M. (1996). Predicting the effect of cognitive therapy for depression: A study of unique and common factors. *Journal of Consulting and Clinical Psychology, 64*, 497–504.

Charone, J. K. (1981). Patient and therapist treatment goals related to psychotherapy outcome (Doctoral dissertation, Yeshiva University, 1981). *Dissertation Abstracts International, 42*(1-B), 365.

Chefetz, R. A. (2015). *Intensive psychotherapy for persistent dissociative processes: The fear of feeling real*. Norton.

Cooper, G., Hoffman, K., Powell, B., & Marvin, R. (2005). The Circle of Security intervention: Differential diagnosis and differential treatment. In L. J. Berlin, Y. Ziv, L. Amaya-Jackson, & M. T. Greenberg (Eds.), *Enhancing early attachments: Theory, research, intervention, and policy* (pp. 127–151). Guilford Press.

Crastnopol, M. (2001). The analyst's participation: A new look [Commentary]. *Journal of the American Psychoanalytic Association, 49*, 386–398.

De Wolff, M., & van IJzendoorn, M. H. (1997). Sensitivity and attachment: A meta-analysis on parental antecedents of infant attachment. *Child Development, 68*, 571–591.

Diamond, D., Clarkin, J. F., Stovall-McClough, K. C., Levy, K. N., Foelsch, P. A., Levine, H., & Yeomans, F. E. (2003). Patient–therapist attachment: Impact on the therapeutic process and outcome. In M. Cortina & M. Marrone (Eds.), *Attachment theory and the psychoanalytic process*. London: Whurr.

Diamond, D., Clarkin, J., Levine, H., Levy, K., Foelsch, P., & Yeomans, F. (1999). Borderline conditions and attachment: A preliminary report. *Psychoanalytic Inquiry, 19*, 831–884.

Diamond, D., Stovall-McClough, C., Clarkin, J. F., & Levy, K. N. (2003). Patient–therapist attachment in the treatment of borderline personality disorder. *Bulletin of the Menninger Clinic, 67*, 227–259.

Dozier, M. (2003). Attachment-based treatment for vulnerable children. *Attachment and Human Development, 5*, 253–257.

Dozier, M., & Bates, B. C. (2004). Attachment state of mind and the treatment relationship. In L. Atkinson & S. Goldberg (Eds.), *Attachment issues in psychopathology and intervention* (pp. 167–180). Erlbaum.

Dozier, M., Cue, K. L., & Barnett, L. (1994). Clinicians as caregivers: Role of attachment organization in treatment. *Journal of Consulting and Clinical Psychology, 62*, 793–800.

Dozier, M., & Tyrrell, C. (1998). The role of attachment in therapeutic relationships. In J. A. Simpson & W. S. Rholes (Eds.), *Attachment theory and close relationships* (pp. 221–248). Guilford Press.

Eagle, M. N. (2006). Attachment, psychotherapy, and assessment: A commentary. *Journal of Consulting and Clinical Psychology, 74*, 1086–1097.

Farber, B. A., & Geller, J. (1994). Gender and representation in psychotherapy. *Psychotherapy, 31*, 318–326.

Farber, B. A., Lippert, R. A., & Nevas, D. B. (1995). The therapist as attachment figure. *Psychotherapy, 32*, 204–212.

Ferber, R. (1990). Sleep schedule-dependent causes of insomnia and sleepiness in middle childhood and adolescence. *Pediatrician, 17*, 13–20.

Ferber, R. (2006). *Solve your child's sleep problems* (rev. ed.). New York: Fireside.

Flaskerud, J. H. (1990). Matching client and therapist ethnicity, language, and gender: A review of research. *Issues in Mental Health Nursing, 11*, 321–336.

Fonagy, P., Gergely, G., Jurist, E. L., & Target, M. (2002). *Affect regulation, mentalization, and the development of the self*. New York: Other Press.
Freud, S. (1912a). The dynamics of transference. In J. Strachey (Ed. and Trans.), *The standard edition of the complete psychological works of Sigmund Freud* (Vol. 12, pp. 97–108). Hogarth Press.
Freud, S. (1912b). Recommendations to physicians practising psycho-analysis. In J. Strachey (Ed. and Trans.), *The standard edition of the complete psychological works of Sigmund Freud* (Vol. 12, pp. 109–120). Hogarth Press.
Freud, S. (1913). On beginning the treatment (Further recommendations on the technique of psycho-analysis I). In J. Strachey (Ed. and Trans.), *The standard edition of the complete psychological works of Sigmund Freud* (Vol. 12, pp. 123–144). Hogarth Press.
Freud, S. (1915). Observations on transference-love (Further recommendations on the technique of psycho-analysis III). In J. Strachey (Ed. and Trans.), *The standard edition of the complete psychological works of Sigmund Freud* (Vol. 12, pp. 157–171). Hogarth Press.
Freud, S. (1918). The taboo of virginity (Contributions to the psychology of love III). In J. Strachey (Ed. and Trans.), *The standard edition of the complete psychological works of Sigmund Freud* (Vol. 11, pp. 191–208). Hogarth Press.
Goodman, G. (2006, November). [Discussant, *The perspectives of attachment theory and psychoanalysis: Adult psychotherapy*]. In M. Eagle & D. L. Wolitzky (Chairs), *The perspectives of attachment theory and psychoanalysis: Adult psychotherapy*. Symposium conducted by Adelphi University and the New York Attachment Consortium, Garden City, NY.
Goodman, G. (2010). *Transforming the internal world and attachment: Clinical applications* (Vol. 2). Lanham, MD: Jason Aronson.
Goodman, G. (2025a). *Practical applications of transforming the attachment relationship to God: Using attachment-informed psychotherapy*. Routledge.
Goodman, G. (2025b). *Using psychoanalytic techniques to transform the attachment relationship to God: Our refuge and strength*. Routledge.
Granqvist, P. (2020). *Attachment in religion and spirituality: A wider view*. Guilford Press.
Greenberg, J. (2001). The analyst's participation: A new look. *Journal of the American Psychoanalytic Association, 49*, 359–381.
Greenson, R. R. (1965). The working alliance and the transference neurosis. *Psychoanalytic Quarterly, 34*, 155–181.
Griffith, J. L. (2010). *Religion that heals, religion that harms: A guide for clinical practice*. Guilford Press.
Hoffman, I. Z. (1994). Dialectical thinking and therapeutic action in the psychoanalytic process. *Psychoanalytic Quarterly, 63*, 187–218.
Hoffman, K. T., Marvin, R. S., Cooper, G., & Powell, B. (2006). Changing toddlers' and preschoolers' attachment classifications: The Circle of Security intervention. *Journal of Consulting and Clinical Psychology, 74*, 1017–1026.
Holmes, J. (1996). Psychotherapy and memory: An attachment perspective. *British Journal of Psychotherapy, 13*, 204–218.
Holmes, J. (1998). The changing aims of psychoanalytic psychotherapy: An integrative perspective. *International Journal of Psycho-Analysis, 79*, 227–240.
Horvath, A., & Greenberg, L. (1989). Development and validation of the Working Alliance Inventory. *Journal of Counseling Psychology, 36*, 223–233.
Horvath, A., & Symonds, B. (1991). Relation between working alliance and outcome in psychotherapy: A meta-analysis. *Journal of Counseling Psychology, 38*, 139–149.

Jones, E. E. (2000). *Therapeutic action: A guide to psychoanalytic therapy.* Northvale, NJ: Jason Aronson.

Kantrowitz, J. (1995). The beneficial aspects of the patient–analyst match. *International Journal of Psycho-Analysis, 76,* 299–313.

Kantrowitz, J. L. (2001). The analyst's participation: A new look [Commentary]. *Journal of the American Psychoanalytic Association, 49,* 398–406.

Kobak, R. R., Cole, H. E., Ferenz-Gillies, R., Fleming, W. S., & Gamble, W. (1993). Attachment and emotion regulation during mother–teen problem solving: A control theory analysis. *Child Development, 64,* 231–245.

Luborsky, L. (1994). Therapeutic alliances as predictors of psychotherapy outcomes: Factors explaining the predictive success. In A. O. Horvath & L. S. Greenberg (Eds.), *The working alliance: Theory, research, and practice* (pp. 38–50). New York: Wiley.

Luborsky, L., Singer, B., & Luborsky, L. (1975). Comparative studies of psychotherapies: Is it true that "everyone has won and all must have prizes"? *Archives of General Psychiatry, 32,* 995–1008.

Lyons, L. S., & Sperling, M. (1996). Clinical applications of attachment theory: Empirical and theoretical perspectives. In J. M. Masling & R. F. Bornstein (Eds.), *Psychoanalytic perspectives on developmental psychology* (pp. 221–256). Washington, DC: American Psychological Association.

Mackie, A. J. (1981). Attachment theory: Its relevance to the therapeutic alliance. *British Journal of Medical Psychology, 54,* 203–212.

Mahler, M. S., Pine, F., & Bergman, A. (1975). *The psychological birth of the human infant: Symbiosis and individuation.* New York: Basic Books.

Main, M., & Goldwyn, R. (1994). *Adult attachment scoring and classification systems* (6th ed.). Unpublished manuscript, University College, London.

Mallinckrodt, B. (2000). Attachment, social competencies, social support, and interpersonal process in psychotherapy. *Psychotherapy Research, 10,* 239–266.

Mallinckrodt, B., Gantt, D. L., & Coble, H. M. (1995). Attachment patterns in the psychotherapy relationship: Development of the Client Attachment to Therapist Scale. *Journal of Counseling Psychology, 42,* 307–317.

Mallinckrodt, B., King, J. L., & Coble, H. M. (1998). Family dysfunction, alexithymia, and client attachment to therapist. *Journal of Counseling Psychology, 45,* 497–504.

Mallinckrodt, B., Porter, M. J., & Kivlighan, D. M., Jr. (2005). Client attachment to therapist, depth of in-session exploration, and object relations in brief psychotherapy. *Psychotherapy: Theory, Research, Practice, Training, 42,* 85–100.

Martin, D. J., Garske, J. P., & Davis, M. K. (2000). Relation of the therapeutic alliance with outcome and other variables: A meta-analytic review. *Journal of Consulting and Clinical Psychology, 68,* 438–450.

Mitchell, S. (1999). Attachment theory and the psychoanalytic tradition: Reflections on human relationality. *Psychoanalytic Dialogues, 9,* 85–107.

Nelson, M. L., & Neufeldt, S. A. (1996). Building on an empirical foundation: Strategies to enhance good practice. *Journal of Counseling and Development, 74,* 609–615.

New International Version. (1978). *The Holy Bible, new international version.* Grand Rapids, MI: Zondervan.

Parish, M., & Eagle, M. N. (2003). Attachment to the therapist. *Psychoanalytic Psychology, 20,* 271–286.

Reis, B. F., & Brown, L. G. (1999). Reducing psychotherapy dropouts: Maximizing perspective convergence in the psychotherapy dyad. *Psychotherapy, 36,* 123–136.

Roisman, G. I., Holland, A., Fortuna, K., Fraley, R. C., Clausell, E., & Clarke, A. (2007). The Adult Attachment Interview and self-reports of attachment style: An empirical rapprochement. *Journal of Personality and Social Psychology, 92,* 678–697.

Rosenzweig, S. (1936). Some implicit common factors in diverse methods of psychotherapy. *American Journal of Orthopsychiatry, 6*, 412–415.
Safran, J. D., & Muran, J. C. (2000). *Negotiating the therapeutic alliance: A relational treatment guide.* New York: Guilford Press.
Sandler, J. (1960). The background of safety. *International Journal of Psycho-Analysis, 41*, 352–356.
Schafer, R. (1983). *The analytic attitude.* New York: Basic Books.
Slade, A. (1999). Attachment theory and research: Implications for the theory and practice of individual psychotherapy with adults. In J. Cassidy & P. R. Shaver (Eds.), *Handbook of attachment: Theory, research, and clinical applications* (pp. 575–594). Guilford Press.
Szajnberg, N. M., & Crittenden, P. M. (1997). The transference refracted through the lens of attachment. *Journal of the American Academy of Psychoanalysis, 25*, 409–438.
Talley, P. F., Strupp, H. H., & Morey, L. C. (1990). Match-making in psychotherapy: Patient–therapist dimensions and their impact on outcome. *Journal of Consulting and Clinical Psychology, 58*, 182–188.
Tyrrell, C. L., Dozier, M., Teague, G. B., & Fallot, R. D. (1999). Effective treatment relationships for persons with serious psychiatric disorders: The importance of attachment states of mind. *Journal of Consulting and Clinical Psychology, 67*, 725–733.
Wallin, D. J. (2007). *Attachment in psychotherapy.* Guilford Press.
Weiss, J., & Sampson, H. (1986). *The psychoanalytic process: Theory, clinical observation, and empirical research.* New York: Guilford Press.
Westen, D., & Gabbard, G. O. (2002). Developments in cognitive neuroscience: II. Implications for theories of transference. *Journal of the American Psychoanalytic Association, 50*, 99–134.
Zetzel, E. R. (1956). Current concepts of transference. *International Journal of Psycho-Analysis, 37*, 369–375.

Chapter 9

Final Reflections

Seven Models of Spiritual Intervention

Part I: Models of Spiritual Intervention Conducted by Lay Ministers

Stephen Ministry

Stephen Ministry is a nondenominational Christian model of spiritual intervention founded in 1975 by Kenneth Haugk to carry some of the burdens of pastoral care often borne by the pastor (see Table 9.1). Stephen Ministers meet with their care receivers individually on a weekly basis for an hour and "come alongside" (Bretscher, 2020, p. 127) them for a circumscribed period of time, typically one to two years. Stephen Ministers are explicit in their use of spirituality, sometimes quoting Bible verses of encouragement and praying for their care receivers, but they focus on the process of caring rather than the outcome. The tools of Stephen Ministry include reflective listening, empathy, unconditional positive regard, and genuineness but not confrontation or interpretation. By using these tools, Stephen Ministers create a secure base for care receivers to explore their minds and relationship to God. Care receivers typically present with problems of adjustment such as divorce, loss of significant others, health crises, and the responsibilities of elder care. Stephen Ministers must go through a careful vetting process by a Stephen Leader or pastoral care clergy and then complete 50 hours of training, which includes didactic instruction as well as role-plays. Because Stephen Ministers are volunteers through their church, this caring ministry is free and, in some circumstances, is open to persons outside the church who are struggling and want Christian-focused pastoral care.

Spiritual Direction

Spiritual Direction is a model of spiritual intervention typically associated with early Christianity but practiced by most faith traditions (see Table 9.1). For example, the Shalem Institute program director, who is Episcopalian, has a spiritual

Table 9.1 Features of the Seven Models of Spiritual Intervention at a Glance

Features	SM	SD	12-Step	GP	SG	SIP	AIP
Religious affiliation	Christian	Most faith traditions	None	Christian	None	None	None
Individual/group	Individual	Individual or group	Group/individual	Group	Group	Individual	Individual
Goal	Come alongside struggling Christian	Attend to present moment to experience union with God	Stop addictive behavior	Experience God's presence through Bible stories	Revise God/parent/self-representations	Find spiritual meaning by addressing spiritual struggles	Restore secure attachment relationships to God/significant others
Explicit/implicit spirituality	Explicit	Explicit	Explicit	Explicit	Explicit	Explicit or implicit	Explicit or implicit
Safe haven/secure base	Provides reflective listening	Provides reflective and contemplative listening	Emotionally available 24/7	Facilitates creative exploration	Facilitates exploration of mental representations	Facilitates spiritual and mental exploration	Facilitates spiritual and mental exploration
Inclusion/exclusion	Problems of adjustment	Desire for deeper connection to the Divine	Desire to stop addictive behavior	Sunday school attendance (ages 3–12)	Desire to explore spirituality in group setting	Symptomatic; searching for spiritual meaning	Symptomatic; searching for spiritual meaning

(Continued)

Table 9.1 (Continued)

Features	SM	SD	12-Step	GP	SG	SIP	AIP
Caregiver training	50 hours	2 residencies (19 days); 4 Zoom intensives (24 hours); 15 monthly 2-hour peer group supervisions (30 hours)	Working the 12 steps with a sponsor	18 hours	Mental health degree/divinity degree and license	Mental health degree and license	Mental health degree and license
Frequency	Weekly[a]	Monthly[a]	Weekly[b]	Weekly	Weekly[a]	Weekly[a]	Weekly[a]
Meeting length	60 minutes	45 minutes	60–90 minutes	45–60 minutes	45 minutes	45 minutes	45 minutes
Cost[c]	Free	Free–$150/session	Free	Free	Free–$250/session	$150–250/session	$150–250/session

Notes: SM = Stephen Ministry. SD = Spiritual Direction. 12-Step = 12-Step programs. GP = Godly Play. SG = spirituality groups. SIP = Spiritually Integrated Psychotherapy. AIP = Attachment-Informed Psychotherapy.
[a] Frequency can vary. [b] Members attend as frequently or infrequently as needed. Meetings with a sponsor are scheduled separately. [c] Estimates are based on 2025 norms.

director who is a Buddhist nun. Regardless of faith tradition, the spiritual director helps the directee to attend to the present moment to experience union with God, as the directee understands God. Spiritual directors are explicit about their use of spirituality, usually opening a session with a prayer and silent meditation and maintaining the focus on the feeling of God's presence (or absence) during the session. How is God (or the Spirit) communicating to the spiritual director and directee in the present moment? Has the spiritual director created the mind-quieting conditions under which both participants can hear God's "still small voice" (I Kings 19:12, King James Version)? The tools of Spiritual Direction include reflective listening (like Stephen Ministry) as well as contemplative listening—sitting in silence and listening for the Spirit to "speak." By using these tools, spiritual directors create a secure base from which the directee can explore their heart in search of the One Who has always been there, waiting for them. Unlike Stephen Ministers, spiritual directors sparingly use confrontation and interpretation as interventions. Spiritual directees do not typically present for direction in a crisis but, instead, become increasingly aware of a desire for a deeper connection to the Divine. Training to become a spiritual director is rigorous and includes extensive reading, paper writing, two residencies, four Zoom intensives, and 15 monthly peer group supervisions. Spiritual directors typically meet with their directees on a monthly basis, sometimes offering their services free of charge but at other times charging up to $150 per session.

Twelve-Step Programs

Alcoholics Anonymous (AA) and other 12-step programs have no religious affiliation but explicitly acknowledge spirituality by codifying belief in a Higher Power in their 12 steps, their suggested program of recovery (see Table 9.1). Founded by Bill W. and Dr. Bob in 1935, AA spawned the establishment of at least 43 12-step programs at least partially patterned after AA. All 12-step programs seek to help the addict who still suffers from their addiction to acknowledge their powerlessness over the addictive behavior and the resulting unmanageability of their lives because of this disease (Step 1) and turn their will and their lives over to the care of a Higher Power of their own understanding (Steps 2 and 3). The tools of recovery include attending 12-step meetings, reading 12-step literature, and developing a relationship to a sponsor, who has worked the 12 steps and wants to help the sponsee to work them. The sponsor becomes the sponsee's lifeline, offering their availability for support 24 hours per day, 7 days per week—whenever the urge to engage in the addictive behavior becomes too strong for the sponsee to inhibit. In attachment language, the sponsor offers a safe haven when the existential threat of the addictive behavior becomes overwhelming. The sponsee seeks the sponsor's (as well as a Higher Power's) proximity, which provides a sense of protection against this threat and comfort. Anyone who has a desire to stop their addictive behavior can become a member. A sponsee becomes a sponsor by having worked the 12 steps with their own sponsor. A sponsee typically attends free weekly group meetings as well as separately scheduled free meetings with their sponsor. All 12-step programs are self-supporting, and their help is always free.

Godly Play

Godly Play is a nondenominational Christian model of spiritual intervention founded in the early 1970s by Jerome Berryman to enliven Sunday school teaching of children ages 3–12 through the playful telling of Bible stories and liturgical events (see Table 9.1). Berryman and his wife, Thea, moved to Bergamo, Italy, to study at the Center for Advanced Montessori Studies, which provided them with the methods that they would later incorporate into their so-called "Christian language system" of four linguistic genres: sacred stories, parables of Jesus, liturgical actions, and contemplative silence. The Berrymans wanted children to experience God's presence through storytelling with props and "I wonder" questions, with an opportunity to respond to this storytelling through a free play time in which they could express their feelings to God. Godly Play makes spirituality explicit through children's confrontation of four existential limits: death, the need for meaning, the threat of freedom, and aloneness. The four linguistic genres of Godly Play provide children with a language—the Christian language—that they then internalize and carry with them throughout life to help them confront these existential limits. Through their attitude of total acceptance of the children's responses, Godly Play teachers provide a secure base from which the children can creatively explore their experiences of and feelings about God and communicate with God, knowing that they are safe to do so. Any child who attends Sunday school can participate in Godly Play, which does not require church membership. Training to become a teacher requires a minimum of 18 hours of didactic instruction as well as role-plays. Because Godly Play teachers are volunteers through their church, this model of spiritual intervention is free.

Part II: Models of Spiritual Intervention Conducted by Licensed Professionals

Spirituality Groups

Spirituality groups are a therapeutic model of spiritual intervention, led by a licensed mental health professional and a chaplain or pastor, that explores a specific topic (see Table 9.1). In my Chapter 6 illustration, group members explore their mental representations of God, parents, and self, but other topics are available to explore in this model such as loss, divorce, parenting special needs children, or aging. Group members can come from many different settings such as psychiatric units, prisons, Veterans Administration (VA) centers, unhoused shelters, oncology units, and, of course, churches. Having two group leaders with different skill sets ensures that both psychology and spirituality are explicitly incorporated into the participant experience. Group members want to change their mental representations of God, parents, and self, as well as their mental representations of a spiritual struggle such as clergy betrayal. Group leaders provide a secure base from which participants can explore their various mental representations without fear of judgment or internal or external threat. These groups are open to anyone who wants to explore their spirituality in a group setting if they have experience with the specific topic, such as being a special needs parent. Group leaders must have attained either a mental health license (minimum of 2 years of graduate-level training) or a master of divinity degree (minimum of 3 years of graduate-level training). If offered as part of a patient's psychiatric care (e.g., in a psychiatric unit), spirituality groups are free. If offered as a service within a church mental health counseling center, however, the patient would pay up to $250 per session.

Spiritually Integrated Psychotherapy

Spiritually Integrated Psychotherapy (SIP) is a therapeutic model of spiritual intervention in which a licensed mental health professional listens for opportunities to address the patient's spirituality, either explicitly or implicitly (see Table 9.1). Authors such as Kenneth Pargament and James Griffith have suggested that even nonreligious persons seek spiritual meaning and bring spiritual struggles to the SIP therapist. These spiritual struggles can produce or be produced by psychiatric symptoms, and the SIP therapist must be alert to these connections and be prepared to address them. The SIP therapist demonstrates to the patient, through careful listening, a nonjudgmental attitude and, through nonreactivity, an unconditional acceptance of the patient's entire being. This therapeutic attitude creates not only a safe haven for patients to find comfort but also a secure base from which to explore their spiritual and mental struggles. The therapist leverages the developing therapist–patient relationship to help the patient understand their expectations in the relationship. These therapeutic experiences give the patient the freedom to restore their relationship to a Higher Power, which for the patient can be a profound sense of transcendence, boundlessness, or the eternal. In contrast to the spiritual directee, who is considered psychologically well-adjusted and seeking a deeper connection to a Higher Power, the ideal patient in SIP is someone experiencing psychiatric symptoms and searching for spiritual meaning, whether explicitly or implicitly. SIP therapists must earn a mental health degree (minimum of 2 years of graduate-level training) and pass the licensure examination in their state. Having earned a certification specifically in SIP is also helpful in practicing this model of spiritual intervention. Because psychotherapy takes place with a licensed mental health professional, SIP is seldom free. Typically,

SIP costs between $150 and $250 per session, depending on the therapist's level of experience as well as geographical location.

Attachment-Informed Psychotherapy

Attachment-Informed Psychotherapy (AIP) is a specific model of SIP that focuses on attachment relationships that the patient has developed to their caregivers during childhood, to a Higher Power, and to the therapist (see Table 9.1). The AIP therapist seeks to change the patient's attachment relationships to caregivers, significant others, and a Higher Power from insecure to secure by not only observing but also participating in the patient's attachment relationship to the therapist. Through the phenomenon of transference, the AIP therapist creates the conditions under which the patient begins to perceive the emotionally responsive therapist as stronger and wiser—the criteria for establishing a person as an attachment figure. The AIP therapist can address the patient's spirituality explicitly or implicitly, always listening for opportunities to address the patient's spiritual struggles exacerbated by an insecure attachment relationship to a Higher Power. As with SIP, the AIP therapist creates not only a safe haven for patients to find comfort but also a secure base from which to explore their spiritual and mental struggles, focusing on their attachment relationships. The AIP therapist evaluates the patient as belonging to one of four attachment relationship models (secure, anxious-avoidant, anxious-resistant, disorganized/disoriented) and uses gentle challenge to move the patient out of their insecure mode of relating into a secure mode of relating. As with SIP, the ideal patient in AIP is someone experiencing psychiatric symptoms and searching for spiritual meaning, whether explicitly or implicitly. Like SIP therapists, AIP therapists must have earned a mental health degree (minimum of 2 years of graduate-level training) and passed the licensure examination in their state. The cost for AIP is also similar to the cost for SIP.

Comparisons Between Lay Ministers and Licensed Professionals

I want to end this book by comparing the models of spiritual intervention conducted by lay ministers with those conducted by licensed mental health professionals, because clergy and licensed mental health professionals need to be aware of which referral option is best suited to the person who presents for help. Psychotherapy is focused on relieving patients of their psychiatric symptoms. Some writers suggest that psychiatric symptoms are byproducts of an individualistic society shaped by late-stage capitalism. According to this argument, psychotherapy plays a role in maintaining the status quo because it "becomes a substitute for social change, a way of encouraging adjustment and so reducing discontent" (Leech, 1977, p. 104). Psychotherapy even "perpetuat[es] injustice by its lack of awareness of social and political dimensions" (p. 104). By contrast, spiritual direction, conducted by lay ministers, is focused "not so much on the prevention and treatment of sickness as on the achievement of salvation" (p. 96). According to this view, spiritual direction is a superior model of spiritual intervention because it focuses on cultivating what is eternal—the human soul—while psychotherapy focuses on adjusting to the prevailing social conditions. I am reminded of I John 2:17 (New International Version [NIV]): "Do not love the world or anything in the world. ... The world and its desires pass away, but whoever does the will of God lives forever." Psychotherapy seems to facilitate a greater love of the world through conformity, whereas spiritual direction seems to facilitate a greater love of God through an awareness of the eternal. Palmer (1990) even suggests that licensed mental health professionals promote and perpetuate "a silent conspiracy to stay in business by making sure that society never runs out of the problems that [licensed mental health professionals] know how to solve" (pp. 43–44).

Although I sympathize with this criticism of psychotherapy, spiritual direction and other lay ministries must also struggle with addressing problems that plague people in the world and still "not conform to the pattern of this world" (Romans 12:2, NIV). In fact,

> without first locating ourselves and, in some measure, shifting our location ... our ministry simply maintains relationships of dominance under the guise of ministry. ... In such a case, the ministry of spiritual direction becomes a tool to enforce and maintain "business as usual." (Reed, 2000, p. 97)

Thus, psychotherapy is not the only model of spiritual intervention potentially adapted to cultural and social norms at the expense of searching for meaning in the transcendent.

In Chapter 3, Julie is struggling to figure out how to support her family if she loses her job. She experiences anxiety and perhaps also depression. Taking away her anxiety and depression might not make her a better employee, but it just might give her the courage and mental energy to explore other job options such as ministry. Leech (1977) and Palmer (1990) suggest that an implicit dualism exists between models of spiritual intervention conducted by licensed mental health professionals and models of spiritual intervention conducted by lay ministers: psychotherapy treats patients so that they become more efficient cogs in the machinery of an oppressive society, whereas spiritual direction and other lay ministries help patients to focus on what is truly important—a deeper connection to God. Jesus's ministry, however, contains no such dualism. In the story of the feeding of the 5,000, Jesus shows compassion for the crowd that has gathered from faraway places to hear him preach by feeding them fish and bread

(Matthew 14:13–21; Mark 6:30–44; Luke 9:10–17; John 6:1–14, NIV). Palmer (1990) suggests that,

> human beings are such a complex interaction of body and spirit that they can never be fully satisfied in body alone. Surely the five thousand were satisfied because Jesus had addressed them as whole persons, honored them at every level of authentic human need. (p. 132)

Jesus views the crowd's needs as simultaneously physical and spiritual: there is no dualism. The practice of silent meditation would draw Julie closer to God and simultaneously quiet her mind by helping her to detach from the feared outcomes that cause her so much anxiety.

How can psychotherapy not address spiritual needs? How can spiritual direction not address psychological needs? In spiritual direction, the lay minister "enters the areas of psychological disturbance and psychological health; it concerns itself with issues of distress, inner conflict and upheaval, and mental pain" (Leech, 1977, p. 105). I propose that all models of spiritual intervention—whether conducted by lay ministers or licensed professionals—must address both spiritual and psychological needs. Lay ministers and licensed professionals cannot afford to ignore the spiritual or the psychological dimension, both of which constitute our humanity. Cultural and social norms can also co-opt all models of spiritual intervention, diverting both caregivers and care receivers from the search for meaning in the transcendent.

Even though both lay ministers and licensed professionals must address both spiritual and psychological needs, it appears that psychotherapy emphasizes deficiencies in the psychological dimension, while lay ministries such as Stephen Ministry and Spiritual Direction emphasize deepening the spiritual dimension. Each model has its strengths and weaknesses. Leech (1977) suggests that a SIP therapist can prepare a person for Spiritual Direction by helping them to become "free and autonomous" (p. 119). Obviously, not everyone is ready for Spiritual Direction: "Some people ... are not sufficiently mature for the kind of adult relationship which [spiritual] direction implies, and for them the attempt at such a relationship can be harmful" (p. 119). The SIP therapist can "enabl[e] the individual to become open to the activity of the Spirit, and to become more truly human" (p. 99). A colleague in my Spiritual Direction peer supervision group is working with a spiritual directee who, during contemplative prayer times in their sessions, dissociates from her surroundings. She has a history of childhood trauma. I suggested that this person first seek a course of SIP, conducted at a frequency higher than Spiritual Direction typically affords, before graduating to Spiritual Direction with my colleague. At least, this spiritual directee should attend SIP simultaneously with Spiritual Direction. My colleague is not a licensed professional and thus has no training to address her spiritual directee's trauma or dissociative symptoms.

Barbara Holmes (2017) observes,

> Those who have been traumatized ... may be uncomfortable with reflective and meditative activities. ... Those who have buried [systematic abuse] in the center of their souls are not anxious to participate in activities that will bring the memories and pain back to consciousness. (p. 7)

For situations such as these, spiritual directors should leave the work to the licensed professional—at least initially. After the symptoms subside, the patient is then able to tolerate, and even welcome, the contemplative silence associated with Spiritual Direction and listen to God's still small voice without dissociating.

Final Reflections

I want to make a final comment about the techniques used by lay ministers and licensed professionals related to their respective emphases on spiritual and psychological needs. In Chapters 2 and 3, I suggest that Stephen Ministry and Spiritual Direction primarily use Rogerian techniques such as unconditional positive regard, empathy, and genuineness (Rogers, 1957) to accomplish their aims. In Chapters 6, 7, and 8, I suggest that spirituality groups, SIP, and AIP use a wider range of clinical techniques such as confrontation and interpretation to accomplish their aims. While Rogers champions unqualified acceptance in psychotherapy, which lay ministries have since adopted for their own purposes, Buber (1965) champions confrontation and acceptance of personal responsibility in psychotherapy. We observe this technique in Chapter 8, as the AIP therapist provides a "gentle challenge" (Dozier & Bates, 2004, p. 174; see also Dozier, 2003, p. 254) to help move the patient from an insecure to a secure attachment relationship. Buber recognizes that the therapist encounters a patient in conflict with themselves.

During my training to become a child and adolescent psychoanalyst many years ago, I remember treating a 10-year-old girl and presenting an early session to my supervisor, Delia Battin. The girl repeatedly tossed a baby doll into the air and dropped it. I pretended to voice the baby doll: "Ow, that hurts! Mommy, stop dropping me!" The girl's behavior continued. Later that week, in supervision, my supervisor asked me, "Did you consider taking the girl's point of view? Perhaps it feels good to drop the baby." I was so invested in the victim/baby doll's point of view that I never considered the victimizer/girl's point of view. This girl needed to identify with her aggressor (the mother), which made her feel good because she was actively reversing the roles between her mother and her. She was no longer the drop-ee; she was now the drop-er.

I use this story to illustrate the fact that our minds contain many mental representations in conflict with each other. At certain times, we identify with a specific mental representation; at other times, we identify with a different one in conflict with the first. Lay ministers who try to empathize with their care receivers must decide which parts of them to empathize with. I was empathizing only with the baby part of my patient's mind and not empathizing with the mommy part. Empathy and validation can take a caregiver only so far. Knowing which mental representations to empathize with at which moments requires considerable skill and empathy for the totality of a patient, not just the parts that speak to us in their immediacy. Licensed professionals have presumably acquired the skill necessary to interpret these different parts to the patient and to help the patient to empathize with their unacceptable parts. The caregiver's empathizing with all parts of the care receiver's personality is sometimes best achieved with a gentle challenge, not empathy applied indiscriminately. My voicing the baby doll's feelings was not wrong but one-sided. I could have also commented that it feels good to drop the baby, thus voicing the sadistic mommy part of this girl. These are the initial steps that I took to cultivate this girl's compassion for her baby parts and mommy parts simultaneously.

In this book, I tried to demonstrate that each of these seven models of spiritual intervention meets both spiritual and psychological needs but tends to emphasize one over the other. A care receiver seeks spiritual intervention possessing a particular personality structure, level of spiritual maturity, and set of immediate needs that often suggest one specific model of spiritual intervention. Despite the differences inherent in these seven models, they should all model love, acceptance, and grace. Ultimately, lay ministers and licensed professionals must follow their spiritual intuition in both listening and responding to the person's verbal and nonverbal communications, especially their emotional expressions, when making the referral to one of these models of spiritual intervention. This is what I personally seek in a model of spiritual intervention:

> Be transformed by the renewing of your mind. (Romans 12:2, NIV)

> Jesus sought me when a stranger
> Wandering from the fold of God
> He to rescue me from danger
> Interposed His precious blood
> Prone to wander, Lord, I feel it
> Prone to leave the God I love
> Here's my heart, O take and seal it
> Seal it for Thy courts above. (Robinson, 1758)

> We need a bond of love
> That takes away the fear
> A bond that spans the distance
> Between me and You. (Goodman, 1985)

References

Bretscher, J. P. (Ed.). (2020). *Stephen Minister training manual, Volume 1*. Stephen Ministries.
Buber, M. (1965). *The knowledge of man: Selected essays*. Harper & Row.
Dozier, M. (2003). Attachment-based treatment for vulnerable children. *Attachment and Human Development, 5*, 253–257.
Dozier, M., & Bates, B. C. (2004). Attachment state of mind and the treatment relationship. In L. Atkinson & S. Goldberg (Eds.), *Attachment issues in psychopathology and intervention* (pp. 167–180). Erlbaum.
Goodman, G. (1985). Trying to find a home [Song]. Grimm Music.
Holmes, B. (2017). *Joy unspeakable: Contemplative practices of the black church* (2nd ed.). Fortress Press.
King James Version. (2017). *The Holy Bible, King James version*. Thomas Nelson.
Leech, K. (1977). *Soul friend: The practice of Christian spirituality*. Harper & Row.
New International Version. (1978). *The Holy Bible, new international version*. Zondervan.
Palmer, P. J. (1990). *The active life: A spirituality of work, creativity, and caring*. Harper & Row.
Reed, J. (2000). Can I get a witness? Spiritual direction with the marginalized. In N. Vest (Ed.), *Still listening: New horizons in spiritual direction* (pp. 93–104). Morehouse.
Robinson, R. (1758). Come Thou fount of every blessing [Song]. In the public domain. https://en.wikipedia.org/wiki/Come_Thou_Fount_of_Every_Blessing
Rogers, C. R. (1957). The necessary and sufficient conditions of therapeutic personality change. *Journal of Consulting Psychology, 21*, 95–103.

Author Index

Aafjes-van Doorn, K. 185
Ackerman, A. 103
Ainsworth, M. D. S. 12–14, 97, 116, 164
Akers, I. B. 40, 44, 47, 101
Alexander, B. K. 92
Alexander, F. 164, 194, 200
Allen, J. P. 93
Allers, R. 73
Allison, E. 43
Amini, F. 183
Anderson, N. 163
Arizmendi, T. 191
Arvidson, J. 43
Astin, H. S. 152
Au, N. C. 171
Au, W. 171

Barnett, W. S. 119
Baron-Cohen, S. 189
Barrett, J. L. 21, 149
Barry, W. A. 65
Bateman, A. 76
Bates, B. C. 41, 73, 192, 195–197, 199, 200, 217
Benjamin, J. 187
Bernier, A. 192, 195, 197, 199
Berryman, J. W. 108–117
Berzins, J. I. 191
Beutel, M. E. 63, 191
Beutler, L. E. 20
Bishop, S. R. 57, 58, 70
Blakney, R. 55, 67
Blatt, S. J. 20, 138, 166
Blinder, B. J. 63
Bordin, E. S. 185
Bouwhuis-Van Keulen, A. J. 163

Bowlby, J. 9, 11, 12, 14, 20, 67, 68, 70, 71, 78, 95, 100, 103, 115, 130, 161, 182, 183, 188, 189, 194
Bradley, D. F. 150
Bradley, R. 185
Brand, B. L. 199
Bretscher, J. P. 11, 33, 36, 38–40, 45, 60, 208
Briggs, J. R. 2
Brown, C. 72–73
Brown, L. G. 191
Bryant, A. N. 152
Buber, M. 217
Bullock, S. L. 167
Burke, L. A. 152
Burns, P. 184
Burtchaell, J. T. 54, 65–66, 77

Captari, L. E. 163
Carlson, E. A. 13, 14
Carnes, P. 82, 83, 85–86
Cassian, J. 64
Cassibba, R. 127
Cassidy, J. 190
Castonguay, L. G. 201
Charone, J. K. 191
Chefetz, R. A. 199
Chryssavgis, J. 64
Clarkin, J. F. 183, 193, 195
Cohen, J. 162
Cohen, L. 66
Cole, B. S. 162
Cole, M. 120
Cooper, G. 190, 193
Cooper-White, P. 6
Crastnopol, M. 190
Crittenden, J. 103

Crittenden, P. M. 195
Crocker, M. M. 93
Cuthbertson, A. 69

Daniel, S. I. F. 14–19, 41, 94–97
de Dreuille, M. 64
de Wit, H. F. 53, 55, 56, 58, 62–63, 67–68, 71, 75
De Wolff, M. 189
Dent, V. 118, 121
DeSteno, D. 91
Diamond, D. 183, 192, 193, 195
Doehring, C. 6
Dougherty, R. M. 62, 65
Dozier, M. 41, 73, 164, 192–197, 199–200, 217
Dykstra, R. C. 6, 8–10

Eagle, M. N. 183, 184, 189, 190, 193
Edwards, T. 53, 54, 56, 58–62, 64, 75–77
Eichberg, C. G. 13
Exline, J. J. 4, 148–152, 154, 156, 161, 163, 165, 170

Fairbairn, W. R. D. 134
Farber, B. A. 183, 186, 187
Felsen, I. 20, 166
Ferber, R. 186, 202
Fisher, J. W. 112
Flaskerud, J. H. 191
Flora, K. 82
Fonagy, P. 20, 43, 76, 93, 112, 137, 189
Ford, R. 20
French, T. M. 164, 194, 200
Freud, S. 10, 35, 57, 59–61, 73, 111, 153, 183–185, 191, 195, 197, 201, 202

Gabbard, G. O. 185
Gallagher, R. E. 129
Garvey, C. 111
Geller, J. 187
George, C. 14
Gerkin, C. V. 173
Goldwyn, R. 14, 70, 137, 191, 192
Goleman, D. 70
Gonçalves, J. P. B. 162
Goodman, G. 2, 6, 12, 13, 15, 20, 39, 85, 86, 93, 100, 118, 121, 129, 130, 137, 138, 155, 158–160, 162, 166, 172, 186, 187, 189, 192–194, 197, 198, 200, 202

Granqvist, P. 4, 19, 41, 69, 96, 127–129, 165, 198
Grant, B. 111, 112
Greenberg, J. R. 37, 184, 198
Greenberg, L. 43, 185
Greenson, R. R. 184
Grice, H. P. 161
Griffith, J. L. 4, 148–149, 154, 159, 165, 167, 199
Gustafson, W. 148

Harlow, H. F. 12
Harwood, T. M. 20
Haugk, K. C. 11, 33, 36, 39–40, 44, 46, 47, 60, 101
Hawkins, I. L. 167
Hay, D. 111
Hayes, J. A. 151
Hayes, S. C. 57, 58
Hesse, E. 10, 14, 137, 161, 166
Hoffman, I. Z. 190, 193, 198
Holmes, B. 217
Holmes, J. 183
Horowitz, H. A. 93
Horvath, A. 43, 185
Hyde, B. 112

Ingraham, C. L. 157

Jacobvitz, D. 93
Jaoudi, M. 66
John of the Cross 59, 77
Johnson, C. V. 151
Jones, E. E. 24, 190
Jones, J. M. 3
Jones, R. S. 77, 148, 154, 165

Kabat-Zinn, J. 57, 70
Kantrowitz, J. L. 190, 198
Karen, R. 13
Keating, T. 59
Kelly, J. F. 82
Kennedy, R. E. 4, 19
Kernberg, O. F. 57, 135, 137
Kirkpatrick, L. A. 96, 128, 137, 165
Kobak, R. R. 191, 192, 194, 200
Kohut, H. 92
Kraus, S. W. 143

Laird, M. 53, 55, 66, 68
Landreth, G. L. 173

Lanzetta, B. 63, 67, 172
Lartey, E. Y. 6, 7, 10, 15
Leech, K. 66, 214–216
Lewis, C. S. 150
Lichtenberg, J. D. 151
Luborsky, L. 185, 191
Lyons, L. S. 183
Lyons-Ruth, K. 13, 14

Mackie, A. J. 183, 184
Mahler, M. S. 184
Maier, K. E. 63
Main, M. 10, 13–14, 70, 137, 164, 191, 192
Mallinckrodt, B. 183
Martin, D. J. 185
Marure, C. C. 22
May, G. G. 53, 55, 58, 68, 77
Mehrabian, A. 110
Merton, T. 64
Mesman, J. 14–15, 164
Midgley, N. 97
Mikulincer, M. 161
Minkoff, R. 73
Minor, C. V. 111, 112
Mitchell, S. A. 183
Moon, H. 10
Mullen, J. A. 114
Muran, J. C. 185
Muratori, F. 112
Murphy, P. E. 151
Murray-Swank, N. A. 162

Neimeyer, R. A. 152
Nelson, M. L. 191
Neufeldt, S. A. 157, 191
Nicolopoulou, A. 120
Nkara, F. 127
Novac, A. 63
Nye, R. 111

Paley, V. G. 119, 120
Palmer, P. J. 215, 216
Pargament, K. I. 4, 96, 148–152, 154–156, 158–163, 165, 170, 171
Parish, M. 183, 184, 189
Park, C. L. 152
Pattison, E. M. 161
Patton, J. 6–8
Peale, N. V. 34
Pfiffner, K. 113
Propst, L. R. 158

Ramsay, N. J. 6
Reed, G. M. 86
Reed, J. 215
Reis, B. F. 191
Reynolds, N. 152
Rieger, K. L. 130
Riggs, S. A. 93
Rizzuto, A.-M. 114, 127, 128, 155
Roan, C. 1
Roberto, J. 113
Robinson, R. 218
Rockland, R. H. 39
Rogers, C. R. 6, 39, 52, 159, 160, 217
Rohr, R. 66
Roisman, G. I. 93, 165, 195
Rosenstein, D. S. 93
Rosenzweig, S. 111, 191
Rosmarin, D. H. 151
Roth, A. 20
Rubin, J. B. 71–72

Safran, J. D. 185
Sampson, H. 183
Sandler, J. 115, 183
Sarna, N. 117
Schafer, R. 183
Scheib, K. D. 2, 6
Schuengel, C. 14
Schwartz, G. E. R. 70
Sedlar, A. E. 150
Shahar, G. 20
Shapiro, S. L. 70
Shedler, J. 73
Singh, K. D. 68, 72
Skinner, B. F. 153
Slade, A. 14, 19, 41, 164–166, 192
Smith, T. B. 162
Snodgrass, J. L. 153, 154
Solomon, J. 13, 164
Sperling, M. 183
Sterba, R. F. 57
Sting 54
Stovall-McClough, K. C. 164, 183, 192
Sue, S. 157
Sullivan, H. S. 9
Sunderland, R. H. 22
Symonds, B. 185
Szajnberg, N. M. 195

Talley, P. F. 191
Thomas, M. 172

Thurman, H. 63
Tisdale, T. C. 158
Townsend, L. 153
Tyrrell, C. L. 192, 194–195, 197, 199, 200

Ulanov, A. B. 164

van der Kolk, B. A. 36, 78
van Gogh, V. 69
van IJzendoorn, M. H. 13, 189
Vennard, J. E. 119, 121
Vidrine, A. 59
Vygotsky, L. S. 115

Walker, A. 163–164
Wallin, D. J. 10, 182

Wang, Z. 117
Ward, A. F. 78
Waters, E. 14, 164
Watson, J. B. 153
Weiland, C. 119
Weiss, J. 183
Westen, D. 16–19, 185
Winnicott, D. W. 59–60, 127, 136
Wittig, B. A. 13
Wolf, E. S. 92

Yoshikawa, H. 119

Zapf, J. L. 93
Zetzel, E. R. 185
Zigler, E. F. 119

Subject Index

Bolded page numbers indicate a table; *italicized* page numbers indicate a figure

acceptance, deep 160
addiction 86
   defined 87
   diagnostic criteria 86–87
Adolescent Attachment Prototype
      Questionnaire (AAPQ) 16
Adult Attachment Interview (AAI) 14,
   128, 192, 194, 195
African Americans 7–8, 20, 152, 163–164
Alcoholics Anonymous (AA) 82, 85, 94,
   97–99, 211
   founding 88. *See also* Big Book;
      Bill W.
alcoholism
   religion and the psychodynamics of 86.
      See also Alcoholics Anonymous;
      Bill W.
aloneness 110. *See also* existential limits
ambiguity, intolerance of 159
American Association of Pastoral
      Counselors (AAPC) 153
Anthony the Great 64
anxious-avoidant attachment pattern 16–17
   and the practice of contemplation 70–71
   in spiritual intervention 42
anxious-resistant attachment pattern 17–18
   in spiritual intervention 42–43
arts-based spiritual care (ABSC) 130
Association for Clinical Pastoral
      Education (ACPE) 153, 156,
      168–169, 172
atheists 153
   spiritual struggles 150–151. *See also* Blair
attachment concepts applicable to therapist–
   patient relationship 183, **184**

Attachment-Informed Psychotherapy
   (AIP) 37, 164, 178, 188–189,
   196, 202
   description of 214
   features **209–210**
   essence of 197
   indications for 199–200
   Pilgrim and 37
   Séamus and 199–200
   Spiritual Direction and 73, 74, 76, 78,
      209–210
   spiritually curious persons and 166
   Spiritually Integrated Psychotherapy
      (SIP) and 163, 166, 200,
      209–210, 214
   training requirements to become AIP
      therapist 200
attachment needs, therapist's secure
      base provision and patient's
      underlying 189–199
attachment patterns 13–19
   assessment 16. *See also* Adult At-
      tachment Interview; Strange
      Situation
   interpersonal markers that discriminate
      among. *See* interpersonal markers
   matched with models of spiritual inter-
      vention 19–21
   in spiritual intervention 41–44
Attachment Q-Set (AQS) 192
attachment representations 14
attachment strategies of therapist and
      patient, secondary
   interaction structures based on **197**,
      197–198

Subject Index

attachment theory 9, 183
  application as an organizing framework 11–12
  Godly Play viewed in the context of 115–116
  role across cultures 14–15
  role in individualizing spiritual care 12–14
  Spiritual Direction viewed in context of 67–73
authenticity 158, 159. *See also* therapeutic change
availability of caregiver 183

Berryman, Jerome W. 108–117, 122, 212
Berryman, Thea 113–114, 212
Bible 108, 188. *See also* Jesus; New Testament
Big Book (AA) 84, 90, 99, 103, 104
  on character of those who fail to recover in AA 88
  on ego and surrender 86
  and other 12-step programs 85, 90
  on resentment 83
  on sponsorship 91, 100, 101
  Step 1 in 85
Bill W. (co-founder of AA) 82, 94–96, 99
  autobiography 87, 89, 90
  God and 87, 89, 90, 96, 97
  hospitalizations 87
  Oxford Group and 88–90, 96
  on prayer and meditation 89–90, 97
  on reading recovery literature 90
  spiritual conversion 87–88
  and surrender to Higher Power 85
  12-step model and 87–91, 94–98. *See also* Big Book; *Twelve Steps and Twelve Traditions*
Black Lives Matter (BLM) movement 7
blacks. *See* African Americans
Blair, case of
  atheism 142–145, 157
  case conceptualization introduction 142
  Goodman's spirituality and therapeutic process 145
  interventions 144
  presenting issues and diagnosis 143
  session excerpts 144–145
  spiritual assessment 143
Boison, Anton 9
bond (subscale of Working Alliance Inventory) 185

borderline personality disorder (BPD) 129, 135–138. *See also* spirituality groups
Buddhism 4, 70–73, 143

"California" (Roan) 1
care receivers 33. *See also specific topics*
caregiver–infant attachment relationship
  as metaphor for therapist–patient relationship 182–185
  limitations 185–187
  reflections on 187–189
caregivers 33
  availability 183
  types of 4–5, **5**. *See also* lay ministers; licensed professionals
Catholicism and Catholic Church 131–133
Catholics 127–128
chaplains 139
Christian-based recovery programs 21–22
Christian caring, principles of distinctively 38–40
Christian linguistic genres 108
clergy–laity collaboration 22
client-centered therapy. *See* person-centered therapy and interventions
clinical paradigm of pastoral care 6
Color Purple, The (Walker) 163–164
communal contextual paradigm of pastoral care 6–7
compensation hypothesis (God representations) 128, 129, 135–138
compensation pathway 196, 198
complementary vs. noncomplementary therapeutic dyads 191–197, **197**, 199–201
complex spiritual struggles 151
confession 89
conflict management 96. *See also* interpersonal markers
contemplation
  anxious-avoidant attachment and the practice of 70–71
  Christian 63–64, 66, 75–77
  H. F. de Wit on 62–63, 67, 68, 71, 75
contemplative literature 54, 55, 62–63, 66–69, 77
contemplative prayer 49, 50. *See also* meditation

contemplative silence 75–76, 108
continuing education (CE) requirements 169
correspondence hypothesis (God representations) 127–129, 135–138
correspondence pathway 128, 196, 198
counseling-inspired Spiritual Direction 61
countertransference 10, 159, 181
   description of 10, 52
   transference and 10–11, 52, 182

de Wit, H. F. 55, 56, 62, 68
   contemplation and 62–63, 67, 68, 71, 75
   on Spiritual Direction 53, 63
deactivating attachment strategy 191–195, **197**, 197–198, 200
death, as existential limit 110. *See also* existential limits
delayed grief in a care receiver 33–38
demonic struggles 150
Dent, Valeda 7–8, 118, 119
dependence/independence 70, 94, 191–193. *See also* interpersonal markers
detachment, theoretical problems with 67–69
discipling 61
dismissing attachment strategy 191–193, 196, **197**
disorganized/disoriented attachment pattern 18–19
   in spiritual intervention 43–44
Dittes, James 9, 10
divine struggles 150
doubt struggles 150
Dowling, Edward 98
dualism 215–216

Ebby T. 88
Eckhart, Meister 55, 67
ecologist 182
ego/false self
   addiction and 86
   attachment and 67
   description of 53–55, 67
   God and 53–55, 67, 86
   separateness and 54, 68
   sin and 54, 55
   surrender/death of 53, 55, 61, 67, 86
eldering 61
emotion regulation 97, 183. *See also* interpersonal markers

empathy 6, 173, 218
   attachment patterns and 15–18. *See also* interpersonal markers; Stephen Ministry program: interventions; therapeutic change
encouragement 40, 41. *See also* Stephen Ministry program: interventions
epistemic trust 43–44
existential anxiety 150, 161. *See also* spiritual struggles
existential limits 110, 114–117
expectations of others. *See* interpersonal markers

false self. *See* ego/false self
feelings, strong 183
Florence, case of
   case conceptualization introduction 145
   Goodman's spirituality and therapeutic process 147–148
   interventions 146–147
   presenting issues and diagnosis 146
   session excerpts 147
   spiritual assessment 146
forgiveness 179–181
freedom, threat of 110. *See also* existential limits
Freud, Sigmund
   attachment and 183–185, 197
   on technique 59–61, 191, 201
   on transference 183–185

gay patients. *See* Séamus
"gentle challenge" 41, 61, 70, 73, 196, 214, 217, 218
Gentle Path Through the Twelve Steps, A (Carnes) 82, 83, 85, 100
"gentle whisper" 172, 193
genuineness. *See* authenticity; therapeutic change
gifted spiritual direction 61
goal (subscale of Working Alliance Inventory) 185
God
   anthropomorphic 21
   Bill W. and 87, 89, 90, 96, 97
   as "Curegiver" 11, 36, 39, 40, 46, 60
   ego/false self and 53–55, 67, 86
   Jesus and 35, 54
   relationship with 77. *See also under* surrender

secure attachment 93–94
transference 9–10
separation from 54, 67–68
silence and 59, 60, 65
silent prayer and 49, 51–52, 56. *See also* Higher Power; Hudson; Jasmine; Julie; twelve-step programs; *specific topics*
God representations. *See* mental representations: of God
Godly Play (GP)
  description of 212
  definition 108–110
  features **209–210**
  purpose 110–111
  empirical evidence supporting the effectiveness of 111–113
  history 113–114
  indications for 116–118
  training requirements to practice 118
  viewed in the context of attachment theory 115–116
grace 160
grandiose self 96, 135, 137. *See also* narcissism
grief, delayed 33–38
group Spiritual Direction 62

help, attitude to seeking and receiving. *See* interpersonal markers
Higher Power 12. *See also* God
Holy Spirit 77
  defined 52
  Spiritual Direction and 52–53, 59, 65
homosexuality. *See* Séamus
Hudson, case of 133–135
  God and 129, 133–136
  drawing of her representation of God 131, *132*
humanistic psychology 6, 39
hyperactivating attachment strategy 191–195, **197**, 198, 200

Images of Pastoral Care (Dystra) 8–11
implicit spiritual assessment 156
implicit spiritual interventions 142
implicit spirituality 142
informal relationships 61–62
insight, cultivation of 53–54
interaction structures (Sullivan) 9
intercultural paradigm of pastoral care 7

internal working models 14
interpersonal markers (that characterize attachment patterns)
  attachment patterns and 15–19, 41–43
  Bill W. and 97
  description of 14, 94
  12 steps and 94–97
interpersonal struggles 150
interpretation 59–61, 77, 173

Jasmine, case of
  abusive childhood 134
  God and 130–136
  drawing of her representation of God 130, **131**
Jesus 6, 171, 218
  attachment security and 68
  children and 110–111
  death and 110
  on death of ego 55
  detachment and 69
  God and 35, 54
  Godly Play and 117, 122
  human divinity and 66
  nondualism and 215–216
  parables 65, 108
  quotes v, 6, 35, 55, 66, 68, 69, 117, 145
  resurrection 110–111
  Stephen Ministers and 38
Julie, case of 49, 215
  areas of concern in her life 49
  excerpt from second session 49–51
  God and 49–52, 56, 60, 65, 66, 78, 216
  meditation and 50, 56, 59
  and silent prayer and meditation 49, 51–52, 56, 216
  Spiritual Direction and 49, 51–52, 56, 59–61, 65, 66, 78
  transference and countertransference 51, 52

lay ministers **5**, 5–7, 55
  compared with licensed professionals 5, **5**, 214–217
  defined 5. *See also specific intervention models*
Lewis, C. S. 144, 150, 157
licensed professionals 168
  compared with lay ministers 5, **5**, 214–217

defined 5. *See also specific intervention models*
Lion King, The (film) 73

malpractice insurance 153
master–disciple relationship 61
meaning, need for 110. *See also* existential limits
meditation 50, 57
  12-step programs and 89–90, 96
mental health professionals. *See* licensed professionals
mental representations
  defined 184
  of God 68, 69, 127–129, 134–138, 164
    drawings of God 130, 131, **131**, *132*
mentalization 189
mentorship 64. *See also* sponsorship
mindfulness 53, 57, 58, 70–71
Montessori, Maria 113–115, 122
moral dilemmas 170–171
moral inventory, taking a 95
moral struggles 150
Mustard Seed, parable of the 107–109
mutual Spiritual Direction 62

narcissism 86, 91, 102, 135–138
  grandiose self and 96, 135, 137
New Testament 1, 3, 39–40, 64, 108, 188. *See also* Jesus
noncomplementary therapeutic dyads
  defined 192. *See also* complementary vs. noncomplementary therapeutic dyads
nondualism 215–216

object representations
  God representations and 127–129, 134–138. *See also* mental representations
Old Testament 3, 108, 188
open-mindedness 53, 54. *See also* unknowing
openness 94, 136, 137, 158. *See also* interpersonal markers
Original Sin 54, 56, 66, 67
Oxford Group 88–90, 96

parables 107, 108
  Parable of the Mustard Seed 107–109
  Parable of the Prodigal Son 65

parental representations and God representations 127–129, 134–138
Park Street Church 1, 2, 4, 6, 10
particularity 183, 184
pastoral care
  defined 6
  Images of Pastoral Care (Dystra) 8–11
  models/paradigms of 6–8
  resources about 6
pastoral counseling 152–154
person-centered therapy and interventions 6, 39, 40, 44
Pilgrim, case of 40, 47
  attachment patterns 37, 40–41
  background 33–34
  delayed grief in a care receiver 33–38
  relationship with Goodman 37–38
prayer
  12-step programs and 89–90, 96. *See also* silent prayer
preoccupied attachment strategy 191, 192, 196, **197**
presence, reassuring 160
problem-solving 60–61
Prodigal Son, parable of the 65
proximity-seeking 96–97, 183. *See also* interpersonal markers
psychodynamic therapy (PDT) 57, 71, 73. *See also* Sam; *specific topics*
psychotherapists. *See* licensed professionals
psychotherapy outcome research 191

questioning (in therapy) 173

racial identity 157. *See also* African Americans
reading recovery literature 90
reassuring presence 160
recovery literature, reading 90
Reeves, Dianne 172
religion
  defined 4
  spirituality and 4. *See also specific topics*
religious beliefs. *See* spiritual beliefs
religious or spiritual-adapted psychotherapy (R/S-adapted psychotherapy) 163
repetition compulsion 35–36

Subject Index

sacred, the 4, 148, 160
    definitions 4, 148, 166
sacred qualities of therapeutic relationship 160–162
sacred stories 108–110
Sam, psychoanalytic treatment of 71–72
    reflections on the 72–73
Samantha, case of 133, 134
Séamus, case of 158–159
    attachment relationships 199–200
    commentary on psychotherapy process 181–182
    homosexuality 178–180, 188
    presenting issues and diagnosis 178–179
    session excerpt 179–181
secure attachment to God, 12 steps of recovery from addiction and 93–94
secure base 12, 97, 121–122, 182–183
    therapist providing secure and safe base 165, 166
    therapist's secure base provision and patient's underlying attachment needs 189–199
securely attached persons 15–16
Seekers 1
Seinfeld (TV program) 91, 103
self-centeredness 86
self-disclosure 94. *See also* interpersonal markers
self-image/self-esteem 94, 96. *See also* interpersonal markers
self-knowledge, cultivation of 53–54
self-representation 128, 135, 136. *See also* grandiose self
separateness 54, 66–68
separation protest 183
separations from caregiver 13
Sex Addicts Anonymous (SAA) 143
Shalem Institute 62, 64, 74, 75
silence
    contemplative 75–76, 108
    God and 59, 60, 65
    in psychoanalysis 60
silent meditation 59, 75–76, 211, 216
silent prayer
    God and 49, 51–52, 56
    Julie and 49, 51–52, 56
sin 54, 55, 89
    definitions 54, 55. *See also* Original Sin
sociocultural context 7–8, 10

Soldiers in the Parade mindfulness exercise 57–58
somatic symptom disorder (SSD) 179
Spirit 172
"Spirit-undercurrents" 201, 202
spiritual assessment
    clinical examples 143, 146
    conducting a 155–156, 169
spiritual awakening 97, 102. *See also* Bill W.: spiritual conversion
spiritual beliefs 20–21
spiritual bias 159
spiritual cockiness 159
spiritual companion 53
"spiritual companion" 53. *See also* Spiritual Direction
spiritual directee 53. *See also* Spiritual Direction
Spiritual Direction (SD) 76–78
    Attachment-Informed Psychotherapy (AIP) and 73, 74, 76, 78, **209–210**
    contraindications to 78
    definitions 52–53
    description of 52–56, 75–76, 208, 211
    features **209–210**
    discernment in 65–67
    goals of 53–54
    history of 64
    indications for 74
    literature on 76–77
    models of 61–62
    practical application of 56–64
    presuppositions of 54
    vs. Spiritually Integrated Psychotherapy (SIP) 77
    training requirements to practice 74–75
    viewed in context of attachment theory 67–73
spiritual directors 53
    qualities 76
    themes characterizing the meaning of their experience 63. *See also* Spiritual Direction
Spiritual Directors International (SDI) 74, 75
spiritual intervention
    defined 4
    explicit vs. implicit 4–5, **5**
spiritual intervention models 4–5, **5**, 21–23, 208, 211–214

features of **209–210**
what Goodman seeks in 218. *See also* implicit spiritual interventions; *specific topics*
spiritual myopia 159
spiritual overenthusiasm 159
spiritual radar 171
spiritual strivings 148, 149
spiritual struggles 159, 160, 163
　atheists' 150–151
　categories of 150, 151
　description of 149–150
　existential struggles and 161
　psychological/psychiatric symptoms and 151–152. *See also* Spiritually Integrated Psychotherapy
spiritual timidity 159
spirituality
　definitions 4, 148–149, 155, 156
　essence of 4
　as innate quality of humanity 54. *See also specific topics*
spirituality groups (SG) 129–134, 139–140
　description of 212–213
　features **209–210**
　indications for 138–139
　training requirements to become spiritual group leader 139
"spiritually integrated." *See* spiritually integrated therapists
Spiritually Integrated Psychotherapy (SIP) 170
　Attachment-Informed Psychotherapy (AIP) and 163, 166, 200, **209–210**, 214
　basic therapist stance toward 170–171
　core SIP competencies 169
　description of 148–152, 213–214
　features **209–210**
　empirical evidence supporting the effectiveness of 162–163
　history of 152–154
　indications for 167–168
　practical application of 155–163
　sacred qualities of therapeutic relationship 160–162
　SIP certificate program 172–174
　vs. Spiritual Direction 77
　therapist qualities facilitating and hindering 156–160
　training requirements to practice 168–169
　viewed in the context of attachment theory 163–166. *See also specific topics*
spiritually integrated therapists 149, 158
sponsorship (twelve-step groups) 101
　requirements to become a sponsor 99–101
　working on the 12 steps with a sponsor 91–92
Stephen Leader 33
　training requirements to become a 45–46
Stephen Leader Training Course (SLTC) 45
Stephen Minister(s) 33, 41, 44–45, 99, 101, 208
　description of 33
　Goodman as a 33, 35, 36
　and principles of distinctly Christian caring 38–40
　training requirements to become a 45–46
Stephen Ministry program (SM)
　critique of 40–41
　description of 208
　features of **209–210**
　indications for 44–45
　interventions 40, 41, 44
Storytelling/Story-Acting play intervention (STSA)
　as alternative to Godly Play 118–121
　applying STSA to Godly Play storytelling 121
　history and process of STSA in Uganda 119–121
Strange Situation (Ainsworth) 10, 13
stronger/wiser caregiver/attachment figure 9–12, 20, 161
　Higher Power as 95
　sponsor as 91, 100, 103
　therapist as 161, 183, 184, 214
substance use disorder (SUD) 93, 94
suggestion 61
Sundermeier, Tony 66
Surprised by Joy (Lewis) 144, 150, 157
surrender
　to God/Higher Power 53–55, 58, 85, 92, 94–95, 102
　case illustration from Goodman's experience 82–86. *See also under* ego/false self

task (subscale of Working Alliance Inventory) 185
Thatcher, Ebby ("Ebby T.") 88
theory of mind (ToM) 189
therapeutic alliance 185. *See also* working alliance
therapeutic change, Rogers's core conditions for 6, 39, 159, 160, 167
therapeutic relationship
  sacred qualities of the 160–162. *See also* working alliance
therapist–patient matching and mismatching 191. *See also* attachment needs
therapists. *See* licensed professionals
Tiebout, Harry M. 86
transference 185, 214
  components 184–185
  and countertransference 10–11, 52, 182
  definition and nature of 10, 52
  Freud on 184–185
  to God 9–10. *See also* working alliance
transmission gap 190
trauma 35–37, 73, 199, 216–217
trust 43–44, 95. *See also* interpersonal markers; Pilgrim
"trust servants," leaders and sponsors as 103

twelve-step groups
  attending 12-step meetings 92–93
  features **209–210**
  requirements to become a 12-step member 99. *See also* sponsorship
twelve-step programs (12-step)
  analysis of the 12 steps 94–97
  and attachment to God 93–94
  description of 211–212
  essential ingredients of 89–94
  history of 12-step movement 87–89
  indications for 97–98
  as a spiritual intervention 86–87. *See also* Alcoholics Anonymous
Twelve Steps and Twelve Traditions 90, 91, 97

ultimate meaning struggles 150
unknowing, mind of 76–77

validation. *See* Stephen Ministry program: interventions

Wilson, Bill (co-founder of AA). *See* Bill W.
working alliance 184, 185, 194

Zen Buddhism 71–73

For Product Safety Concerns and Information please contact our EU
representative GPSR@taylorandfrancis.com
Taylor & Francis Verlag GmbH, Kaufingerstraße 24, 80331 München, Germany

www.ingramcontent.com/pod-product-compliance
Lightning Source LLC
Chambersburg PA
CBHW050532300426
44113CB00012B/2065